The Cheer Reader

Terry and Jan Todd Series on Physical Culture and Sports
Edited by Sarah K. Fields, Thomas Hunt, Daniel A. Nathan, and Patricia Vertinsky

ALSO IN THE SERIES

Scott Beekman, *The Last Gladiator: William Muldoon and the Making of American Sports*

Richard L. Cleary, *The Architecture of the Playing Field: Shaping Space in Sport*

Maureen M. Smith, Daniel A. Nathan, and Sarah K. Fields, eds., *Sports through the Lens: Essays on 25 Iconic Photographs*

Jonathan Silverman, ed., *Astros and Asterisks: Houston's Sign-Stealing Scandal Explained*

Adam Berg, *The Olympics That Never Happened: Denver '76 and the Politics of Growth*

Michella M. Marino, *Roller Derby: The History of an American Sport*

Ronald A. Smith, *The Myth of the Amateur: A History of College Athletic Scholarships*

Andrew R. M. Smith, *No Way but to Fight: George Foreman and the Business of Boxing*

Jason P. Shurley, Jan Todd, and Terry Todd, *Strength Coaching in America: A History of the Innovation That Transformed Sports*

Kevin Robbins, *Harvey Penick: The Life and Wisdom of the Man Who Wrote the Book on Golf*

John Hoberman, *Dopers in Uniform: The Hidden World of Police on Steroids*

John D. Fair, *Mr. America: The Tragic History of a Bodybuilding Icon*

Thomas M. Hunt, *Drug Games: The International Olympic Committee and the Politics of Doping, 1960–2008*

# The Cheer Reader

## INSIDE AN AMERICAN INSTITUTION

*Edited by Natalie G. Adams*

University of Texas Press *Austin*

Printed in the United States of America
First edition, 2026

The photographs in chapter 1 are used with the permission of Oregon State University, Special Collections Research Center.



♾ The paper used in this book meets the minimum requirements of ANSI/NISO Z39.48-1992 (R1997) (Permanence of Paper).

Library of Congress Cataloging-in-Publication Data

Names: Adams, Natalie G. editor
Title: The cheer reader : inside an American institution / edited by Natalie G. Adams.
Other titles: Terry and Jan Todd series on physical culture and sports
Description: First edition. | Austin : University of Texas Press, 2026. | Series: Terry and Jan Todd Series on Physical Culture and Sports | Includes index.
Identifiers: LCCN 2026003528 (print) | LCCN 2026003529 (ebook)
ISBN 978-1-4773-3456-0 hardcover
ISBN 978-1-4773-3457-7 paperback
ISBN 978-1-4773-3458-4 pdf
ISBN 978-1-4773-3459-1 epub
Subjects: LCSH: Cheerleading | Cheerleading—History | Cheerleading—Social aspects | Cheerleading—Sex differences | Cheerleaders—In mass media | Sports—Political aspects—United States | LCGFT: Essays
Classification: LCC GV706 .C44 2026 (print) | LCC GV706 (ebook)
LC record available at https://lccn.loc.gov/2026003528
LC ebook record available at https://lccn.loc.gov/2026003529

doi:10.7560/334560

To Pam Bettis.

Your name may not be on this book, but your playful presence is hiding throughout. Thanks for being my cheer partner for twenty-five-plus years.

# Contents

# Illustrations

# The Cheer Reader

INTRODUCTION

# Cheer Obsession

*Natalie G. Adams*

You keep going until you get it right, and then you keep going until you can't get it wrong.
Coach Monica Aldama, Navarro College cheer team

On January 8, 2020, Netflix released *Cheer*. The docuseries follows the Navarro College cheerleaders of Corsicana, Texas, as they prepare for the National Cheerleaders Association (NCA) collegiate championship, held every April in Daytona Beach. These are not stereotypical cheerleaders. They are not the mean, vicious, super-popular girls who make everyone else's life pure hell, as so often featured in popular culture; nor are they the silly and shallow Spartan Cheerleaders of *Saturday Night Live* fame. The team's death-defying, two-minutes-and-fifteen-seconds routine does not remotely resemble the highly sexualized moves of the Dallas Cowboys Cheerleaders.

No one uses the phrase "all-American girl next door" to describe these cheerleaders. Lexi Brumback is a formerly incarcerated high school dropout. La'Darius Marshall and Jerry Harris are Black, male, and openly gay. Morgan Simianer was an abandoned teen living with her brother in rural Wyoming until her grandparents rescued her. Gabi Butler, who never cheered on a high school team, has been a "cheerlebrity" for her entire teenage life, with a pre-*Cheer* Instagram following of over eight hundred thousand. As the series unfolds, we watch this eclectic group of cheerleaders sweat, bleed, tumble, climb, fall, jump, and stumble as they compete fiercely for a position on the mat.

When *Cheer* dropped, America was in the midst of a presidential impeachment trial; a waning trust in institutions of all kinds; vitriolic debates over immigration, reproductive rights, race relations, and climate change; and the beginning of what would become a worldwide coronavirus pandemic. *Cheer* seemed to be just what a country suffering the loss of national unity needed. Rich and poor, Black and white, and gay, straight, and queer Americans embraced *Cheer*. And if only for a short period, we caught a glimpse of the America we longed for—one personified by cheerleading itself: strength during crisis, unity around common causes, optimism about the future, and a country where everyone belongs. But the popularity of *Cheer* extended beyond the United States. Soon an international audience was obsessed with Coach Monica Aldama and her scrappy squad, who persevere through pain and heartbreak to win their school's fourteenth collegiate national championship. It turns out that it wasn't just Americans who needed a big cheerleading hug—the rest of the world did as well.

*The Washington Post* was the first to review the series, with the headline "The Documentary That Hard-Working Cheerleaders Have Long Deserved."[1] For the thousands of cheerleaders involved in competitive cheerleading, *Cheer* offered a realistic portrayal of their sport. It was public confirmation of the blood, sweat, and tears of competitive cheer. Its focus on cheerleaders as athletes displaced tired stereotypes of cheerleaders as ditzy blonds in short skirts on the sidelines yelling, "Rah, rah, rah!" But the appeal of *Cheer* spread beyond a niche market of cheer-friendly viewers. The show's spotlight on competitive cheerleading, the intensity of its athletes, and the injuries associated with the sport attracted a much wider audience, including individuals who heretofore had no interest in cheerleading—people like Greg Whiteley, *Cheer*'s creator, director, and executive producer, who told *The Wrap*, "Cheerleaders are the toughest athletes I've ever seen."[2]

Since the release of *Cheer*, gym owners have experienced a surge in their competitive cheer teams. College girls are donning their old All Star T-shirts, and former cheerleader naysayers are flooding social media with their newfound love of cheer. The lovefest with *Cheer* may suggest that this fascination with cheerleading is new. It is not. From its inception in 1869 as an all-male activity to its feminization in the 1950s, its sexualization in the 1970s, and the introduction of competition-only All Star teams in the 1990s, cheerleading has evoked criticism, adulation, contempt, and celebration. In 1911, when all yell leaders were male, the president of Harvard University attacked "organized cheering" as a deplorable avenue for respectable college men to express emotion.[3] By the 1920s, cheerleading was so popular on college campuses that the *Literary Digest* declared, "The position of cheer-leader nowadays is fraught with great responsibility and rated as a high honor, so much so that in many colleges competitions and examinations are held to select the cheer-leaders."[4] When Title IX was passed in 1972, feminists were certain cheerleading was all but dead. But it survived by becoming more athletic, more entertaining, and more competitive—so much so that in the 1990s, young men began returning to a sport they had dominated a hundred years earlier. In 2000, Hollywood, which has always had a fascination with cheerleaders, released the blockbuster cheerleading movie *Bring It On*, ushering in a new era of obsession with cheerleading as an intensely competitive and athletic sport.

In the twenty-five years since *Bring It On*, cheerleading has suffered some image problems. In 2008, Lifetime released a less-than-complimentary movie called *Fab Five: The Texas Cheerleader Scandal*. It was based on a true story of some high school cheerleaders who gained notoriety when they posted pictures of themselves, in uniform, simulating sexual acts in front of a Condoms to Go store. In 2017, Coastal Carolina University suspended its entire cheerleading team after revelations surfaced about CCU cheerleaders working for an escort service, earning $100 to $1,500 per date. In 2010, a federal judge upheld the formal position of the National Collegiate Athletic Association (NCAA) and dozens of high school athletic associations: Cheerleading is not a sport and cannot count as such under Title IX guidelines. In 2014, professional cheerleaders representing several National Football League teams filed lawsuits against their franchises for wage discrimination. In September 2020, *USA Today* published a scathing exposé about registered sex offenders working directly with cheerleaders in cheer gyms throughout the United States. And in July 2022, *Cheer* cast member Jerry Harris was sentenced to twelve years in federal prison for possession of child pornography and solicitation of sex from a minor.

Can cheerleading survive sex scandals, the #MeToo movement, and internal conflict within the cheer industry? Will cheerleading finally be recognized as a sport? And if it is, given that Title IX is based on the gendered segregation of sports, will we see the elimination of coed teams at the high school and collegiate levels? Does cheerleading's close entanglement with hyperfemininity and sexuality hinder its fight for sport legitimacy? How is the image of cheer changing to accommodate a more diverse group of participants? Ironically, will it be cheerleading, long maligned and trivialized, that forces conversations about the limitations of the gender binary in sports? Does cheer have a promising future?

In the pages that follow, we probe these questions and others but do so from a unique perspective. While cheerleading is ubiquitous in American culture and has an expansive global following, it is noticeably absent in scholarly research. This book addresses this omission by bringing together a multidisciplinary group of scholars who provide a critical and nuanced analysis of cheerleading in the United States. As Pamela Grundy points out in her history of North Carolina sports, "the most successful cultural institutions have been those that can support multiple meanings, be put to many ends."[5] Cheerleading is one such cultural institution. What then can we learn by studying the multiple meanings of this American cultural institution? The contributors to this volume delve into a myriad of cheer-related topics to demonstrate how a serious study of cheerleading offers a glimpse into broader areas of social and cultural life, such as race, class, gender, and sexuality.

In part I, "Made in the USA: The Gendered and Raced Politics of Cheer," the authors map out the 160-plus-year history of cheerleading. Birthed on Ivy League campuses in the late 1860s, cheerleading has evolved to reflect changing gender roles, norms, and expectations in the United States. In chapter 1, Dwaine Plaza, Kathleen Stanley, and Michelle Inderbitzin examine the evolution of cheerleading from a male-dominated, masculine activity to a feminized activity symbolizing ideal femininity through a case study of cheerleading at Oregon State University from the early 1920s to the present.

In chapter 2, Amira Rose Davis and Paulina A. Serrano explore cheerleading's role in the desegregation of our nation's schools. While the integration of football and basketball on college campuses has been widely recorded, the selection of cheerleading teams has received scant attention—even though, as Grundy notes, it was "one of the most volatile issues of school desegregation."[6] Focusing on the experiences of Black and Brown cheerleaders from the 1950s to the 1970s, the authors explore how race, resistance, and politics converged in the selection and representation of cheerleaders during school desegregation.

In chapter 3, Amy Moritz and Natalie G. Adams examine the debate around whether cheerleading is a sport. And spoiler alert: It is not—at least according to the NCAA, Title IX, and a federal court judge. As the authors illustrate in their discussion of cheer's evolution from a sideline activity to a competitive athletic activity—one whose participants rival football players in their injury rates—cheerleading's complicated history with feminists and Title IX and its close entanglement with sexuality have deterred its twenty-five-plus-year quest to be recognized as a sport.

In chapter 4, Emily West and Laura Grindstaff extend the conversation of cheer's legitimacy as a sport by explicating the gendered politics *within* cheerleading. Drawing on ethnographic research and hundreds of interviews with cheerleaders, they discuss the tensions between the feminized performance and appearance demanded of female cheerleaders and the threat this performance presents to cheer's legitimacy as a sport, and how cheerleaders (both male and female) respond to these seeming contradictions.

Part II of the book, "The Other Cheerleaders: Sex, Work, and Protest," delves into cheerleaders who look and act, in many ways, very differently from the high school, collegiate, and All Star cheerleaders discussed in the first section. The section begins with two chapters focusing on professional cheerleaders. How did professional cheerleaders become the sexual pinups of their day? In Chapter 5, Lauren R. Nowosatka answers that question through an examination of the most iconic professional cheerleading team: the Dallas Cowboys Cheerleaders. While the origins of the team and its iconic uniform are debatable, one fact is undisputable: The Dallas Cowboys Cheerleaders birthed an entire professional cheerleading industry built, in part, on the tension between piety and sexuality. In Chapter 6, Lauren C. Hindman further complicates the image of professional cheerleaders through her discussion of them as activists who, before the #MeToo movement, filed numerous lawsuits against their franchises, forcing them to acknowledge and in some cases address a pervasive hostile work environment and abysmally low wages.

In chapters 7 and 8, Laura Grindstaff takes us into a different dimension of cheerleading by focusing on alternative groups whose origins lie explicitly in politics and activism. In chapter 7, Grindstaff explores a network of queer-friendly adult performance teams, of which she was a member. Her autobiographical account of being part of Cheer Sacramento challenges assumptions about the purpose of cheerleading and who can wear the cheerleader moniker. In chapter 8, she takes us into the world of radical cheerleading, whose heyday was in the early 2000s. Drawing from interviews with participants, Grindstaff examines the rise of radical cheerleaders, their subversive form of political protest, and their eventual demise.

In part III, "Not Just Any Girl: Mediated Representations of Cheerleaders," the authors examine how cheerleaders are represented in popular media, how cheerleaders make sense of these representations, and how they represent themselves. In Chapter 9, Barbara J. Brickman undoes the simplicity of the cheerleader archetype as the heterosexual girl and object of male desire through a close analysis of the 1999 cult classic film *But I'm a Cheerleader*. In chapter 10, Caitlyn M. Jarvis and Ashleigh N. Shields turn our attention to how cheerleaders navigate the pressure to maintain the thin, perfect cheerleader body. Drawing from Michel Foucault's notion of surveillance, they discuss the regulatory discourse of cheerleaders and coaches in online cheer communities. In chapter 11, Isabelle Bennington invites us into the inner world of cheerleading and reveals how cheerleaders themselves seek to be represented. Drawing from over a decade of personal experience as a cheerleader and from interviews with current and former cheerleaders, Bennington discusses how cheerleaders balance the barrage of criticism they face with their intense love for the sport.

In the fourth and final part of the book, "Cheer Trouble," the authors lead us far away from the typical places we find cheerleaders, to courtrooms, multimillion-dollar high-rises, and backroom board meetings. In chapter 12, Zoie Comer and Stanley J. Murphy describe how one cheerleader's rant on Snapchat about not making the varsity cheer team landed her in front of the Supreme Court in what has been dubbed the "cursing cheerleader case"—one of the most significant student free speech cases in fifty years. In chapter 13, Natalie G. Adams traces the history of the cheer industry from its beginnings in Texas in the late 1940s, to its growth during multiple economic downturns, to its current iteration largely controlled by one company, Varsity Brands. Cheerleading is typically known for its spirit making, not its moneymaking, but Adams's account of the business side of cheerleading reveals an intriguing (yet rarely discussed) story about innovation, capitalism, greed, jealousy, and power.

In the conclusion, Adams examines key themes discussed throughout the volume and returns to the central thesis of the book: Cheer matters. She explains how cheer has enjoyed success as a malleable, adaptable institution that has responded well to social and cultural changes, and why cheer has a cheery future.

Interspersed throughout the book are "Cheer Notes"—fun facts, quizzes, and activities that will augment your understanding of cheer and its specific language, rituals, and customs. You will learn some cheer trivia and test your knowledge of cheer's close association with other significant areas of American life.

Now we invite you to join us in a playfully serious look at cheerleading: its history, its place in the sports regime, its appearance in various forms of popular media, its close entanglement with sexuality, and its contemporary problems. You will find that the conflicts, crises, and contradictions inherent in this beloved and vilified American institution have implications far beyond the mat.

## Notes

1. Hank Stuever, "Netflix's 'Cheer' Is the Documentary That Hard-Working Cheerleaders Have Long Deserved," *Washington Post*, January 8, 2020, https://www.washingtonpost.com/entertainment/tv/netflixs-cheer-is-the-documentary-that-hardworking-cheerleaders-have-long-deserved/2020/01/08/2f8ee890-2e59-11ea-bcb3ac6482c4a92f_story.html.

2. Margeaux Sippell, "'Last Chance U' Director on Cheerleaders in Netflix's 'Cheer': Toughest Athletes I've Ever Filmed," *The Wrap*, January 6, 2020, https://www.thewrap.com/last-chanceu-director-talks-debunking-stereotypes-in-netflixs-cheer-toughest-athletes-ive-ever-filmed/.

3. "Organized Cheering," *The Nation* 92 (January 1911): 6.

4. "November Yells That Win Games," *Literary Digest*, November 4, 1924, 34–40.

5. Pamela Grundy, *Learning to Win: Sports, Education, and Social Change in Twentieth-Century North Carolina* (University of North Carolina Press, 2001), 7.

6. Grundy, *Learning to Win*, 285.

CHEER NOTE #1

# The Big Cheer Umbrella

The term "cheerleading" is broad and encompassing, as you will discover in this book. Broadly speaking, five different types of cheerleaders fall under the larger cheerleading umbrella.

1. "Sideline cheerleaders" describes the bulk of cheerleaders in the United States at the middle and high school levels (a type of cheer sometimes called "traditional" or "classical" cheerleading). These squads, primarily girls, perform the traditional role of cheering for other athletes and serving as ambassadors for their school. If sideline cheerleaders compete, it is secondary to these other responsibilities. Many collegiate squads also fall under this category.

2. "All Star cheerleaders" are not affiliated with any school or university. They are sponsored by private cheer gyms and do not perform any of the traditional roles of cheerleaders. In the United States, there are both coed and all-girl All Star teams. To date, no all-boy All Star cheer teams compete in the United States, although a few have emerged internationally. All Star is sometimes referred to as Club Cheer or Show Cheer.

3. "Competitive cheerleading" broadly describes the collegiate, All Star, and high school teams who compete for state, regional, national, and international championships. They train, work out, and practice year-round. The term "competitive cheerleading" is meant to emphasize the sport-like nature of cheerleading, rather than its traditional supportive role. But the name is a bit ambiguous, because although many cheerleading teams spend much of their time preparing for national championships, they also perform the traditional duties of cheerleaders (i.e., cheering at football games and performing at community events). The Navarro cheer team featured in *Cheer* is an example of a competitive team at the collegiate level that also fulfills the role of supporting other school athletes. Globally, competitive cheer is the most popular form of cheerleading and typically includes mixed-gender teams.

4. "Professional cheerleaders" are affiliated with professional basketball and football franchises. Originally, they were all women and were more akin to dance teams than traditional cheerleaders. Recently, professional cheerleading has undergone some significant changes, both in gender composition and performance style. As their name implies, professional cheerleaders are adults who are financially compensated for their time and work.

5. "Alternative cheerleaders" refers to a disparate group of teams that incorporate many of the characteristics of traditional cheer teams while disrupting, parodying, or changing conventional notions of cheerleading. The most well-known group of alternative cheerleaders is CHEER San Francisco, which began in 1980 as the world's first LGBTQ+ cheer squad.

PART I

# Made in the USA

## THE GENDERED AND RACED POLITICS OF CHEER

CHAPTER 1

# From Campus Leaders to Rowdy Boys

## MASCULINITY IN COLLEGE CHEERLEADING

*Dwaine Plaza, Kathleen Stanley, and Michelle Inderbitzin*

OAC, our hats are off to you,
Beavers, Beavers, fighters thru and thru,
We'll cheer for ev'ry man,
We'll root for ev'ry stand
That's made for old OAC
Rah, rah, rah!

"Hail to Old OAC: A Rooter's Song," original Oregon State University fight song, 1907

Cheerleading emerged as an outgrowth of collegiate sports, especially football, at elite colleges and universities in the late nineteenth and early twentieth centuries. Although frequently derided as ungentlemanly, barbaric, and dangerous, football flourished. As its popularity grew, so too did the rituals and traditions associated with the game. Collegiate sports created institutional identities around which students could demonstrate loyalty to their schools. Colleges selected team colors and adopted mascots, while the students developed cheers and rituals that gave the institution a unique identity.[1] Elite colleges were generally all male, and even at coeducational state schools, women were excluded from prominent leadership roles on campus. Not surprisingly, the first cheerleaders—or yell leaders, as they were more commonly called—were men. Yell leaders were regarded as campus leaders, chosen by other male students, and played public roles at games and on campus.

Over time, women at coeducational colleges and universities were given some recognition as "rooters" for the team. Still, their roles remained subordinate to those of the male yell leaders, especially as cheering began incorporating acrobatic stunts to entertain and excite the fans. But the early decades of the twentieth century were a time when women's roles were changing. Women were attending college in larger numbers, seeking academic knowledge and degrees. Politically, women organized to pursue suffrage, finally winning the right to vote in 1920. Small numbers of women entered cheerleading in the early decades of the twentieth century, typically as "rally girls," but it was not until the 1940s that women entered cheerleading in large numbers. As men marched off to war, women assumed many traditionally masculine roles as workers, as heads of households, and, on college campuses, as cheerleaders.

Men never disappeared completely from cheerleading, nor did they regain their dominant position. During the postwar era, cheerleading became strongly associated with feminine qualities and physical attractiveness. This emphasis on physical attractiveness has remained a prominent feature of cheerleading, even as female cheerleading has become more athletic. Over time, men's roles within the larger world of cheerleading have become secondary to those of female cheerleaders. Male cheerleaders, with their booming voices, augmented with megaphones, and physical strength when performing complicated lifts, are often portrayed as assistants to the "real," female cheerleaders. As men's roles on cheerleading squads declined, their involvement in cheering focused on their roles as costumed mascots and as participants in boisterous cheering sections in stadiums and arenas.

The history of collegiate cheerleading at Oregon State University (formerly called Corvallis College, Oregon Agricultural College, and Oregon State College) parallels its history in the United States more generally. Through a content analysis of photographs appearing in the student yearbook at OSU, changes in the meaning of cheerleading over time can be understood through the lens of the participants themselves. Of particular interest are the related issues of gender and sexuality in cheerleading. Photographs in the school yearbook, *The Beaver*, provide a glimpse into the changing meanings and practices of masculinity and femininity at OSU and on college campuses across the United States. While most research on cheerleading has focused on girls and women,[2] our focus in this chapter is on men, the original cheerleaders. We chart the representation and role of men in cheerleading at OSU, from their early dominance, to their near extinction as cheerleading became a feminine activity, to their reintegration as adjutants to female cheerleaders in later decades. These local changes in gendered performances and practices reflect larger historical transformations in gender relationships, roles, and norms in the United States.

## A Word About Methodology

A total of 426 photographs appearing in the OSU yearbooks were analyzed using a content analysis methodology spanning a ninety-year period from 1912 to 2002. Photos for inclusion were selected using two sampling criteria: (1) individuals were depicted wearing cheerleading uniforms, and (2) the accompanying text identified them as yell leaders, rooters, or cheerleaders. The photographs represent the collective efforts to define and record understandings of cheerleading from three distinct social groups. The first group is the cheerleaders themselves, who exert some control over how they will appear in public through their uniforms, mannerisms, and the cheers they perform. The second group is the photographers who chose the specific moments to record and the specific subject matter of each photograph. The third group is the editors of the school yearbooks, students themselves, who made decisions each year about which photographs to include in the annual publication. This collection of photographs is, therefore, a social construction reflecting individual and shared understandings of the meaning of cheerleading at a particular moment in time. Examining these photographic representations provides insight into how these meanings, including the relationship between gender and cheerleading, were created and transformed.

Our content analysis incorporated numerical counting of men and women in the photographs and textual analysis of the written captions accompanying the pictures. This analysis revealed four major periods in the evolution of cheerleading at OSU (fig. 1.1). In period 1 (1912–1942), cheerleaders were exclusively or predominantly men. In period 2 (1943–1955), cheerleading became a coed activity that was quickly becoming identified as a primarily female activity. Period 3 (1956–1970) was a time of mostly female cheerleaders. Male cheerleaders, when present, were not the primary focus of photos, as cheerleading increasingly became a feminine activity associated with both girl-next-door wholesomeness and sex appeal. In period 4 (1971–2002), cheerleading became more athletic, pro-

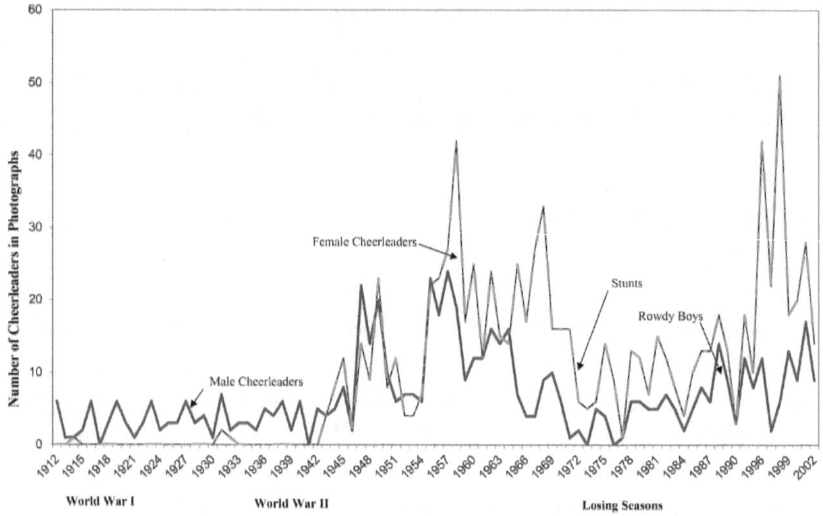


FIGURE 1.1. *Cheerleading trends at Oregon State University, based on an analysis of college yearbook photographs, 1912–2002.*

viding men opportunities for fuller participation in cheerleading, albeit in new roles, largely as support for their female teammates. As men's formal role as cheerleaders declined, new ways for men to show support for the team emerged in the form of mascots, überfans, and what we call "rowdy boys."

## The Masculine World of Cheerleading

The history of cheerleading at OSU dates to the early twentieth century, when men began to play a crucial role in forming and developing the university's cheerleading tradition. The early yell leaders, exclusively men, led the crowds with chants, pep songs, and simple, straightforward cheers to rally support for the football and basketball teams.[3] Their role was to create excitement, using megaphones and other tools to amplify their voices. Only male students were allowed to elect or serve as yell leaders.[4] Yell leaders, selected from each class following public tryouts, were popular, charismatic, and generally members of the Greek system of fraternities. For fraternities, having a yell leader elected from their chapter was a badge of honor and prestige, and as organized social groups, the more prestigious fraternities had considerable influence on the selection process.[5] As illustrated in the following excerpt from the 1914 Oregon Agricultural College annual, yell leaders were expected to organize the cheering activities of their class, along with school-wide pep rallies and other pregame spirit events, such as the serpentine parade and annual campus bonfire:

> He has, in large quantities, that element most necessary to the success of a college yell leader, namely personal magnetism. Almost any college man of ordinary ability can stand in front of a bunch of rooters and wave his arms up and down in time with a yell, but something else is needed to keep five hundred rooters cheering fiercely on the bleachers during a driving hailstorm.[6]

Cheerleading was a central component of student government at this time, and yell leaders were listed with other class officers in the yearbook. Although female students might be recognized as rooters, their role was secondary and more of an organizational support role for the male yell leaders. These gendered distinctions were not confined only to activities like cheerleading. Still, they reflected the subordinate position of women throughout society, with few opportunities for formal leadership positions in other social institutions.

Photographic representations of cheerleaders at OSU began in 1912. In contrast to more contemporary photographs of stoic male cheerleaders, male yell leaders expressed joy and exuberance, with big smiles and poses celebrating male camaraderie. Kewpie Green, the Varsity Rooter King, for example, appears as an almost circus-style entertainer (fig. 1.2).[7] This is reflected in his uniform of sweater, hat, and striped trousers, and in his posture. His nickname, Kewpie, is evocative of doll-like qualities. Although recognized at the time as an important student leader, by today's standards Kewpie seems neither muscular nor athletic. But the Rooter King was still regarded as masculine. He was required to "possess lungs of ox hide, vocal cords of high carbon steel, and the temperament and enthusiasm of a Mexican general inciting a new revolution."[8]

As was true at other colleges, by the 1920s, athletic ability was becoming a more important component of the yell leader's role at what was then the Oregon Agricultural College, with synchronized cheers and acrobatic tumbling stunts incorporated into sideline performances. Yearbooks from the 1920s show admiration for the creativity and leadership of the Yell King and his yell leaders (fig. 1.3): "Many visitors commented that never before had they seen such acrobatic yell leading with such effective results

FIGURE 1.2. *Kewpie Green, the Varsity Rooter King, 1916.*

[from] the Yell King and his assistants. The student body at all times gave their support to the yell leaders and the athletic team."[9] By 1925, the Oregon Agricultural College yell leaders had established a national reputation for their acrobatic stunts. The yearbook exhorts, "Our yell leaders have made a national name for themselves. They delighted the crowds with their antics and led them in mighty cheers. The untiring efforts of this acrobatic, yell-leading duet have contributed more than their share to the success of the Orange and Black athletic teams."[10]

During the 1920s and 1930s, women began joining cheer squads, albeit in small numbers. Mary Ellen Hanson argues that "women's participation as collegiate cheerleaders may have resulted from factors which developed on campus in the 1920s: fraternity and sorority dominance in student culture, and the increasing emphasis on physical attractiveness and its conspicuous display as a value in coeducational student life."[11] This transition was also connected to recently introduced beauty pageants, Hollywood motion pictures, and the use of feminine sex appeal in advertising.[12] Women were still excluded from the elite universities where cheerleading first emerged, but at state-supported universities, they were admitted at earlier dates. Women's

FIGURE 1.3. *The Yell King and his assistants, 1929.*

societal roles were changing as more women gradually assumed a greater role in public life, particularly after winning the right to vote in 1920. Women's rising numbers in higher education and their expanded economic and political roles were reflected in their slow but ultimately successful attempts to assume greater prominence within cheerleading.

Nevertheless, men dominated cheerleading throughout this period, particularly in leadership roles. Two early manuals on cheerleading, written in 1927, refer exclusively to the cheerleader as "man," "chap," and "fellow."[13] Gamma Sigma, a national honorary fraternity for yell marshals, selected an annual all-American cheerleading squad. As late as 1939, women were excluded from the squad.[14] Numerous reasons account for the absence of women on cheerleading squads. Men outnumbered women on college campuses, traditionally feminine emotional and physical traits were not considered appropriate for yell leaders, and there was the perception that any involvement in masculine pursuits would psychologically harm women.[15]

At Oregon Agriculture College, women had been admitted since 1870, and they constituted 25 percent of the student body by the 1920s. As their numbers on campus grew, women became more involved in cheerleading but were never designated as yell leaders or captains. Even though women were now active participants, photographs from the 1930s continue to highlight the central importance of men in cheerleading. A photo from 1931 features five male yell leaders, with the squad captain clearly identified in the center, wearing a distinct insignia (fig. 1.4). Juxtaposed with this photo is a depiction of the rally squad, composed of eight men and seven women (fig. 1.5). Men were of higher status as cheerleaders than as members of the coed rally squad.

FIGURE 1.4. left *Male yell leaders, 1931.*

FIGURE 1.5. below *Coed rally squad, 1931.*

## Cheerleading Goes Coed

World War II ushered in a dramatic transformation of gender roles throughout society. As men went to war, some women joined the military as support staff. Women on the home front entered wartime industries as paid employees and assumed the full responsibility for running a household and maintaining it financially. For the first time, middle- and upper-class women stepped outside of their traditional homemaker roles, taking on a greater public presence and leadership opportunities. Not surprisingly, these changes at the societal level significantly affected higher education and were reflected in cheerleading.

By the 1940s, cheerleading was well established at most high schools and colleges, with tens of thousands of participants nationwide. As the United States was drawn into the war and young men enlisted, college women had new opportunities, such as hosting pregame pep rallies, teaching cheers, and decorating the school with banners and other memorabilia to boost the campus spirit. These were roles formerly occupied by the Yell King and his assistant men. Rather than being part of a large group of rally boys and girls tasked with organizing pregame activities to build excitement for the men's teams, women had the chance to take on more prestigious positions. Women found new opportunities in cheerleading, and their new roles were celebrated. According to a 1941 article in *Life* magazine, "the girl cheerleader is establishing her ability to evoke unprecedented vocal energies from any grandstand she confronts."[16]

The shortage of men at what was now Oregon State College allowed women to assume various roles from which they had previously been excluded. This also included senior leadership roles in student government. For the first time, by the mid-1940s, the number of female cheerleaders at the college was higher than the number of male cheerleaders. In 1944, Peg Mahaffy was elected as the school's first female yell leader:

> In keeping with Oregon State College's penchant for women leaders in 1944, friendly, energetic Peg Mahaffy carried the megaphone as Yell Queen for the Beavers. . . . To bolster anemic school spirit, the Rally men and girls were on hand to cheer, cheer, and cheer at all games. . . . Jim Healy and Joe Olsen were added in the winter term to increase the male contingent.[17]

FIGURE 1.6. *Oregon State University cheerleaders in high heels and short shorts, 1959.*

It is worth noting that men were now underrepresented as cheerleaders, and there was thought to be a need to boost their numbers.

Following the war, men returned to campus and to cheerleading, but in smaller numbers. Cheerleading as an activity had been fundamentally transformed. Cheerleading was now a way to showcase femininity rather than masculine leadership. Female cheerleaders demonstrated the ideals of femininity: women as youthful, physically attractive, and emotionally open. Cheerleading was a sign of popularity and femininity, attracting women from across campus to try out for the squad and conferring high status and desirability on those who made the team. Women were eager to become cheerleaders. In contrast, for men, the 1950s were marked by significant fear and persecution of those who displayed any feminine tendencies. This period witnessed the moral panic commonly referred to as the Lavender Scare. Ultimately, the stigma of being labeled as feminine caused many men to avoid the once-prestigious role of the yell leader who cheered on the success of hypermasculine men on the court or playing field. A note from the 1957 yearbook suggests that at least fifty women were members of junior cheerleading squads, hoping to be selected eventually for the top team. The junior squads held summer training camps and operated like a farm team where younger high school cheerleaders could practice difficult routines in the hope that they could make a future run for a spot on the main cheer squad.

New trends in the cheering style contributed to the decline in men's

FIGURE 1.7. *The Tail Flappers ("Look at those rally girls, Howie"), 1959.*

participation.[18] During the late 1950s, dancing became an integral part of cheerleading and a new way of entertaining the fans. Tumbling and acrobatic stunts, long the province of male cheerleaders, were replaced by rhythmic marching band music and swaying hips. Cheerleading skirts were shorter to accommodate dance moves, and sweaters became tighter to highlight women's physical attributes. The uniforms for the men remained very similar to those of earlier times and resembled casual street clothes, consisting of trousers, shirts, and sweaters. Yearbook photos illustrate the sexualization of cheerleading and the emphasis on women's bodies during this period (fig. 1.6).

The postwar 1950s was a time of heightened concern around gender roles, and cheerleading became a way to emphasize gender differences. Female cheerleaders epitomized not just sex appeal but also, somewhat contradictorily, a girl-next-door wholesomeness. As cheerleading became associated with femininity, men's participation was suspect. Heightened fears of latent homosexuality during this time encouraged men to find ways to demonstrate their heterosexuality through hypermasculine behaviors such as taunting, catcalling, and openly objectifying women (fig. 1.7). If men failed to play this degrading game or showed any sign of gendered weakness, they ran the risk of being labeled as soft, a sissy, or queer among their peer group of other men.[19]

## Cheerleading Takes Flight

By the 1970s, a new trend in cheerleading began to emerge: group stunting. Prior to this, cheerleading included more individual moves, like rolls, backflips, cartwheels, and splits. Following the passage of Title IX in 1972, as women's opportunities in collegiate athletics grew, cheerleading also became more athletic. Stunting became more elaborate, with the introduction of human pyramids, paired lifts, throws, and other moves designed to entertain the crowd. These more athletic movements required a different type of cheerleader, opening the door for a transformed male role in cheerleading. The ideal female cheerleader was often an accomplished gymnast, while male cheerleaders had to be strong and muscular. Male cheerleaders played a more supportive role in this new style of cheerleading. They became the base to help the female cheerleaders execute complicated stunts and acrobatics. At OSU, male cheerleaders receded into the background, sometimes even into invisibility (fig. 1.8).

Over time, cheer teams began to compete at regional and national cheer competitions. The emphasis on athleticism had opened new opportunities for men in cheerleading, but in roles circumscribed by gender. Individual cheerleaders, particularly the men, tended to be less visible on campus than campus leaders. This is a marked difference from the original male yell leaders a century ago, who were chosen by their peers and regarded as key members of student leadership groups. Bodies and physical appearance defined cheerleading roles for both women and men, but in ways that continued to highlight ideologies of gender difference, even as gender roles were being transformed throughout society. The shift toward a more athletic and competitive form of cheerleading, which includes complex and demanding stunts, has required a greater emphasis on strength and power for male cheerleaders. Their ideal body type became more muscular, while the women's body type became more petite and athletic.

Evidence of the gendered division of labor in cheer can be found in the OSU yearbook photographs from 1970 onward. No photographs showed male cheerleaders involved in dancing routines or showing great emotion while cheering. Men's physical strength was displayed through their role in lifting, throwing, and catching the female cheerleaders and serving as anchors for the pyramids. In photographs, the men's faces are often blurred, as if they are literally fading into the background. As Laura Grindstaff and Emily West argue, cheerleading constitutes a public stage for "doing gender" in ways that highlight normative, taken-for-granted notions of gender difference and heterosexuality.[20] Cheerleading has, from

FIGURE 1.8. *Oregon State University cheerleaders, 1992.*

its inception, been a vehicle for the enactment of hegemonic masculinity in contrast to femininity, and this has remained true even as men's and women's roles within cheerleading have been transformed.

The antiestablishment mood on college campuses by the 1970s led to a decline in the popularity of cheerleading, along with lower regard for the Greek fraternity and sorority houses that had long been integral to cheerleading at many colleges and universities. This transition at OSU resulted in the dramatic decline in male and female cheerleaders in the early 1970s (see fig. 1.1). Cheerleading did not, however, disappear completely at OSU or elsewhere. It continued to reflect and reproduce dominant ideas about masculinity and femininity, even as cheerleading became more athletic. Female cheerleaders were small, light, and flexible, while male cheerleaders were physically strong supports whose presence ensured the safety of the female flyers. The new style of cheerleading has continued to be a prominent vehicle for the demonstration of gender difference and assumed heterosexuality.

## Alternative Masculine Cheerleading Pursuits

In addition to serving as cheerleaders for the athletes on the field or court, collegiate men have created other outlets to demonstrate their masculinity on the sidelines. The college mascot is the most well known; however, other iterations, such as the "rah-rah boys," emerged in the 1920s and 1930s.[21] At OSU, Billy Beaver, the Tail Flappers, rowdy boys, and (most recently) the überfan have provided an alternative to cheerleading for men who want to take a more active and visible role in a sporting event.

### MASCOTS

The origins of university football mascots can be traced back to the late nineteenth century, when colleges and universities began adopting symbols to foster school spirit and unity among students. Initially, the concept of a mascot was not formally recognized within the realm of sports; rather, it was a broader cultural phenomenon. The earliest mascots were children or animals, and both were associated with good luck. By the 1890s, mascots had become deeply embedded in the identity of colleges and universities across the United States. One of the earliest recorded mascots in college sports was Handsome Dan, a bulldog from Yale University who debuted in the 1890s. Many early university mascots were derived from local history or stereotypes, prominently featuring Indigenous imagery and other cultural references.[22]

At OSU, much of the social history of mascots parallels what was going on at other institutions in the late nineteenth century. In 1893, the first mascot for what was then Corvallis College was a live coyote named Jimmie. In 1909, the live coyote was replaced with Doc Bell, a Corvallis pastor and former regent of the college who wore a beaver-skin coat and led a pregame procession of students to a local river, where he would toss in his hat prior to a football game. In 1921, the human mascot was replaced by a seven-hundred-pound bronze statue of a beaver that was transported to games on a wooden cart and served as a focal point for school spirit throughout the 1920s.[23] In the 1930s, an injured young beaver was rescued from a nearby river and nursed back to health, becoming Bevo Beaver. Bevo was stolen as a prank and never seen again, and was succeeded in 1935 by another live beaver, Billy, who died within two years. Depictions of beavers in yearbooks and on cheerleading uniforms in the 1940s are based on Billy's image. The current mascot, Benny Beaver, got his start in the 1940s as a paper-mache replica of the bronze beaver statue from two decades prior. Benny was the first mascot on the West Coast to feature a performer inside a costume (fig. 1.9).[24]

Benny Beaver underwent several transformations in the following decades as costumes wore out and marketing strategies changed. Benny's most extreme changes happened in the early 1980s, when Benny gained weight, became more cartoonish, with a rounder physique and larger smile, and found a girlfriend (then wife), Bernice (fig. 1.10). Bernice wore a wedding dress to every homecoming game, while Benny donned a tuxedo. In this manner, through the domestication of the university's costumed mascots, the OSU students who were playing these characters tacitly endorsed not only traditional paternalistic values but also heterosexual norms and practices of finding a partner of the opposite sex and marrying them as a rite of passage on the road to maturity.[25]

Bernice disappeared for a time but has reemerged in the past few years as Benny's hip, glammed-up girlfriend who cuts in with the cheerleaders and dance team in choreographed routines where she is the feature. In this gendered role, Bernice can show emotions through her dances, shaking her hips, and doing most of the routines in a sexually provocative manner. Benny, on the other hand, has also metamorphosed; he has gone from a

FIGURE 1.9. *Benny Beaver, 1951.*

FIGURE 1.10. *Benny and Bernice, circa 1980s.*

happy beaver to a series of angry beaver designs. The super-macho Benny is a buff, athletic mascot who struts on the sidelines, frequently mocks the opposing mascot, and runs the chainsaw to celebrate big plays and touchdowns at football games. Unlike Bernice, Benny never moves his hips or dances on the field.

## TAIL FLAPPERS AND ROWDY BOYS

For men who wish to root for their team, there have long been alternatives to cheerleading. At OSU, men participated in the Tail Flappers, an all-male rooting section of upperclassmen established in the 1920s and celebrated for their prominent role in promoting school spirit. The group's mission, as explained in the 1958 annual, was "to promote spirit and good sportsmanship at athletic contests. The men all wore a similar uniform: white shirts with tails out, white cords, and orange and black rooter lids."[26] They led chants and school cheers from the stands (fig. 1.11; see fig. 1.7).

The Tail Flappers were an exclusive male club that received official college recognition for their support role in school spirit. But there was a darker side to their activities. As a variant and continuation of the "rah-rah boys" of the 1920s at other schools, who were often drunk and obnoxious during games,[27] the Tail Flappers were known to yell harassing and derogatory statements about the opposing team's masculinity, sexuality, and virility. This might also come in the form of taunting individual players by making fun of their last name, hairstyle, uniform, and walking or running style. These behaviors were designed to rile up the crowd and distract opposing teams and players.

The Tail Flappers established a sense of belonging and camaraderie among male fans. They united around a common cause governed by rituals and shared values.[28] In moments of triumph, the Tail Flappers shared a collective euphoria; in moments of loss, they consoled each other, reinforcing a sense of mutual care. The Tail Flappers provided a community for male fans and an outlet for toxic masculine behaviors impermissible for cheerleaders. The Tail Flappers had a sense of symbolic collective resistance and adopted an us-versus-them mentality, striving against rival teams and unfair officiating. They viewed themselves as actively contributing to the success of the OSU football and basketball teams and developed bonds that offered participants a sense of identity and purpose.

The Tail Flappers' newest incarnation is what we call "rowdy boys." These young men sit front and center in the student cheering section, paint themselves in the school colors of orange and black, don costumes, and

FIGURE 1.11. *The Tail Flappers, 1961.*

generally engage in boisterous, occasionally transgressive behavior. As an unofficial group, they have been free to engage in a performative version of hypermasculinity that distinguishes them from both feminine and masculine cheerleaders. While women may sit near the rowdy boys in the stands, their participation is generally limited, and the focus is on male fans and displays of masculinity. The rowdy boys are sometimes silly, sometimes obnoxious, but always entertaining.

The rowdy boys are not unique to OSU. On campuses across the United States, we can find evidence of men engaging in the same performative behaviors. At the University of Texas, for example, a group of men formed the Longhorn Hellraisers, who provide fervent support from the south end zone of the stadium.[29] At Louisiana State University and the University of Georgia, the Painted Posse and the Paint Line, respectively—men with bare chests painted to spell out the team's name—are a fixture of fandom in the stands.[30] More recently, a few women wearing sports bras or bikini tops have joined the men in body painting. The inclusion of women leads to greater noticeability and a degree of sexual titillation.

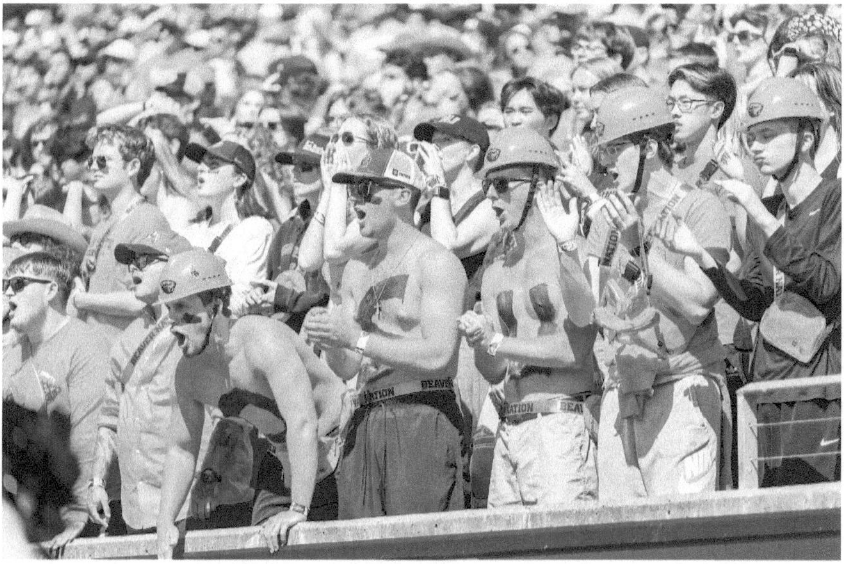

FIGURE 1.12. *Oregon State University rowdy boys, 2022. Photo by Maya Kirschenbaum. Used with permission from* The Daily Barometer, *the student newspaper of Oregon State University, 2022.*

At OSU, even on the coldest and rainiest game days, the rowdy boys take off their shirts, put on body paint, and use their bodies as a canvas to spell out the school's name in a demonstration of masculine bravado (fig. 1.12). Costumes allow other men to express themselves creatively and to step into alternative personas during games. We refer to these types of rowdy boys as "überfans." They organize themselves for each game, arriving early to claim their spot in the student section.[31] In addition to hyping up the crowd, a primary goal is to be noticed by film crews and photographers. Given their antics, it is not surprising that rowdy boys are frequently shown during television broadcasts of games and in photographs.

## Cheer and the Everyday Doing of Gender

As cheerleading and our understanding of gender roles changed and diversified, widely different images of cheerleaders proliferated in American culture. The first cheerleaders were privileged college men seen as magnetic and respected figures, part of the masculine world of competitive sport. These cheerleaders exemplified leadership and popularity. As female students joined the cheerleader ranks in the 1940s, the role of the cheerleader came to be viewed in feminized terms, as supportive and entertaining rather than reflecting heroic leadership.

In the more contemporary period, the mass media's emphasis on images such as erotically packaged professional cheerleaders tends to reinforce perceptions that cheerleading is a feminine realm where men should play little role. As a result of these historical processes, male cheerleaders at OSU and nationally have adapted in new ways, reentering cheerleading as supportive partners to their female squad members while still asserting their sense of masculinity.

In addition to occupying the formal role of cheerleaders, men have created alternative ways to cheer on the team while still adhering to the basic rules of masculinity. In an earlier period, they came as Tail Flappers and mascots. At OSU, the original mascots were male. In the 1980s, the addition of a female mascot highlighted gender differences in sports and cheering and the heterosexuality of the participants.

All-male cheering sections like the Tail Flappers morphed into rowdy boys and überfans. The rowdy boys and the überfans can be seen as a manifestation of men returning to cheerleading in a reimagined masculine role. These roles are adjacent to cheerleaders; they are not trying to replace the cheerleaders or the dance team, but, rather, they are helping to boost enthusiasm and inspire other student fans. For these men, the wild behavior, partial nudity, costumes, and body paint become a performance of hypermasculinity that is designed to spotlight the audience and their important role in helping to win the game.

Gender permeates social relationships and institutions. An examination of men's roles in cheerleading and its historical transformations illustrates how gender difference is created and reproduced and how it is subject to change throughout society. Our analysis using school yearbook photos has provided a window into those changes and the meanings that everyday participants ascribe to gender, and how they make sense of historical changes.

## Notes

1. John Watterson, *College Football: History, Spectacle, Controversy* (Johns Hopkins University Press, 1990); Eric A. Moyen and John R. Thelin, *College Sports: A History* (Johns Hopkins University Press, 2024).

2. Natalie G. Adams and Pamela J. Bettis, "Commanding the Room in Short Skirts: Cheering as the Embodiment of Ideal Girlhood," *Gender and Society* 17, no. 1 (2003): 73–91; Natalie G. Adams and Pamela J. Bettis, *Cheerleader! An American Icon* (Palgrave Macmillan, 2003); Mary Ellen Hanson, *Go! Fight! Win! Cheerleading in American Culture* (Bowling Green State University Popular Press, 1995); Gary Fine and Bruce Johnson, "The Promiscuous Cheerleader: An Adolescent Male Belief Legend," in *Manufacturing Tales: Sex and Money in Contemporary Legends*, ed. Gary Fine (University of Tennessee Press, 1992), 179–194; George Kurman, "What Does Girls' Cheerleading Communicate?," *Journal of Popular Culture* 20, no. 2 (1986): 57–64; John Hawkins, *Texas Cheerleaders: The Spirit of America* (St. Martin's Press, 1991); Nancy Lesko, "'We're Leading America': The Changing Organization and Form of High School Cheerleading," *Theory and Research in Social Education* 16, no. 4 (1988): 263–278.

3. Benjamin Forgard, "Benny's Family Tree," *The Messenger* 27, no. 1 (2012).

4. *Oregon Agricultural College Student Handbook* (Associated Students of Oregon Agricultural College, 1927), 40.

5. Forgard, "Benny's Family Tree."

6. *The Orange* (Oregon Agricultural College, 1916), 204.

7. *The Orange* (Oregon Agricultural College, 1912), 166.

8. *The Beaver* (Oregon Agricultural College, 1923), 246.

9. *The Beaver* (Oregon Agricultural College, 1929), 244.

10. *The Beaver* (Oregon Agricultural College, 1925), 246.

11. Hanson, *Go! Fight! Win!*, 17.

12. Adams and Bettis, *Cheerleader!*; Hanson, *Go! Fight! Win!*

13. Hanson, *Go! Fight! Win!*, 17.

14. Adams and Bettis, *Cheerleader!*, 14.

15. Adams and Bettis, *Cheerleader!*, 13.

16. "High School Cheerleaders: Agile Trio at Whiting, Ind. Specialize in Rhythmnastics," *Life*, November 10, 1941, 58.

17. *The Beaver* (Oregon State College, 1944), 69.

18. Hanson, *Go! Fight! Win!*

19. Laurel Davis, "Male Cheerleaders and the Naturalization of Gender," in *Sport, Men, and the Gender Order*, ed. Michael Messner and Donald Sabo (Human Kinetics, 1990).

20. Laura Grindstaff and Emily West, "Hegemonic Masculinity on the Sidelines of Sport," *Sociology Compass* 5, no. 10 (2011): 559–581.

21. W. H. Cowley, "Explaining the Rah Rah Boy," *New Republic* 46 (1926): 242–245.

22. Jeff Vrabel, "History of Mascots: Lions and Tigers and Bears (and Zips and Banana Slugs and Purple Cows)—Oh, My!," *NCAA Champion*, August 8, 2017; Moyen and Thelin, *College Sports*, 55–56; Laurel Davis, "The Problems with Native American Mascots," *Multicultural Education* 9, no. 4 (2002): 11–14; S. P. Morris, "The Trouble with Mascots," *Journal of the Philosophy of Sport* 42, no. 2 (2015): 287–297, https://doi.org/10.1080/00948705.2014.997740.

23. Forgard, "Benny's Family Tree," 21.

24. Forgard, "Benny's Family Tree," 21.

25. Gary Gennar DeSantis, "Collegiate Symbols and Mascots of the American Landscape: Identity, Iconography, and Marketing" (PhD diss., Florida State University, 2018).

26. *The Beaver* (Oregon State College, 1959), 289.

27. Hanson, *Go! Fight! Win!*, 13.

28. *The Beaver* (Oregon State University, 1961), 95.

29. "About Us," Longhorn Hellraisers, April 21, 2009, https://www.tumblr.com/longhornhellraisers/98484307/about-us.

30. Ethan Stenger, "Who Are the LSU Fans That Paint Their Chests? Meet the Painted Posse," *Reveille*, February 10, 2025, https://lsureveille.com/247263/sports/how-did-lsus-painted-posse-begin/; Olive Deffes, "The LSU Painted Posse Has Been Bringing the Spirit to Tiger Stadium for More than 50 Years," *225*, August 1, 2025, https://www.225batonrouge.com/our-city/lsus-painted-posse-has-been-bringing-the-spirt-to-tiger-stadium-for-more-than-20-years; Tori Mcelhaney, "How 'Terrible Idea' Turned into Georgia Tradition," *DawgNation*, November 17, 2017, https://www.dawgnation.com/football/georgia-football-uga-paint-line/.

31. *The Oregonian*, May 31, 2023, https://www.oregonlive.com/beavers/2023/05.

CHAPTER 2

# Sidelined No More

## CHEERLEADING, EMBODIED ACTIVISM, AND THE POLITICS OF RACIAL BELONGING

*Amira Rose Davis and Paulina A. Serrano*

*¡Somos fieles a ti, Bowie High!*
*¡Somos fieles a ti, Bowie High!*
*¡Lucharemos por ti, si es preciso hasta el fin!*
*¡Somos fieles a ti, Bowie High!*
*¡Eres número uno, Bowie High!*
*¡Eres número uno, Bowie High!*
*A los Osos no hay quien los pueda negar.*
*¡Somos fieles a ti, Bowie High!*

"La canción de la Bowie," Bowie High School fight song

In April 1969, a group of Black students gathered in front of West Senior High School in Rockford, Illinois, carrying signs that proclaimed, "Black Cheerleaders to Cheer Too." Among a swelling crowd of nearly two hundred protesters, Black cheerleaders argued that segregation was alive and well on the sidelines of West High. It was a complaint that echoed across the nation as Black students, from Illinois to Georgia, from North Carolina to Minnesota, walked out in protest of segregated cheer squads. And they weren't the only ones. In December of that same year, Mexican students also walked out of school in Crystal City, Texas. They carried signs that said, "Brown Legs Are Beautiful Too, WE DEMAND CHICANA CHEERLEADERS."[1]

In addition to the demands *for* Black and Brown cheerleaders, students also used their status *as* cheerleaders to engage in various forms of protest. From the 1950s to the mid-1970s, Black and Chicana girls, along with their families and communities, fought for the integration of cheerleading squads in schools across the country. The sideline became a key, yet oft-overlooked, space from which battles over racial integration, contested citizenship, gender norms, and institutional belonging were waged.

By 1969, the American public was well aware of activist athletes. Olympic medal stand protests, press conferences, boycotts, and petitions helped shape a public image of an "athletic revolt" centered on Black male athletes.[2] These iconic images of the activist athlete of the late 1960s have come to dominate our historical imagination. In recent years, scholars have located other examples of activist athletes, including women, by considering different temporalities and geographies to chart a longer, more expansive genealogy of athletic activism.[3] But the football field and the basketball court have dominated discussions of activist athletes. By simply turning our gaze from the field to the sidelines, new narratives, possibilities, and histories come into view.

Centering the experience of both Black and Chicana cheerleaders allows for a comparative analysis that illuminates intersections and divergent points in their shared history of cheer. Their parallel protests for cheerleaders is but one part of this story. The juxtaposition also reveals the nuances of racial segregation—the limits of integration and the different meanings placed on cheerleading as both groups turned to the sidelines to assert a sense of belonging.

Drawing upon a historical examination of Black and Chicana cheerleaders, this chapter tracks the way joy, resistance, and politics collided on the sidelines during a moment fraught with social and cultural change. From Rockford to Crystal City, cheerleading functioned as a layered site of play, recreation, performance, and competition. Cheer provided cultural capital for students in ever-changing educational and social spaces. Like football teams, cheerleading squads became a site for the struggle over representational power and social change. This chapter expands our view of the sporting landscape by demonstrating the integral role that battles over cheer squads played in formal and informal expressions of protest and politics. Indeed, considering the activism both on behalf of cheerleaders and by the cheerleaders themselves reveals new ways of thinking about the racial and gendered contours of the sport, the possibilities of embodied activism, and the contested and multiple meanings of cheer.

**Cheer Across the Color Line**

Cheerleading in postwar America was a key component of the developing image of the nation, and the image was undeniably white. On the sidelines of football fields and in gyms across the country, the hyperfeminine, all-American girl smiled and cheered for the sporting heroes who embodied the strength and vigor of the country.[4] The athletes on the field projected the might and power befitting an emerging superpower. And the cheerleaders were the feminine ideal that supported it. Television and print media amplified and circulated these images as a key feature of a national culture in formation. State-sanctioned segregation meant that schools and sporting spaces were largely racial monoliths. But cheerleading existed on both sides of the color line. While a hegemonic image of cheerleading was developing nationally, Black and Mexican girls also flocked to the sidelines to articulate their own meanings of cheer.

For Black and Chicana cheerleaders, the sport functioned both as an athletic opportunity and as a conferral of social status. As for their white counterparts, cheerleading was a pathway to popularity and acceptance in high school. "Being a cheerleader was really important to me," recalls Margo Jefferson, author of the award-winning memoir *Negroland*. "If you [were] a cheerleader . . . you're almost designated like really cute . . . really pretty and really successful."[5]

The pages of Black newspapers and yearbooks confirm Jefferson's recollections. Headlines heralding the "beauties of the game" or profiling the featured coed of the month frequently mentioned that the honoree was a cheerleader.[6] These features painted a portrait of respectability—a young woman whose social mobility was going to "bring the race along rapidly."[7] The respectability of cheerleading intersected with prevailing ideas about race pride and mobility, where social activities, hair, style, mannerisms, and especially skin tone were valued by Black institutions as a strategic method of combating white supremacy.

"When I got to high school I realized there was this color caste system," recalls Aurie Pennick, who attended a Black high school in 1961. "I tried out for cheerleading . . . but they were all fair-skinned. You couldn't be my color and cheer. . . . I could be a majorette, but I clearly couldn't be a cheerleader."[8] "You had to have the right hue of skin," Reverend Constance Jackson similarly recalls about her high school.[9]

Cheerleaders in Black high schools may have carried a similar social status as their white counterparts, but the cheer itself looked very different. Stylistically, Black cheerleading had its own aesthetic. "Our cheerleading had a lot of hip action," recalls one former cheerleader.[10] Black cheerleading emphasized rhythmic movements, stomping, clapping, and "soul-swinging."[11] Cheer squads, along with majorettes and drumlines, were key features of Black sporting traditions. Black squads used creative cheers that integrated popular Black music and call-and-response.[12] "Let's take our hats off to the girls in the short skirts, satin and gold braid," wrote one Black sportswriter. "The game just can't be played without the pretty cheer leaders and the cuties who twirl batons and strut in front of the band."[13]

In predominantly Mexican schools, girls enjoyed a similar social boost from cheer. Like Black newspapers, Spanish-language newspapers and borderland periodicals such as the *El Paso Times* frequently spotlighted high-achieving, reputable girls from the community; overwhelmingly, these selections were quickly noted to be cheerleaders. Bowie High School, located in El Paso, Texas, near the border with Mexico, said that their cheerleaders "exemplified the never-say-die-spirt of the school."[14] The yearbook, local newspapers, ROTC sweetheart announcements, and homecoming court selections similarly underscore the social importance of cheerleaders in Mexican communities.[15]

Unlike cheerleaders at Black high schools, Mexican girls on cheer squads generally did not develop different cheer aesthetics or styles. Indeed, cheerleading was a way to assert citizenship and belonging under the performance of quintessential American iconography. The limits of this were clear when the predominantly Mexican high schools competed against white high schools. The social status gained from being a cheerleader did not insulate Mexican girls from being discriminated against and harassed by their white counterparts, who did not see them as equal. One Bowie High cheerleader recalls cheering in towns that hung signs that said, "No Mexicans or Dogs Allowed." Another cheerleader who went to Bowie in the 1950s recalls having ice and water thrown on them.[16]

The ability of predominantly Mexican high schools to play against white schools also highlights the nuances of school segregation. In border states like Texas, Mexicans' legal status was "other white."[17] This not-quite-white designation created porous color lines where Mexican Americans were able to legally access white schooling spaces, but it also required an appeal to and performance of whiteness as political and social strategy. Assimilating to the hegemonic high school culture—through cheerleading, for example—was one manifestation of this social strategy. Yet as Mexican students found themselves integrating into Anglo schools, the otherness of their fragile legal whiteness was clear. Consider the case of Olga Castillo, the first Mexican cheerleader at Roy Miller High School in Corpus Christi, Texas.

Olga Castillo and her family moved to Corpus Christi from Sinton, Texas, in 1940, when she was eight years old. Sinton was a predominantly Mexican town where Olga had attended a Mexican school and received instruction in both English and Spanish. Corpus Christi, on the other hand, was a melting pot for Mexican, Black, and white families. The Castillo family moved to the Navarro housing projects, a multiethnic, working-class unit located across the street from military housing. "We were a tri-ethnic group playing together during the summer, but when school started all my white friends were there and we were there, but the Black kids weren't there," Olga recalls.[18]

In the Navarro housing projects, Olga and her brother benefited from the various recreational opportunities sponsored by the city parks department. Olga was a skilled athlete and even earned money playing baseball with the Navarro Tigers to supplement her family's income.[19] But few athletic opportunities were offered for girls at her high school, so Olga migrated to cheerleading.

At Roy Miller High School, Olga and other Mexican students experienced their own de facto color line. Mexican Texans may have been considered white in the eyes of the law, but socially they encountered rampant discrimination. Although the school was integrated, Mexican students were barred from certain extracurricular spaces. By senior year, Olga challenged these unwritten rules and put her name in the running for the all-white cheerleading squad. Her selection to the squad was met with immediate resistance. After her principal, Charles Gregg, announced her position, members of the squad protested her selection. "They brought in their lawyers," Olga recalls. Ultimately, Gregg refused to concede to their protest, and Olga Castillo remained on the team.[20] Her teammates, however, challenged her place on the team on various occasions. During her tenure as a cheerleader on the Roy Miller squad, Castillo endured continuous aggression from her teammates, who protested her selection, limited her presence in the school yearbook, and excluded her from public appearances.[21]

On a trip to Brackenridge High School in San Antonio, the cheer squad stopped at a local hotel so the girls could change into their uniforms for the game. Castillo's teammates refused to let her into the room and forced her to change in a lobby closet. While Olga was changing clothes in the lobby, the team bus departed, leaving her behind and excluding her from appearing with the team. Later, the team chaperone confronted Olga and asked why she had stayed behind with her boyfriend, a lie her teammates had made up. While it may be easy to dismiss this lie as merely a petty high school prank, the accusation played into tropes of hypersexual Mexican women that dated back to the early years of the film industry and carried strong racist undertones.[22] Mexicanas and Latinas, more broadly, were overrepresented as prostitutes and spitfires in films and other media. The insinuation that Olga had abandoned the team to have sex with her boyfriend recycled a familiar racist trope to further ostracize her from the team by contrasting her against the idea of the pure, virginal, and respectable image of white cheerleaders.

Olga's experience at Roy Miller underscores the social importance placed on athletics and cheerleading. Although the school was open to Mexican students, the image of the school, as popularized by its social identity, was tightly drawn around whiteness. What was so threatening about a Mexican cheerleader? As the historian Frank Andre Guridy demonstrates, the mid-century emergence of the white football hero with a white beauty queen or cheerleader on his arm symbolized an idealized notion of white masculinity and femininity.[23] Olga's presence on the sidelines challenged that ideal. As Black girls began to gain access to white schools in the coming years, they would experience similar internal color lines. Schools were integrating, but the squads remained segregated.

Thirteen hundred miles north of Corpus Christi and well outside of the Jim Crow South, some Black girls were also able to break the color line in cheer. In 1950, Harriet Bowman started her junior year of high school with a plan. Her older brother, Earl, had just graduated. His athletic success in baseball and football was still celebrated in the halls of Minneapolis Central High School, but this was the year she would emerge from his shadow and leave her own legacy. With similar athletic ability but far fewer options, Harriet decided that there was one clear path to matching her brother's accolades: She had to become a cheerleader. There was just one problem. Central High School had never had a Black cheerleader before. There were no integrated cheer squads in all of Minnesota.[24] Harriet set out to change that.

Minnesota was segregated, but some Black families were able to slip through the cracks of the color line. While the city of Minneapolis had racially restricted covenants and maintained segregated schools, Black homeowners could safely exist in some parts of the city. The Bowmans were part of a handful of Black kids who attended Central High. Harriet's friend Gwen Morrow attended a different white school in the northern part of the city. Together the girls decided to try out for their respective cheerleading squads. They both made it and broke the cheerleading color line together.

In Minnesota, Harriet and Gwen navigated de facto segregation. Their ability to integrate local schools and their cheerleader squads reminds us that the color line in the North could be a bit more porous than the violently and legally maintained one in the Jim Crow South. Like Olga, however, they were not challenging the aesthetics or style of the cheer squads they were integrating. Their cheer belonging was rooted in assimilation and access.

Olga, Harriet, and Gwen may have navigated different sides and complexities of the color line, but placing their experiences together allows us to see the way cheerleading, its social space and symbolic function, was used to maintain hegemonic femininity and particular cultural aesthetic norms. For Black and Chicana girls, cheerleading was a way to assert social belonging, experience athleticism and concomitant opportunities, and lay claim to dominant notions of femininity and Americanness so often denied to both groups. The fight to integrate cheer squads demonstrates the social significance of the sideline among changing institutions in the shadow of desegregation.

Harriet, Gwen, and Olga were high school girls who wanted to cheer. Their fights to integrate cheer squads were not necessarily grounded in a larger project of political activism. As school desegregation fumbled and bumbled along, Black and Chicana girls used cheerleading to assert their place in an ever-changing racial landscape. Access to cheerleading became a way to claim belonging not just to their respective schools but to their own version of postwar femininity and rah-rah Americana. It was also about their personal quest for enjoyment. As the country moved deeper into the 1960s, protests for Black and Brown cheerleaders would also become protests *by* Black and Brown cheerleaders.

## "They Don't Want Our Girls to Cheer for Them": Visible Limits of Integration

As news about the pivotal 1954 *Brown v. Board of Education* Supreme Court decision rippled across America, many people wondered about the breadth and reach of its implications. For *Chicago Defender* columnist Enoch Waters, the "ramifications were vast," but he found himself wondering what would become of Black schools, especially ones that boasted names of cultural heroes like Booker T. Washington and Frederick Douglass. Would integration be a one-way street? Waters asked, "How enthusiastic could white cheerleaders be chanting such 'siss boom ba, Booker T., Booker T.'[?]"[25]

Waters's concern about the direction of integration and its impact on formerly segregated schools and their students, including cheerleaders, was profound, considering how school desegregation was implemented in the fifteen years after *Brown*. In 1954, the Supreme Court had declared in a unanimous decision that racial segregation was unconstitutional in public schools and had created a legal foundation for desegregation efforts across the country. The process and enforcement of desegregation, however, was largely left to local school districts and controlled by all-white school boards and civic leaders. As a result, desegregation was a "one-way street," where Black schools, teachers, and administrators bore the cost of integration. Many Black high schools closed or were converted to elementary or junior high schools, and Black students sent to the previously all-white high schools were expected to assimilate into their rituals, practices, and traditions.[26]

When juxtaposing post-*Brown* agitations for Black and Brown cheerleaders on previously all-white squads, the convergences and divergences are clear. While Black and Brown parents both targeted cheer as an important social site, their tactics, goals, and experiences were different. In both cases, cheer, homecoming court, student council, and access to other extracurricular activities became fights that defined the fabric and identity of the school. While many of these extracurricular sites were important, cheer became the most visible site of this conflict. Cheerleaders were visible representations of the school; they were at events that encompassed the entire community, and they were a key part of sporting landscapes that dominated cultural interest.

As school integration began, Black teachers, administrators, band directors, cheer coaches, and other school personnel faced rampant job loss as Black schools were reduced, closed, and gutted.[27] Black schools had boasted their own athletic culture and traditions. Black high school and college sporting events were community affairs. These "sporting congregations" featured athletes, fans, cheerleaders, dance squads, beauty queens, drumlines, school administrators, and reporters, and they connected the local community to the institution.[28] Waters's concern about white cheerleaders at Black-named schools would soon be irrelevant, for it was Black students who found themselves moved and shuttled to the formerly all-white schools.

The integration of schools created a new push for inclusion on previously segregated cheerleading squads and dance teams. Black high school students, athletes and nonathletes, parents, and community members advocated for Black cheerleaders in schools across the country. For Black folks, protests about Black cheerleaders went hand in hand with criticisms about the cost of integration, the continued dearth of Black professionals in the schools, and the ongoing exclusion of Black students in a variety of extracurricular activities.

During the 1950s and early 1960s, high school students and their parents relied on a variety of protest tactics to "take a strong stand to secure a Negro cheerleader," including appealing to local school boards and undertaking direct-action protest.[29] In Pennsylvania, Black families from multiple townships utilized support from local NAACP chapters to threaten legal action against schools that failed to integrate cheer squads. Eighty juniors at Rankin High School in Georgia staged a walkout, followed by a two-day strike, to protest homework requirements and to "inform school officials that they resented the fact that [the] school did not have any Negro Cheerleaders or Majorettes."[30]

The clear valuing of Black male athletic labor on the football fields and basketball courts and the devaluing of Blacks girls on the sidelines also underscored the extraction occurring in the wake of integration. As one student from Gastonia, North Carolina, noted during a student walkout, "They want our boys to play on their teams and win the games for them but they don't want our girls to cheer for them."[31] While white schools that were invested in fielding competitive athletic teams began recruiting Black athletes to their schools, they had no such desire to include Black cheerleaders. "All this turmoil started when they tried to mix up the cheer squad," one white parent in Cairo, Illinois, lamented.[32] White-only cheerleading squads remained the norm even after football and basketball teams became integrated. "We had Blacks on the football team, basketball team, we ran track," recalls a former student from Winona, Texas, "but we never had any . . . Black girls . . . as cheerleaders."[33]

Mexican students and parents also advocated for integrated cheer squads, yet the political strategies in the wake of *Brown* varied for Black and Mexican communities. Despite the 1947 decision in *Mendez v. West-*

*minster*, a legal precursor to *Brown* that shared similar concerns about school segregation, many Mexican American political leaders sought to distance themselves from formal desegregation efforts based on racial discrimination.[34] Instead, Mexican parents and political leaders charged schools with discrimination based on national origin and language.

The Mexican American strategy of claiming legal whiteness meant that solidarity with Black Americans troubled that claim to white racial identity. In other words, if *Brown* applied to them and they filed a racial discrimination suit, it was an admission that Mexicans were not white and a threat to the dominant approach to Mexican civil rights up until that point. Black Americans wanted to dismantle the entire system of Jim Crow schools, while Mexican American political leaders wanted to change their positionality within the system. When the Texas Legislature passed House Bill 231 to oppose *Brown*'s reach, the NAACP sought allies in the League of United Latin American Citizens, the leading Mexican American political organization. The response from LULAC leadership was to "let the Negro fight his own battle," with the president of LULAC insisting, "We are white and we will become Americans."[35]

For Mexican communities, similar concerns over representation in extracurriculars existed. As schools became more mixed, the overrepresentation of white students in high-status positions was of particular concern. One study of California schools in the 1960s found that in predominantly white schools with Mexican students, the number of Mexican students in cheerleading, student council, and homecoming court was proportional or slightly under their student-body percentage. But when white students made up only 20 percent of predominantly Mexican schools, they were heavily overrepresented on cheer squads.[36]

When Mexican families called for their daughters to be cheerleaders, they galvanized the community by noting that the schools were effectively deeming their girls not white enough or not beautiful enough to be the face of the school. It was about gaining recognition as part of the all-American white feminine ideal, whereas Black parents' insistence on the inclusion of Black cheerleaders was a strategy to critique integration itself. Calls for Black cheerleaders were equally about not having to assimilate to a one-sided integration that devalued their Black aesthetic and cultural expression as much as about the persistence of de facto segregation in the newly integrated schools. Yet for students themselves, a growing consciousness and activism was brewing, and some Chicana cheerleaders would soon embrace civil rights discourse and protest tactics to gain access to the sport.

## Embodied Activism on the Sidelines

Earlier protests for Black and Brown cheerleaders had taken a variety of approaches, including legal challenges and petitions, but by the mid-1960s, students were sitting in and walking out. Energized by the civil rights movement, students embraced grassroots organizing and local protests to try to remove the stench of Jim Crow from their schools in the 1960s. Segregated cheer squads were a galvanizing issue as cheerleaders and their peers raised their voices to chant for change.

In 1956, Dr. John Brown Sr. joined with a few other Black parents to file a lawsuit against the school board in Miami-Dade County to ensure their compliance with the *Brown* decision. His daughter, Gala, had been one of the first Black students to attend Glade View Elementary School and later Miami Edison Junior High School. Gala Brown had felt "disliked and different" during those early years of desegregation.[37] She had felt outcast from the entire school, from the students and teachers to the social activities. Her experience at Miami Edison High School began the same way. But then in 1966, ten years after her dad's initial lawsuit, Miami-Dade County voted to formally desegregate the school district. In Gala's sophomore year, the number of Black students enrolled at Miami Edison rose from three hundred to five hundred. The new influx of students now made Edison High nearly 25 percent Black. Yet the internal de facto segregation remained.

In 1968 Gala Brown decided to try out for the cheerleading team. Despite the increase in Black students at Edison High, the cheer squad had yet to include a Black cheerleader. Now a senior at Edison, Gala tried out but was not selected. The squad would remain all-white. After speaking with her parents, Gala decided to organize a protest in response. Audrey Edmonson, a freshman at the time, recalls hearing about the planned sit-in. "We went over to her home that night, and the word was, 'Don't come unless you bring your parents with you,'" Edmonson recalls, "and, I was afraid but I knew I wanted to go to this meeting."[38] After explaining to her mother that the school had not included any Black girls on the cheerleading squad, Edmonson was granted permission to participate. And she was not the only one.

The following day, sixty students sat down in the hallway to block the door to the main office. Gala's father, a practitioner of nonviolent protest tactics, had advised the students to sit peacefully. "He told us, no matter what, just sit there, don't open our mouths, and do not use any profane language, don't talk back, just sit there. And, that's what we did," recalls Edmonson. As the protest continued throughout the day, the number of protesters grew, with more Black students joining the sit-in. "I think word got around and if you were Black you came and you sat," recalls Edmonson. Soon the news cameras were also on-site documenting the disturbance at Edison High. While the protest took the school by surprise, Enid Pinkney, one of the few Black staff members at the school, explains why the issue was so galvanizing: "It frustrated a lot of the students because they felt that if Gala Brown whose parents are leaders in the community, her father was active in CORE [the Congress of Racial Equality] and well educated. You know if, if a person like Gala can't become a cheerleader, what hope is there for us?"[39]

The sit-in successfully resulted in the integration of the cheer squad in the spring, when Gala's best friend, Diane Dyes, became the school's first Black cheerleader.[40] It also showed that cheerleading discrimination could be a rousing event for the broader community. The disbelief that Pinkney notes in Gala Brown's case was indicative of the logic and allure cheerleading held. Cheer, as a respectable ideal that had long marked the best and brightest girls of the race, was now directly running into the limits of desegregated schooling. Black cheerleaders were still not respectable enough for the white schools in which they found themselves. In this vein, protesting around cheerleading was also a way to assert the value of Black girls, to critique the omnidirectional approach to integration, and to demonstrate the work still to be done in ensuring equitable educational environments.

And it wasn't just in Miami. Across the country, Black students continually targeted the integration of cheer squads as a priority and reason to protest. Over two hundred Black students walked out of Argo Community High School outside of Chicago after demanding that half of the cheerleaders on the team be Black. In nearby Madison, Wisconsin, seventeen Black football players were kicked off their high school team for skipping practice in protest of the lack of Black cheerleaders. In response to their dismissal, nearly 1,300 Black students boycotted public schools for a week until the school board voted to reinstate the players and mandated that half of the cheerleaders had to be Black the following season. As one protesting cheerleader, Priscilla Lindy, stated, "We're black, we're proud and we are out here to get our demands."[41] Although cheerleading is often overlooked as a contentious site in the struggle for civil rights, direct-action protests about cheerleading and protests by cheerleaders themselves were a constant feature of school-based activism. They also served to galvanize the larger community.

Much like the walkouts by Black high school students, Chicana and Chicano students waged their own protests throughout the South and Southwest. One such place was Crystal City, Texas, in 1968. Influenced in part by the thousands of Mexican American students protesting in East Los Angeles, students in Crystal City began their own form of organizing.[42] The Mexican American Youth Organization (MAYO) had established an agenda known as the Winter Garden Project, with the goal of pursuing changes in education across Texas to destabilize Anglo political control. Yet the event that made the powder keg explode was the announcement of the all-white cheerleading squad at Crystal City High School.

Crystal City High School reflected the long-established discriminatory practices of the all-white leadership of the city. Located in the southern part of Texas, about a two-hour drive from San Antonio, Crystal City was a leading center for agribusiness during the first half of the twentieth century. The majority of those living in Crystal City were Mexican or Mexican American, yet the city leadership was still decidedly white. At the high school, officials implemented policies and practices limiting the participation of Mexican American students in extracurricular activities ranging from selection for class superlatives (e.g., Most Beautiful or Most Representative) to band majors, twirlers, and cheerleaders.[43]

Chicanas at Crystal City High had limited opportunities to participate in athletics, as the school offered only two activities for female students: cheerleading and volleyball.[44] As an active high schooler, Diana Palacios participated in both activities. Cheerleading had been a part of her life growing up as a young Mexican American girl in Texas. As early as junior high, Palacios remembers trying out for cheerleading and wanting to hold the coveted spot in high school.[45] As late as 1969, Crystal City High did not allow more than one Mexican American cheerleader on the four-person squad. Anglo girls comprised the remaining three spots. For Palacios and other Chicanas, an informal but well-understood code of exclusion kept them from representing their high school.[46] Among these unwritten rules, it was understood that "the cheerleading squad was made up of three Anglos and one Chicana and that is just the way it always was. The students would try out in front of the whole student body, but the selection would be made by certain teachers."[47]

The selection process for the cheerleading squad and other student honors carried the long-standing racist logic that held Mexican Americans to second-class status in Texas. In this instance, administrators responsible for selecting the squad members considered other factors beyond the audition, such as a girl's previous training. These criteria disproportionately discriminated against Mexican girls because they did not have access to the cheerleading training camps and workshops that the Anglo girls attended.[48] These extra expenses were often too difficult for Mexican American families to afford, as they held low-wage jobs or depended on seasonal work in the fields, meaning that many families followed the crop cycle and therefore missed extracurricular activities like cheerleading camps. Some students even missed tryouts completely.[49]

Student unrest began after the cheerleading selection of 1968. Then freshmen Diana Palacios and Diana Perez tried out for the only spot allotted for Mexican American girls. Diana Palacios hesitated in trying out, as she knew only one cheerleader of Mexican ancestry would earn the spot. She recalls, "I never saw it written down anywhere, we just knew that's the way things were."[50] Perez was selected. The next year, in spring 1969, Palacios again tried out, even though she knew there were no more spots on the team for Mexican American girls. A friend of Palacios convinced her to try out, and "at the last minute I decided to go ahead and do it. . . . A friend of mine encouraged me. A lot of them told me, 'Run, run you never know.'"[51] Eventually she and her good friend Marta Peña tried out but failed to win a place on the squad. In response to Palacios's rejection from the team the previous year and then again in her sophomore year, students at Crystal City High School organized.

On April 29, 1969, a group of nine students led by Diana Palacios and Libby Lara met with superintendent John Billings and presented a list of seven demands, along with signatures from about 350 students:

1. No punishment for students who demonstrated for better education.
2. Teachers should stop taking political sides.
3. Twirlers should be elected by band members.
4. Students should elect most beautiful girl, most handsome boy, most representative boy and girl, and the cheerleaders.
5. The school should have bilingual and bicultural education.
6. The school parking lot should be paved.
7. They needed to buy new band uniforms.[52]

That evening, a large crowd of parents, students, and organizers confronted the school board about their demands. By then, the list had grown to seventeen demands, and in every iteration, the students emphasized the students' role in the selection process for the various honors, including cheerleaders and twirlers.[53] Fearing violence, Board President Ed Mayer adjourned the meeting early. Those in attendance gathered outside the administration building and listened to the students who addressed the crowd: "Now you know what we're going through at school, this is what they do to us, this is what they did to you. . . . We want to walk out."[54] Several months later, they did.

On the morning of December 9, 1969, two hundred students lined up in front of the school, recited a prayer, said the Pledge of Allegiance, and then marched, holding signs that read, "Chicanos Want to Be Heard," "Education and Discrimination Don't Mix," and "Brown Legs Are Beautiful Too, WE DEMAND CHICANA CHEERLEADERS."[55] By the afternoon, students from the neighboring Fly Junior High School joined their fellow students, increasing the total to approximately five hundred students.[56] Parents also joined, as Diana Palacios recounts: "I remember my mom and other moms . . . they would bring us hot chocolate, because we were serious about being there and taking a stand for what we were fighting for."[57] The Crystal City walkout continued until January 4, 1970, and ended after state and federal government representatives investigated the situation. MAYO's choice of tactic paid off when the regional office of the US Department of Health, Education, and Welfare and the Texas Education Agency (TEA) raised concerns over the number of children absent from school, which had reached approximately six hundred students each day. TEA officials worried about the financial implications of these absences. Students had finally achieved something their parents had failed to do. They had made a dent in the pockets of the Anglo majority.

Hailed as one of the most successful walkouts in Texas, the Crystal City action revealed the expansive nature of the broader Chicano/a movement. Sporting spaces became integral to the foundation of the intergenerational coalition built by MAYO leaders. Students rallied around the selection of cheerleaders, band majors, and twirlers because they saw them as sites from which to articulate the broader goals of the movement. These manifested in the multiple iterations of demands presented by the students, which began with seven points and grew to seventeen by the end of the walkout. For the cheer squad, it resulted in the expansion of the squad to six members, and one that better represented the student body (fig. 2.1).

FIGURE 2.1. *Crystal City High School cheer squad, 1971–1972. This was the school's first all-Chicana squad.* The Javelin *(Crystal City High School, 1971), 102. Personal collection of Martha P. Cotera.*

Similarly, protests in support of Black cheerleaders often morphed into larger demonstrations against white supremacy and racial injustice. In 1969, students protested at the newly integrated Walter Williams High School in Burlington, North Carolina, after a Black girl was refused a spot on the cheerleading team. The protest soon grew to include students at nearby Jordan Sellars High School and local colleges. Events escalated following a fight between white and Black students and the governor's subsequent declaration of a state of emergency. At the end of the second day of protests, stores were set on fire, the National Guard and local police had escalated the violence, and a fifteen-year-old Black boy, Leon Mebane, lay dead—unarmed and riddled with gunshots.[58] While the Burlington case is exceptional because of the resulting violence, it illustrates the way the protests about Black cheerleaders quickly mobilized communities.

Burlington and Crystal City show the movement-building possibilities of cheer. While some dismissed the sidelines as unimportant or merely trivial, student protests revealed cheerleading to be a key site of postintegration struggle for both Black and Chicana girls. Community members, parents, and lay students found meaning in what cheer discrimination signaled about their belonging and citizenship. For cheerleaders themselves, the protests were also about gaining access to the sport that brought them joy. "It may seem insignificant the thing about the cheerleaders," Diana Palacios recalls, "but it was important to us."[59]

## Cheerleading and the Politics of Racial Belonging

In the wake of student protests, changes came to the sidelines of Crystal City High School, where students now had the opportunity to express their Mexican American culture. In 1970, the cheerleaders and the drill team donned the nickname Las Adelitas, a direct reference to the women soldiers of the Mexican Revolution.[60] These changes aligned with the goals of the broader Chicano/a movement. The Javelin band also reclaimed the sidelines, when they added the Mexican song "Jalisco" as their second fight song and performed their halftime shows in English and Spanish. The sidelines presented a realized objective; or as the journalist Calvin Trillin noted, they had achieved their goal of "making a Chicano School."[61]

Three hours north, in Austin, a similar fight for the sidelines was brewing. As the designated Black high school in the city, Anderson High School was the pride of the Black community and supported by all. As one Anderson alumnus explains, "Anderson High was the thread that kept the community together."[62] Lula Collins, another alumnus, notes that "everyone in East Austin attended the same high school, cheered for the same teams and had the same traditions. Sporting events were a community gathering place."[63] As part of this tradition, the Anderson Yellow Jacket cheerleaders, much like Las Adelitas, were proud ambassadors for their school (fig. 2.2). Yet, in 1968, the Office for Civil Rights in the federal Department of

FIGURE 2.2. *Anderson High School Yellow Jacket cheerleaders, Austin, Texas, October 31, 1955. ND-55-1753-02A, Austin History Center, Austin Public Library. Photo used with permission.*

Health, Education, and Welfare found that many of Texas's school districts, including Austin, were not in compliance with desegregation mandates.

Anderson High was open to white students as part of the district's "freedom of choice" plan; however, for the 1969–1970 school year, only seventeen white students chose to enroll there. Therefore, in 1970, a federal judge redrew school zones in Austin to make the school district comply with desegregation orders. School attendance for the new school year would be based on these new zones. Anticipating an influx of white students, Anderson High readied their school. They repainted it and added new equipment. What might integration look like in this direction? Current students decided to allow incoming students to assume the offices and positions they had held at their previous schools. As one former board member explains, "In other words, if they had been cheerleaders at their sending institution, they would become cheerleaders at Anderson High."[64]

Despite these efforts to welcome white students, most white families zoned to attend Anderson refused to enroll their students in the school. After just four days, the judge shut down Anderson entirely and ordered Black students to be bused to various white high schools around Austin. This heartbreaking decision shocked Austin's Black community.[65] For Black students, they found their new schools much less welcoming.

Yellow Jacket cheerleaders quickly realized they would not be allowed to cheer at their new schools. "At O. Henry in order to be a cheerleader . . . and wear the little uniform with the back cut out, your hair had to be long enough to cover your back," recalls one former student, calling the rule "very discriminatory."[66] In addition to rules about hair, other criteria, such as the ability to pay out-of-pocket expenses, curtailed participation by incoming Black cheerleaders. At McCallum High School, where many Black students were bused, they were met with racial slurs, epithets, and discriminatory policies and practices. Ostensibly for the purpose of uniformity, the cheerleading squad mandated the use of ponytail wigs and three different uniforms. These required purchases presented an "extraordinary, unexpected expense" for transferring cheerleaders. They were also another reminder that integrating into a white cheer squad meant an abandonment of their Black aesthetic and cheer style. "It became painful for those kids to participate," remarks a former Austin school board member.[67]

The inverse trajectories of Las Adelitas and the Yellow Jackets reveal the desire for culturally affirming cheer spaces, as well as their precarity. Mexican cheerleaders had fought for integration and recognition, but the students at Crystal City High began to explore what an explicitly Chicana style of cheer might look like. Black cheerleaders like the Yellow Jackets had long developed a cheer aesthetic that conveyed a sense of racial belonging in the shadow of the color line. The short-lived integration of Anderson High might have been an opportunity to see what cheerleading looked like when white cheerleaders entered a predominantly Black cheer space. Instead, the closure of the school, and by extension the cheerleading team, along with the hostility faced by the displaced Yellow Jackets at their new schools, made it clear that Black student concerns about integration, cheerleading, and belonging continued to reverberate well into the 1970s.

## Conclusion

In these muddled realities in the decades following *Brown v. Board of Education*, Black and Chicana cheerleaders sought out the sidelines for their personal enjoyment and social mobility. In segregated schools, cheerleading conferred social status and made them leaders in their communities. Their fight to cheer symbolically represented their fight to claim femininity, Americanness, and visible belonging in schools across the country. In fighting for integrated squads in predominantly white schools, both Black and Brown communities rallied around cheerleaders who insisted on full integration. By examining Black and Chicana cheerleaders together, the shared importance of cheerleading emerges. Cheer mattered to both Black and Mexican communities in their quest for civil rights and equality in the mid-twentieth century. But the juxtaposition of their experiences and protests around cheerleading also illuminates key differences in how legal and de facto segregation worked and the varied approaches each group took toward navigating the ever-shifting color line.

While excavating this cheer history can show us the contours of integration, the fight for inclusion can also obscure the joy at the heart of Black and Chicana participation in cheerleading. Indeed, an overemphasis on integration as the goal can obscure the meanings and importance of Black and Brown cheer history. The glimpses of Black and Mexican cheerleaders, separate from integration fights or ideas of whiteness, remind us that their cheer style, aesthetics, and chants had their own meanings and their own history. Black and Mexican cheerleaders and their joys and desires matter even when not attached to political projects or even when dismissed as trivial.

Together, the cheerleaders at the heart of this project underscore how important the sport was for *them*. It mattered politically, yes, but it was also deeply personal. From Olga Castillo to Harriet Bowman. From Diana Palacios to Gala Brown. From Las Adelitas to the Yellow Jackets. Black and Mexican cheerleaders across the country deeply desired to cheer.

Black and Brown cheer history cautions against the dismissal of cheerleading as a point of inquiry by revealing it as an athletic site and an organizing space. But cheerleading should also not be dismissed because it was a space that Black and Mexican girls marked as meaningful because of their own desires. The history of Black and Brown cheerleaders, their love of cheerleading, their fights to integrate squads, and their use of the sideline as a strategy of belonging and a site of activism expands our understanding of Black and Brown girlhood, youth, athletic activism, and integration, and the ideas about cheerleading itself.

## Notes

1. "Mexican," "Mexican American," and "Chicano/a" are overlapping terms with distinct contexts and applications. In this chapter we use "Mexican" and "Mexican American" to refer to people of Mexican ancestry, as well as "Chicana" when speaking about historical actors who used that term to describe themselves in the midst of the Chicano/a movement of the 1960s, when the term was invoked to convey a political and social identity built around cultural pride and the celebration of Mexican heritage.

2. By the end of the 1960s, the press was covering public discussions about Black athletic boycotts. The Cleveland Summit of 1967 brought together prominent Black male athletes, including Muhammad Ali and Bill Russell, followed by a press conference in which they spoke out on race, politics, and the Vietnam War. A year later, the 1968 Olympics saw a number of athletic protests, including the Black Power salute by Tommie Smith and John Carlos on the medals stand that became world news and an iconic image. *Sports Illustrated* ran a three-part series in the summer of 1969, declaring it the year of "Negro athletic revolution." Much of this coverage centered on Black male athletes, who became the face of athletic activism, yet it also obscured the ways other athletes—particularly Black women and other women of color—also used sports to agitate for change.

3. Harry Edwards, *The Revolt of the Black Athlete*, 50th anniversary ed. (University of Illinois Press, 2017); Courtney M. Cox, "The Limits of Smooth Legacies: 1968, Feminist History, and the Tradition of Athlete Activism; An Interview with Amira Rose Davis," *International Journal of Communication* 16 (2022): 4701–4709; Amira Rose Davis, "No More Games: Understanding the Latest Wave of Athletic Activism," *American Historian*, September 2020, https://www.oah.org/tah/history-for-black-lives/no-more-games-understanding-the-latest-wave-of-athletic-activism/; Louis Moore, *We Will Win the Day: The Civil Rights Movement, the Black Athlete, and the Quest for Equality* (Bloomsbury, 2017).

4. Frank Andre Guridy, *The Sports Revolution: How Texas Changed the Culture of American Athletics* (University of Texas Press, 2021); Mary Ellen Hanson, *Go! Fight! Win! Cheerleading in American Culture* (Bowling Green State University Popular Press, 1995); Natalie G. Adams and Pamela J. Bettis, *Cheerleader! An American Icon* (Palgrave Macmillan, 2003).

5. Margo Jefferson (A2017.007), interview by Harriette Cole, January 20,

2017, tape 3, "Margo Jefferson Talks About Societal Beauty Standards," The HistoryMakers Digital Archive.

6. See, for example, "Baton Beauties," *Jet*, January 2, 1964; "Hats Off to Football's Beauties! Where Is the Game Without Them?," *Chicago Defender*, October 30, 1948; H. E. Skip Simmons, "Pageantry and Beauty Mark All Star Game," *Atlanta Daily World*, August 23, 1958; "M'house and 'Skegee to Invade Columbus for Annual Grid Tilt: Bands, Cheerleaders to Add Pageantry and Color to SIAC Battle," *Atlanta Daily World*, October 17, 1963; "Busy Cheerleaders Keep Up Spirit at Arkansas State," *Chicago Defender*, November 29, 1941.

7. Patrick B. Miller, "To 'Bring the Race Along Rapidly': Sport, Student Culture, and Educational Mission at Historically Black Colleges During the Interwar Years," *History of Education Quarterly* 35, no. 2 (1995): 111–133, https://doi.org/10.2307/369629.

8. Aurie Pennick (A2005.223), interview by Larry Crowe, September 29, 2005, tape 2, "Aurie Pennick Recalls Discrimination Based on Skin Color at Englewood High School," The HistoryMakers Digital Archive.

9. Reverend Constance Jackson (A2005.147), interview by Larry Crowe, June 23, 2005, tape 2, "Reverend Constance Jackson Describes High School Football in Texas," The HistoryMakers Digital Archive.

10. Karen Slade (A2014.213), interview by Larry Crowe, July 28, 2014, tape 1, "Karen Slade Recalls Her Extracurricular Activities," The HistoryMakers Digital Archive.

11. Chelsea Mary Elise Johnson, "'Just Because I Dance Like a Ho I'm Not a Ho': Cheerleading at the Intersection of Race, Class, and Gender," *Sociology of Sport Journal* 32, no. 4 (2015): 377–394.

12. Adams and Bettis, *Cheerleader!*, 97–99.

13. "Hats Off to Football's Beauties!," 13.

14. *The Aztec* (Bowie High School [El Paso, Texas], 1950).

15. For example, see "Cadets Pick Sweetheart at Bowie," *El Paso Times*, October 16, 1957; "Football Queen Named," *El Paso Times*, November 12, 1958.

16. R. Gaines Baty, *Champion of the Barrio: The Legacy of Coach Buryl Baty* (Texas A&M University Press, 2015).

17. Brian D. Behnken, *Fighting Their Own Battles: Mexican Americans, African Americans, and the Struggle for Civil Rights in Texas* (University of North Carolina Press, 2011).

18. Olga Gonzales, interview by Moisés Acuña-Gurrola and James Wall, July 12, 2016, Civil Rights in Black and Brown Oral History Project, Portal to Texas History, https://texashistory.unt.edu/ark:/67531/metapth987544/.

19. Paulina Serrano, "A Legacy of Tejana Athleticism: Community, Civil Rights, and Belonging, Since 1930," in *¡Somos Tejanas! Chicana Identity and Culture in Texas*, ed. Norma E. Cantú and Jody Marín (University of Texas Press, 2025), 257–277.

20. Olga Gonzales interview.

21. Olga Gonzales interview.

22. *Latinos Beyond Reel: Challenging a Media Stereotype*, directed by Miguel Picker and Chyng Sun (Media Education Foundation, 2013).

23. Guridy, *Sports Revolution*, 33.

24. Ken Foxworth, "Three Minneapolis Women Who Broke Cheerleading Color Barriers," *Minnesota Spokesman-Recorder*, March 24, 2019, https://spokesman-recorder.com/2019/03/23/three-minneapolis-women-who-broke-cheerleading-color-barriers/; *Polaris* (North High School [Minneapolis, MN], 1949), https://digitalcollections.hclib.org/digital/collection/Yearbooks/id/51745/rec/41; *Polaris* (North High School, 1950), 85, https://digitalcollections.hclib.org/digital/collection/Yearbooks/id/49973/rec/2.

25. Enoch Waters, "Adventures in Race Relations: Another Angle on the Decision," *Chicago Defender*, May 29, 1954.

26. Vincent D. Willis, *Audacious Agitation: The Uncompromising Commitment of Black Youth to Equal Education After Brown* (University of Georgia Press, 2021); Barbara J. Shircliffe, *The Best of That World: Historically Black High Schools and the Crisis of Desegregation in a Southern Metropolis* (Hampton Press, 2006), 1–17; Leslie T. Fenwick, *Jim Crow's Pink Slip: The Untold Story of Black Principal and Teacher Leadership* (Harvard Education Press, 2022).

27. Lani Guinier, "From Racial Liberalism to Racial Literacy: *Brown v. Board of Education* and the Interest-Divergence Dilemma," *Journal of American History* 91, no. 1 (2004): 92–118, https://doi.org/10.2307/3659616; Adam Fairclough, *A Class of Their Own: Black Teachers in the Segregated South* (Harvard University Press, 2009); Fenwick, *Jim Crow's Pink Slip*.

28. Derrick E. White, *Blood, Sweat, and Tears: Jake Gaither, Florida A&M, and the History of Black College Football* (University of North Carolina Press, 2019).

29. "German [Township] High to Have Cheerleader," *Pittsburgh Courier*, November 6, 1954.

30. Amira Rose Davis, "Black Cheerleaders and a Long History of Protest," *Black Perspectives*, African American Intellectual History Society, January 3, 2019, https://www.aaihs.org/black-cheerleaders-and-a-long-history-of-protest/.

31. "All-White Cheerleader Team Causes Walk Out," *New Journal and Guide*, May 10, 1969.

32. Testimony of Jack Greaney, Rye Eves, and Tom Madera, hearing before the US Commission on Civil Rights, Cairo, IL, March 23–25, 1972, https://www.usccr.gov/files/historical/1972/72-002-U.pdf.

33. S. L. Curry, interview by Florine White, June 26, 2001, Parallel and Crossover Lives: Texas Before and After Desegregation, Humanities Texas, https://www.humanitiestexas.org/sites/default/files/page-attachment/Curry_S_L_Interview_0.pdf.

34. Philippa Strum, *Mendez v. Westminster: School Desegregation and Mexican-American Rights* (University Press of Kansas, 2010).

35. Behnken, *Fighting Their Own Battles*, 64–71.

36. US Commission on Civil Rights, *The Unfinished Education: Outcomes for Minorities in the Five Southwestern States* (October 1971), 40–42.

37. Gala Brown Munnings, "Desegregation Pioneer Recalls School Integration in Miami," WLRN, April 29, 2013, https://www.wlrn.org/education/2013-04-29/desegregation-pioneer-recalls-school-integration-in-miami.

38. Audrey M. Edmonson (A2017.035), interview by Harriette Cole, March 10, 2017, tape 2, "Audrey M. Edmonson Recalls Staging a Sit-In to Integrate Her High School Cheerleading Team," The HistoryMakers Digital Archive.

39. Enid C. Pinkney (A2002.064), interview by Samuel Adams, April 16, 2002, tape 3, "Enid Pinkney Describes How Integration Impacted Her Teaching Career," The HistoryMakers Digital Archive.

40. "Civil Rights Activist and Educator Gala Munnings Dies After Brief Illness," *South Florida Times*, June 11, 2011, https://fisku72.com/memorial/BrownGalaArticle.pdf.

41. "No German High Cheer Leader This Year," *Pittsburgh Courier*, November 7, 1953; "German High to Have Cheerleader"; "Clairton School Board Criticized for Tactics Used to Bar Negro Majorettes," *Pittsburgh Courier*, September 24, 1960; "Reforms Promised, as School Strike Ends!," *Pittsburgh Courier*, October 18, 1958; "200 Negroes Walk Out at Argo School," *Chicago Tribune*, September 6, 1968; "Cheerleader Dispute Is Settled; School Boycott in Illinois to End," *New York Times*, November 20 1967.

42. Rodolfo F. Acuña, *Occupied America: A History of Chicanos*, 9th ed. (Pearson, 2019), 303.

43. "Students Air Grievances," *Zavala County Sentinel*, May 1, 1969.

44. *The Javelin* (Crystal City High School [Crystal City, TX], 1971).

45. Diana Palacios, interview by Sandra Enriquez, July 9, 2015, video, Civil Rights in Black and Brown Oral History Project, Portal to Texas History, https://texashistory.unt.edu/ark:/67531/metapth1040173/.

46. Carol Brochin, "The History I Never Learned in School: Diana Palacios Recounts Crystal City in 1969," *LareDOS* (Laredo, TX), October 2001, 34.

47. Gwen Zucker Mercado, Maria E. Cotera, and Karen Getchell, "Crystal City School Walkouts," typescript, personal papers of Martha P. Cotera.

48. John S. Shockley, "Crystal City: La Raza Unida and the Second Revolt," in *Chicano: The Evolution of a People*, ed. Renato Rosaldo, Robert A. Calvert, and Gustav L. Seligmann (Robert E. Krieger 1982), 292.

49. Diana Palacios interview; Miguel A. Guajardo and Francisco J. Guajardo, "The Impact of *Brown* on the Brown of South Texas: A Micropolitical Perspective on the Education of Mexican Americans in a South Texas Community," *American Educational Research Journal* 41, no. 3 (2004): 501–526.

50. Brochin, "History I Never Learned," 34.

51. Diana Palacios interview.

52. "Students Air Grievances," *Zavala County Times*, December 11, 1969, 1.

53. "School Walk Out Continues," 1.

54. Mercado, Cotera, and Getchell, "Crystal City School Walkouts."

55. "School Walk Out Continues," 1; Diana Palacios interview.

56. "School Walk Out Continues," 1.

57. Diana Palacios interview.

58. "It Was a Long Tragic Night for Burlington," *Daily Times-News*, May 17, 1969; "Black Youth Killed in Night of Violence," *Daily Times-News*, May 17, 1969. For more about Mebane's murder and the era's long history of violence, protest, and policing, see Walter C. Stern, "School Violence and the Carceral State in the 1970s: Desegregation and the New Educational Inequality in Louisiana," *Journal of Southern History* 89, no. 3 (2023): 483–534; Elizabeth Hinton, *America on Fire: The Untold History of Police Violence and Black Rebellion Since the 1960s* (Liveright, 2021). See also Pamela Grundy, *Learning to Win: Sports, Education, and Social Change in Twentieth-Century North Carolina* (University of North Carolina Press, 2001), 267.

59. Diana Palacios interview.

60. *The Javelin* (Crystal City High School, 1971), 102.

61. Calvin Trillin, "New Cheerleaders," *New Yorker*, April 9, 1971, 102.

62. Michael Corcoran, "The Pride of East Austin: L. C. Anderson Yellow Jackets," Austin's East End Cultural Heritage District, accessed January 16, 2025, http://www.eastendculturaldistrict.org/cms/schools-education/pride-east-austin-lc-anderson-yellow-jackets-0.

63. Rebekah Dobrasko, "Separate But Equal in Austin: L. C. Anderson High School," *Preservation Austin*, summer 2017, https://www.preservationaustin.org/news/separate-but-equal-in-austin-lc-anderson-high-school.

64. Wilhelmina Delco, interview by Rosalee Martin, May 29, 2001, Parallel and Crossover Lives: Texas Before and After Desegregation, Humanities Texas, https://www.humanitiestexas.org/sites/default/files/page-attachment/DELCO.pdf.

65. Rebekah Dobrasko, "Losing a Community Catalyst: The Closure of L. C. Anderson High School," *Preservation Austin*, fall 2017, https://www.preservationaustin.org/news/losing-a-community-catalyst-the-closure-of-lc-anderson-high-school.

66. Eva Lindsey, interview by Rosalee Martin, May 29, 2001, Parallel and Crossover Lives: Texas Before and After Desegregation, Humanities Texas, https://www.humanitiestexas.org/sites/default/files/page-attachment/Lindsey_Eva_Interview.pdf.

67. Eva Lindsey interview.

CHEER NOTE #2

# The College Mascot

As discussed in chapter 1, college mascots and cheerleaders trace their origins to early school rituals built around football. Despite the many changes to football over the last 150 years, cheerleaders and mascots continue to be instrumental in rallying fans around their teams. How well do you know college mascots and team nicknames? Match the following mascots and nicknames with the college teams they represent.

| | |
|---|---|
| 1. Cardinal and Tree | A. Syracuse University |
| 2. Crimson Tide and Big Al | B. Tulane University |
| 3. Green Wave and Riptide | C. University of Massachusetts |
| 4. Orange and Otto | D. University of Alabama |
| 5. Midshipmen and Bill the Goat | E. Stanford University |
| 6. Fighting Irish and Leprechaun | F. US Naval Academy |
| 7. Minutemen and Sam | G. University of Nevada |
| 8. Golden Hurricane and Gus T. | H. University of Notre Dame |
| 9. Thundering Herd and Marco | I. Marshall University |
| 10. Wolfpack and Wolfie Jr. | J. University of Tulsa |

Bonus: What is unique about these teams' nicknames?
(ANSWERS FOUND ON PAGE 283.)

CHAPTER 3

# Pump It Up

## CHEERLEADING FIGHTS FOR SPORTS LEGITIMACY

*Amy Moritz and Natalie G. Adams*

Cheer's not a sport?
TUCK OFF!
Oh wait, you can't.

Popular cheer T-shirt

Cheerleaders are a ubiquitous part of collegiate basketball and football broadcasts. Without fail, a camera pans the faces of cheerleaders with their perfect makeup and hair styled in glittery bows, rustling their pom-poms and sporting the ever-present cheerleading smile. This is the image of the cheerleader ingrained in our national psyche: hyperfeminine, on the sidelines, supporting the (almost always) male athletes. It is a stereotype frozen in time that has stymied attempts to recognize cheerleaders as athletes and cheerleading as a sport. The purpose of this chapter is to examine cheerleading's complicated relationship with Title IX, cheer's long fight for sports legitimacy, and recent changes foreshadowing (perhaps) a different cheer future. This important part of cheer's history reflects larger historical and contemporary debates about the role of sports in society, normative gender roles and expectations, and the consequences of women transgressing into spheres once deemed appropriate only for men. To understand the context of the current cheerleading-as-sport debate, we need to make a slight detour into the history of women in collegiate sports.

## No Girls Allowed: Women Fight for the Right to Compete

From the inception of institutionalized sports in the United States, men have resisted women's attempts to participate. Begun as a way for men to demonstrate their masculinity and to socialize boys into normative ideas about proper manhood, sports was considered a male-only sacred space for men to bond with each other without the influence of women.[1] By the early 1900s, sports were viewed as the ideal way to cultivate character, moral integrity, and leadership in boys and men. In 1906, the Intercollegiate Athletics Association of the United States was formed to regulate, promote, and govern intercollegiate sports; in 1910, it changed its name to the National Collegiate Athletic Association (NCAA).

As women's roles in public life expanded in the early 1900s, female physical education specialists began advocating for girls' participation in exercise and physical activities, citing the health benefits for girls, women, and society. As a result of their success in promoting the importance of physical activity for the "fairer sex," many upper-class women attending college in the early 1900s participated in such activities as lawn tennis, croquet, bicycling, archery, and rowing.[2] Women's participation in sports was far different from that of their male peers, however, primarily because female physical educators opposed competitive sports for women. Instead, female athletes for much of the twentieth century participated in intramural, club, recreational, and sorority games.[3] These female physical education specialists argued, as did many male academics—most notably Charles Eliot, president of Harvard University from 1875 to 1909—that competitive athletics emphasized the most base elements of American society: crass commercialization, a nondemocratic ethos that only the best deserved to compete, and an excessive and unseemly display of emotions during competitive events.[4] As Senda Berenson, director of physical education at Smith College and creator of the rules for women's basketball, noted in 1901, "Unless we guard our athletics carefully in the beginning, many objectionable elements will quickly come in. . . . The great desire to win and the excitement of the game will make our women do sadly unwomanly things."[5]

After women finally won the right to vote in 1920, they began making some inroads into the sports world, including the addition of women's gymnastics and track and field at the 1928 Olympic Games, boosting female participation to 10 percent of the Olympic events.[6] Nevertheless, women were rarely recognized as serious athletes, and their athletic accomplishments were often overlooked and unrecorded. In 1941, Ohio

State University hosted the first national intercollegiate championship for women, in golf. But the Division for Girls' and Women's Sports of the American Association for Health, Physical Education, and Recreation objected to the competition. As late as the 1950s, most collegiate female athletes still did not have the opportunity to participate in intercollegiate sports competitions. The NCAA, which governed men's collegiate sports in the United States, largely ignored women's sports, and the female faculty and administrators in charge of women's sports continued to de-emphasize winning and intercollegiate competitions, believing their ideas were in line with mainstream American values about women's roles in society. In 1951, Louise Weisiger, director of research at Richmond High School, reported in *School Activities* that most educators did not support interscholastic, competitive athletics for girls. They preferred a sports model that promoted egalitarianism and building relationships and that downplayed aggressive competitiveness. Weisiger writes, "As long as the playing of the game has augmented the health not endangered it, has strengthened old and built up new friendships instead of destroying them, has refreshed and restored the spirit of the players instead of harassing them, the competition engaged in has been educative."[7]

The Cold War, the civil rights movement, and the feminist movement of the mid-twentieth century stoked new conversations about discrimination based on race and gender. Women's inclusion in sports became part of a national debate about equality. In 1966, the Division for Girls' and Women's Sports formed the Commission on Intercollegiate Athletics for Women. The commission recognized the potential growth of women's intercollegiate sports and wanted to be prepared for its governance and regulation. They also sought to protect the two existing national intercollegiate championships for women: golf and tennis.[8] There were mutterings in the sports world that the NCAA knew its exclusion of women was probably vulnerable to an antidiscrimination lawsuit; hence, they began demonstrating a measured interest in women's sports.[9] Concerned about the NCAA's possible encroachment, the Division for Girls' and Women's Sports created a new organization in 1971, the Association for Intercollegiate Athletics for Women (AIAW), to counter any potential NCAA takeover. The Commission on Intercollegiate Athletics for Women was dissolved, and the AIAW assumed all administrative responsibilities for women's sports in the United States.[10] One year later, in 1972, Congress passed Title IX.

For ten years, the AIAW, run primarily by women, governed women's collegiate sports. By 1980, it had grown from 278 charter members to more than 970 institutions, and in 1981–1982, it hosted forty-one national championships for women in nineteen different sports. It secured television deals for women's basketball, thus providing a national stage for women to demonstrate their athleticism.[11] But the AIAW was plagued with internal conflicts and external pressures from the beginning. Continuing a long tradition of female physical educators and administrators distinguishing women's sports from men's, the AIAW initially tried to minimize the competitive nature of sports and to accentuate the social and health benefits for women. In its first few years, it restricted female athletes from receiving scholarships and prohibited off-campus recruiting. The AIAW eventually changed these policies, precipitated in part by *Kellmeyer, et al. v. NEA, et al.*, a gender discrimination lawsuit brought against the AIAW in 1973.

The AIAW was a key supporter of Title IX. The NCAA was not. It fought relentlessly against its passage and then its implementation.[12] In 1976, the NCAA sued the US Department of Health, Education, and Welfare, arguing that Title IX did not apply to athletic programs because athletic departments did not directly receive federal aid.[13] The case was dismissed, and no NCAA member institution joined the suit. The NCAA then quickly changed its position on Title IX and its exclusion of female athletes for several reasons. First, their views about women's sports were not shared by most colleges and universities or by the general public. Second, the significant growth and popularity of women's sports and the expansion of funding for women's athletic programs at many colleges and universities made it a lucrative investment. In 1981, the NCAA officially brought women's sports under its governance and offered its first women's championships in field hockey and cross country. In 1982, in a big blow to the AIAW, three powerhouses in women's basketball (Louisiana Tech, the University of Tennessee, and Old Dominion) opted to play in the NCAA's first women's basketball tournament instead of the AIAW competition. That same year, NBC canceled its contract to air the AIAW basketball championship.[14] In the end, the AIAW simply could not compete financially with the NCAA, and in 1983 it officially dissolved. The NCAA took over the governance of women's collegiate sports.

The demise of the AIAW was most crushing to female coaches and administrators. In 1972, almost every athletic program for women was directed by women. By 1980, over 80 percent of colleges and universities had merged the administration of men's and women's athletic departments into one unit, and 90 percent of them were led by men. Often, the women displaced by these mergers were more qualified than the men—with more experience and higher degrees.[15] By 1978, the year of mandatory Title IX compliance, only 58 percent of women's teams were coached by women, and in 2012 that had fallen to below 43 percent.[16] The long-term effects of the disappearance of women in the highest ranks of collegiate coaching and administration continue today. In 2021–2022, women still held only 42 percent of head coaching positions for women's teams in NCAA Division I sports.[17] And in 2023–2024, in what the NCAA calls a "celebration of progress," there were only fifty-seven female athletic directors of Division I athletic programs.[18]

## Moving Girls Off the Sidelines: Title IX Versus Cheerleading

On June 23, 1972, President Richard Nixon signed into law Title IX, which states that "no person in the United States shall, on the basis of sex, be excluded from participation in, be denied the benefits of, or be subjected to discrimination under any education program or activity receiving Federal financial assistance." The passage of Title IX was the culmination of years of feminist activism to achieve equality for girls and women, particularly in the sports arena. It was intended to open doors to female athletes who longed to play soccer, basketball, hockey, lacrosse, and other sports they had watched their brothers play. Since its passage, opportunities for girls and women to play sports have grown exponentially. Before Title IX, fewer than 32,000 women participated in college sports, or less than 16 percent of all college athletes. By 2020, women represented 44 percent of all NCAA athletes, with 222,920 women playing college sports. The growth is even more pronounced at the high school level. Only 295,000 girls played high school sports in 1972, or just 7 percent of all high school athletes. In 2019, 3.4 million girls, or 43 percent of all high school athletes, played sports.[19]

Women's sports advocates argue that these numbers fail to tell the entire story of Title IX. While more opportunities exist, inequitable treatment continues—including lower budgets, less desirable practice times, and inferior facilities. And while the increase in participation demonstrates women's hunger for competitive athletic opportunities, many colleges and universities remain Title IX noncompliant by failing to offer adequate opportunities and resources for female athletes. In 2022, *USA Today* examined Title IX on its fiftieth anniversary, finding that 87 percent "of colleges and universities are not offering athletic opportunities to women proportionate to their enrollment."[20]

From its beginnings, Title IX pitted cheerleading against "real" sports and feminists against cheerleaders and their supporters. Second wave feminists used the mantra "Let's move girls from the sidelines"—meaning cheerleaders—"to the playing fields" to gain support for Title IX. The feminist argument against cheerleading, prevalent even today, goes like this: Cheerleaders are supplemental, ornamental, and trivial. They exist to support male athletes. They are valued and rewarded for their physical appeal, rather than their athletic abilities. In a culture where girls and women were historically not given meaningful opportunities in athletics, it is no surprise that Title IX advocates pushed hard against classifying cheerleading as a sport. They were concerned that such recognition would give male athletic directors an easy out by calling cheerleaders athletes rather than creating meaningful opportunities for girls and women in basketball and volleyball. In 1975, the US Department of Education's Office for Civil Rights, charged with overseeing the legal implementation of Title IX, issued a memorandum to school administrators that clearly articulated the status of cheerleading: "Drill teams, cheerleaders and the like, which are covered more generally as extracurricular activities . . . are not part of the institution's 'athletic program' within the meaning of the regulation."[21]

Although it remained relegated to the sidelines according to the NCAA and Title IX guidelines, cheerleading evolved in the 1970s and 1980s into an athletic, competitive endeavor that incorporated tumbling, stunting, and pyramid building. With no NCAA-sanctioned competitions or championships available, cheer companies stepped in and began offering state and national competitions. The new form of cheerleading required an athletic prowess that sent cheerleaders to private gyms to hone their skills. These gyms, which had previously catered to budding gymnasts, found a new clientele: cheerleaders who were more interested in competing than in being on the sidelines. Soon these gyms began hosting their own cheer teams and birthed an entirely new type of cheerleading: competitive cheer. All Star cheerleaders, as they are often called, are not affiliated with any school or university. They do not perform any of the traditional cheerleading duties, such as sideline cheering or representing their school at events. Their sole focus is competition, which typically consists of a short, fast-paced, well-choreographed routine combining tumbling, stunting, pyramids, dance, and cheer segments. In 1995, the National Cheerleaders Association (NCA) hosted the first All Star Nationals, a separate competition event exclusively for All Star teams. Today competitive cheer is the fastest-growing segment of cheerleading, both in the United States and globally. In 2025, over 10,500 All Star athletes from twenty-five countries competed in the Cheerleading Worlds (aka Worlds), the top competition nationally and internationally for All Star cheerleaders.

The athleticism of All Star programs influenced cheerleading across the board. Collegiate and high school cheerleaders still appeared on the sidelines at games, but their primary focus shifted to training for and competing in national championships. Reframing cheer as athletic and competitive played a key role in gaining visibility on ESPN, while in turn, championship broadcasts on ESPN gave cheerleading a focal point to be taken seriously as a sport.[22] Many high school and college administrators and state high school athletic associations criticized this change and instituted policies ensuring that cheerleaders performed their roles as school ambassadors and supporters of others, first and foremost. In some cases, universities (e.g., the University of Nebraska) and high school governing agencies (e.g., the Ohio High School Athletic Association) forced cheerleaders back to the sidelines by enforcing "ground bound" rules (i.e., restrictions on tumbling, pyramids, and stunts) and limiting participation in competitions.[23]

Cheerleading's evolution from sideline entertainment to a highly athletic activity has reenergized the cheer-as-sport debate. On one side is an unusual alliance between feminists, women's sports advocates, and the world's largest cheer company. On the other side are physicians, sports researchers, some state legislators, and many cheerleaders and cheer coaches. Let's turn now to the details of the debate, the major players, and their arguments, so you can formulate your own opinion. Should cheerleading be classified as a sport?

## Make Cheerleading Safe by Making It a Sport: The Advocates

In 2006, while performing at a Southern Illinois University basketball game, Kristi Yamaoka fell fifteen feet onto her head from atop a pyramid. The gym fell silent as fans watched Kristi carefully transferred to a stretcher. To break the somber mood, the band broke into the school's fight song. Kristi, with her neck immobilized in a brace, responded with a big thumbs-up and an arms-only performance of the fight song dance as she was whisked away to the hospital. She suffered a concussion and a chipped vertebra from her fall. Days after her injury, Kristi appeared on NBC's *Today Show*, where she was praised for her "loyalty and toughness." Kristi brushed off the compliments and explained, "I'm still a cheerleader—on a stretcher or not. So as soon as I heard that fight song, I knew my job and just started to do my thing."

As Kristi's fall illustrates, cheerleading can be dangerous. Some argue that it is only second to football as the most dangerous sport in the United States. Others argue that the risks associated with cheerleading have been greatly exaggerated. Interestingly, both sides point to data collected by the National Center for Catastrophic Sport Injury Research (NCCSIR), which began reporting in 1982 on sports injuries suffered by high school and collegiate athletes. The NCCSIR gathers injury reports only from high school and college sports, and as they indicate, "catastrophic events are primarily captured through publicly available media reports. Thus, not all catastrophic events are captured."[24] Initially, the NCCSIR did not include cheerleading in its research; however, in 1982 two collegiate cheerleaders suffered serious head injuries. The NCCSIR then decided to include data about cheerleading injuries in their annual research reports and have done so ever since.

So, what does the data say?

If you look at the cumulative data from 1982 to 2019, cheerleading, at the high school level, is the most dangerous female sport in terms of catastrophic injuries. The NCCSIR defines catastrophic injuries as "fatalities, injuries that result in permanent functional disability, and serious injuries that result in temporary functional disability with full recovery."[25] Among both men's and women's sports, cheerleading ranks second, behind football, and ahead of wrestling and baseball. In 2012, the American Academy of Pediatrics published its own data for the years 1982 to 2009. They report that cheerleading accounted for 65 percent of all direct catastrophic injuries to female athletes at the high school level and nearly 71 percent at the college level.[26] According to research published in 2009, concussions are the most common cheerleading injury, followed by ligament sprains, muscle strains, and fractures. Most concussions occur during stunting, particularly the dismount, and often involve cheerleaders coming into hard contact with each other. Cheerleaders in the base role for stunts and pyramids are the most likely to suffer concussions (46 percent), followed by flyers (36 percent) and spotters (10 percent). The report noted that cheerleaders suffer far more concussions at practice than they do at competitions.[27]

Others use the same NCCSIR data to argue that cheerleading is a relatively safe activity. They point to the center's annual reports. According to the 2023 annual report, catastrophic injuries in cheer have decreased 85 percent since 2003. From 2014 to 2023, there were six catastrophic injuries related to cheer, compared to forty-two from 2003 to 2014. Injuries from participating in cheer are comparable to most other girls' sports and lower than football, baseball, boys' wrestling, and girls' and boys' soccer.[28] Another data source often cited is the National High School Sports-Related Injury Surveillance Study, commissioned by the National Federation of State High School Associations (NFHS). Since 2009, cheerleading has been included in this data. In a report in *Pediatrics* analyzing cheerleading injury rates from that study from 2009 to 2014, cheerleading injuries ranked eighteenth out of twenty-two sports. The cheer industry contends that cheerleading has become safer because the industry self-monitored and adopted measures to reduce injuries, such as restricting released twists on surfaces without a mat and prohibiting basket tosses and double full twisting dismounts, regardless of surface, for all elementary, middle school, and junior high cheerleaders.[29]

Proponents of declaring cheerleading a sport point to these injuries and to the hodgepodge of safety guidelines for cheer, which vary greatly not only from team to team but also from state to state and competition to competition. If cheer were to be considered a legitimate sport, it would fall under athletic departments, which must abide by guidelines from the NCAA, state high school athletic associations, and the NFHS. In turn, this would result in safer and more standardized practice conditions, better equipment, improved access to athletic trainers, and more restrictions on practices, training, and competition seasons. It would also mean more scholarships, financial resources, and competent coaches.

Leading the side in favor of cheerleading as a sport are physicians, who began sounding the alarm about cheer injuries over twenty years ago. In 2012, the American Academy of Pediatrics adopted a formal policy designating cheerleading as a sport. Two years later the American Medical Association followed suit. Dr. Georgia Tuttle explained that the association

> recognizes the potential dangers now associated with cheerleading and believes steps should be taken to ensure the health and safety of individuals who participate in the time-honored tradition. By designating cheerleading as a sport, those participating will benefit from the same robust safety protocols as other designated sports, including properly trained coaches and adherence to rules for the proper execution of stunts.[30]

Many state high school athletic associations and some state legislatures have also thrown their weight behind declaring cheerleading a sport. According to the 2018–2019 NFHS Participation Survey, thirty-one state high school associations now recognize cheerleading as a sport.[31] In 2015, the California Legislature passed the California High Schools Expanding Equality Respect and Safety (CHEERS) Act, which classified competitive cheerleading as an interscholastic sport in that state.[32]

But the opponents of cheer's reclassification are an equally strong group, albeit a strange set of bedfellows. Their approaches to the argument range from apprehensions about subverting the spirit of Title IX to concerns about corporate profits.

## Cheer Is Not a Sport, It's Extracurricular: The Opponents

Opponents of designating cheerleading as a sport are concerned, as were earlier women's sports advocates and feminists, that such a move would allow high schools and colleges to subvert the intentions of Title IX. They fear that if schools are able to take an existing extracurricular activity like cheerleading and count it as one of their female sports and its athletes as female athletes, traditional women's sports such as volleyball, soccer, and softball will be eliminated from athletic rosters. This concern came to fruition at Quinnipiac University. In 2009, this small private university located in Hamden, Connecticut, discontinued its women's volleyball team and created a new varsity sports team for women—competitive cheerleading. The volleyball coach, Robin Sparks, and five members of the volleyball team filed a lawsuit against Quinnipiac for violating Title IX. Quinnipiac countered that it was in compliance with Title IX, in part after elevating its cheerleading team to a varsity sport.[33]

As the case wound its way through the court system, women's sports advocates signed on to amicus briefs in support of the volleyball players. Led by the National Women's Law Center, they argued that when Quinnipiac cut women's volleyball and elevated its cheerleading squad to varsity status, it eliminated a competitive athletic opportunity for women while manipulating its rosters to create an appearance of compliance with Title IX. The National Women's Law Center argued that the cheer squad did not provide "athletic participation opportunities that are qualitatively equal to those provided by other varsity teams." In other words, cheerleading did not offer women the same type of athletic opportunity as did volleyball. Put bluntly, cheerleading was not a real sport. The law center conceded that "competitive cheer is, without a doubt, an activity that requires athletic skill. In its current form, however, competitive cheer does not rise to the level of a varsity sport under Title IX because it lacks the organization, competition, and benefits that other varsity sports provide."[34]

In 2012, the US Court of Appeals for the Second Circuit ruled in favor of the volleyball team. The court announced that cheerleading "could not be counted for Title IX purposes because the activity did not yet afford women genuine participation opportunities in a varsity sport."[35] The court cited three reasons why competitive cheerleading is different from other sports: (1) the lack of recruitment efforts, (2) the lack of a standard set of rules, and (3) the lack of regular-season and postseason competitions.[36] The judge ordered the university to reinstate the women's volleyball team for the 2010–2011 athletic season.

The judge conceded that competitive cheer may qualify as a sport under Title IX in the future, but as currently configured, it is "too underdeveloped and disorganized to be treated as offering genuine varsity athletic participation opportunities for students." The ruling made note of the haphazard scoring system used in the thirteen competitions in which the Quinnipiac cheerleading team had participated in 2009–2010 and the inconsistency of the status of their competitors. Sometimes their opponents were similarly configured collegiate competitive cheer teams, but they also competed against sideline collegiate cheer teams, private All Star teams, and, on occasion, high school teams.

One of the key witnesses for Quinnipiac was Jeff Webb, the founder and CEO (at the time) of Varsity Spirit, the world's largest cheerleading company, and the person responsible for first introducing nationally televised cheer competitions. Under oath, Webb, to the surprise of many, unequivocally stated that cheerleading was not a sport:

> ATTORNEY: As you sit here today with your thirty some years of experience in cheerleading, including cheerleading competitions, do you believe that those competitions are sport?
> WEBB: No.
> ATTORNEY: Do you believe they are a varsity sport?
> WEBB: No.[37]

Webb conceded that he had introduced cheerleading competitions as a "publicity vehicle" for his new business to place his products in the hands of thousands of cheerleaders.

Varsity has long held the position that cheerleading is an athletic activity—or, as they say on their website, "Cheerleading is *more* than a sport. [Cheer's] primary purpose is to support high school and college athletic teams. Competition comes second!" Webb's comments in the courtroom drew the ire of many in the cheer world. Critics of Webb and Varsity argue that the company's resistance to reclassifying cheerleading as a sport has more to do with corporate profit than concerns about Title IX.[38] In a 2003 filing with the Securities and Exchange Commission during Varsity's brief stint as a publicly traded company, Varsity stated that "the designation of cheer as a sport and the ensuing increased regulation would likely have a material adverse effect on Varsity's business, financial condition and results of operations."[39] In 2007, Varsity formed USA Cheer, which, according to its website, serves as the "governing body for sport cheering in the United States." Neither the NCAA nor the Second Circuit's ruling in the Quinnipiac lawsuit recognized USA Cheer as such; however, this governance by fiat has allowed Varsity expansive control of cheerleading. Thus Varsity, its critics argue, has a vested interest in keeping cheerleading on the sidelines.

The alliance of feminists, Title IX advocates, coaches of other women's sports, legal scholars, and the largest cheerleading company in the world may seem like an unlikely collective. But these entities joining forces have kept cheerleading in its current iteration from counting as a Title IX equivalency sport. On the global stage, Jeff Webb and Varsity have assumed a very different position.[40]

## Going for Gold: Cheerleading's Journey Toward a World Sports Stage

In 2004, Varsity formed the International Cheer Union (ICU), with Jeff Webb as its president. Its main objective was to introduce cheerleading into as many countries as possible so cheer could achieve formal sports status under International Olympic Committee guidelines. In December 2016, the committee granted provisional status to cheerleading and awarded the ICU $25,000 a year for three years to develop cheerleading as a sport throughout the world.[41] In July 2021, the provisional status was changed to permanent recognition, thus moving cheer one step closer to an appearance in the Olympic Games.[42]

The path to inclusion in the world's largest sports competition is a long one. It must be voted on by the committee and garner a majority vote. The affirmative vote must occur three years in advance of the Games in which the new sport will appear. The International Olympic Committee bases its decision on several criteria, including international participation rates, global popularity, and the value the sport adds to the overall Olympic experience. According to the Olympic Charter governing women's sports, a sport must be practiced widely by women in forty countries on three continents to even be considered for admission into the world's largest multigame sporting event.[43] The ICU hopes that the newly bestowed permanent recognition status will boost participant numbers worldwide, as governmental officials will now be more apt to devote resources to developing cheerleading in their respective countries in hopes of competing at the Olympic level. By 2019, nearly twenty national cheer federations had received National Olympic Committee recognition, according to the ICU General Assembly meeting minutes.[44]

Cognizant of the criticism about cheer's lack of standardized rules and scoring, the ICU has begun addressing these concerns at the global level. Lauri Harris, the executive director of USA Cheer, explains that the organization's

> primary goal is to expand participation in cheerleading locally in the US and to inspire growth globally. To achieve that, it's essential to have organizational structures and governing bodies in place to provide consistency and regulation. The Olympics are just one piece of the picture—our athletes are also engaging in a range of international events, where standardized rules create a level playing field and broader opportunities for growth.[45]

In 2024, the ICU administered fifteen championships with the same rules and standards in eight countries: the United States, Canada, South Korea, Hong Kong, South Africa, Indonesia, Croatia, and Norway.

Why has Varsity, under the auspices of the ICU, led the charge internationally for sports recognition while opposing that move domestically? Varsity's critics contend that it's all about the money. Cheer teams in Europe, Asia, Africa, and South America, unlike those in the United States, are not typically found in secondary schools or universities. Rather, they are akin to All Star cheer squads in the United States—that is, competitive, typically mixed-gender teams associated with private gyms. The only way for

Varsity to expand cheerleading globally is to expand that market. As the global giant in cheer apparel, products, and services, Varsity is well poised to profit from the classification of cheer as a global sport as it expands into dozens of countries with the end goal of becoming part of the Olympics. After all, there is no bigger or better stage for selling a product than the Olympics.

Meanwhile, back in the USA, Varsity has changed its stance on cheerleading as a sport—somewhat.

### Does Cheer Have a Fighting Chance in the United States? Recent Moves for Sports Legitimation

In 2020, the NCAA Committee on Women's Athletics approved a form of competitive cheerleading as an NCAA "emerging sport."[46] This is the first step in a long process to gain official recognition as an "equivalency sport" under Title IX guidelines. An emerging sport can become an NCAA sport at the Division I level if at least forty NCAA-affiliated institutions add the emerging sport within a ten-year period.[47] While not all emerging sports end up making their way to official NCAA status, it does provide credibility for the sport as it makes its case to college and university athletic departments across the country. But this unfolding story of cheer as an NCAA sport is fraught with complications. The sticky point: Two competing organizations are fighting to get their form of cheerleading into colleges and universities as a Title IX equivalency sport.[48]

On one side is a predominantly grassroots effort organized by cheerleading coaches, called the National Collegiate Acrobatics and Tumbling Association (NCATA). In 2010, the group submitted a proposal to the NCAA Committee on Women's Athletics asking that acrobatics and tumbling (often shortened to "acro") be added as an emerging sport. The NCATA is backed by USA Gymnastics, meaning acro coaches and athletes are members of that organization and governed by their rules and regulations. One month after the NCATA submitted its proposal, USA Cheer, affiliated with Varsity, submitted a similar proposal to the NCAA committee, asking that their sport, stunt (often capitalized as "STUNT"), be recognized as an emerging sport.[49] The committee looked at the two proposals and instructed the two organizations to work it out between them. They did not, and over the next ten years they continued to submit separate proposals.[50]

The two organizations claim key differences between their proposed sports.[51] The NCATA distances itself from cheerleading by emphasizing the gymnastics and tumbling components of the sport. The founders of the NCATA, Felecia Mulkey, Mary Ann Powers, Colleen Kausrud, and Kristi Kiefer, knew that the optics of their new sport mattered if they wanted to gain traction in their bid for sports legitimacy. On the other hand, USA Cheer aligns itself with what it calls the "performance" aspects of traditional cheerleading, such as partner stunts, pyramids, jumps, tosses, and tumbling. According to its website, "STUNT is the only discipline designed to meet the US Department of Education Office for Civil Rights (OCR) legal sport requirement for Title IX for schools in the US." But as Bill Seely, the former executive director of USA Cheer and now president of Varsity Spirit, is quick to point out, "STUNT will not come at the expense of traditional cheerleading."[52]

Both the NCATA and USA Cheer host national championships. Differences exist in competition structure and logistics, but the athletes themselves execute very similar athletic skills and performances. At NCATA competitions, meets are broken down into six events, with each event divided into heats. The heats include pyramid building, synchronized acrobatic lifts and tosses, tumbling passes, and a choreographed routine to music. Officials judge each heat, with 10 being the highest possible score.[53] At STUNT competitions, two teams compete head-to-head for four quarters. Each quarter focuses on specific technical and athletic moves and skills, such as partner stunts, pyramids, jumps, tosses, and tumbling. The team that performs best in each quarter receives one point. The team with the most points at the end of play is the winner, and they advance to the next round.[54] Both eschew the glittery makeup, sequined uniforms, big bows, and exaggerated smiles and facial gestures common at traditional cheer competitions.

Which version of cheerleading, if any, will we see at colleges and universities in 2026 and beyond? Will this version finally mean that cheerleading is considered a "real" sport, complete with benefits such as scholarships, air transportation to and from games, higher-paid coaches, and collegiate rings? Will cheer naysayers see such a move as a serious misinterpretation of the intentions of Title IX? And what about the boys? If cheerleading is considered a Title IX equivalency sport, as proposed by advocates of both acro and STUNT, boys will not be allowed to compete. Will the lack of men in competitive cheerleading change the sport?

## Why the Sporting Debate Matters

Proponents and critics provide compelling reasons for and against the formal recognition of cheerleading as a sport. Those pushing for the sport designation point to practical matters. At the collegiate level, the athletic department administers varsity sports, while club sports and activities are typically governed by another department—often student affairs, student life, or student government. Athletic departments typically have bigger budgets and more and better resources. Equipment, uniforms, and travel expenses for competitions are covered. Student athletes qualify for tuition and book scholarships and receive free meal plans. Sports governed by an athletic department have access to quality facilities and equipment for practice and competitions. Student athletes have access to weight rooms and professional staff—from certified trainers and nutritionists to medical personnel that can address injuries and illnesses. Proponents argue that access to these resources, coupled with NCAA administrative oversight and regulation, would make the sport physically, mentally, and emotionally safer for its athletes.

A few examples are illustrative of how cheerleaders may benefit from a formal sport designation. In 2020, the Navarro College cheerleaders, whose story was featured in the Netflix series *Cheer*, received either a $500 scholarship if they lived off campus or a $1,000 scholarship if they lived on campus at the junior college. At Clemson University, a Division I institution, the cheerleaders fare little better than the Navarro team. In 2023, their scholarships were maxed at $1,500 per year; they receive no textbook stipend and are allotted fewer meals than other athletes. Further, they lack a consistent, dedicated space in which to practice and train. This lack of support from their university often takes a toll on the team, as Ava DeStefon related in the school's newspaper: "From time to time, it can be hard doing a year-long season and sometimes feeling undervalued for all we do and the true athleticism is never fully seen. Sometimes the lack of funding and support makes it hard to do all the things we hope and wish for the program."[55]

This differentiation between sport or extracurricular/club activity really hit home with the University of Alabama cheerleading team in 2011, when it won its second National Cheerleaders Association collegiate cheerleading championship. That same year, the Alabama football team won its national championship. But the two national champs were treated very differently. As it has always done, the athletic department bought the football players big, flashy championship rings. The cheerleaders were told they would have to buy their own. To add insult to injury, the university initially denied them the use of the trademarked scripted *A* on the ring. Alabama's athletic department later recanted their earlier statement about preventing the use of the logo, but it did not pay for the rings. Doug Walker, spokesperson for the athletic department, told *The Tuscaloosa News* that the cheerleaders had been aware of Alabama's policy on championship rings: Only athletes who participated in NCAA-sanctioned sports received championship rings.[56]

Critics of the sport designation typically concede that cheerleaders are athletic and that participation requires athletic prowess similar to that of other sports. Cheerleaders train as hard as other athletes, suffer injuries the same as their NCAA-sanctioned sports counterparts, and compete in local, regional, state, and national championships. The critics' concern is how such a designation would circumvent the spirit of Title IX, which has yet to deliver the promise of gender equity in sports. They worry that the inclusion of cheer as a formal sport may result in athletic departments dropping well-established women's sports, thus harming female athletes in other programs. Such concerns are well grounded, as exemplified in the case of Quinnipiac University. Equally problematic is the continued demand for and rewarding of the performance of emphasized femininity in cheer, even within competitive coed cheerleading.

But the heart of the matter has always been about more than just the numbers and compliance with Title IX. The cheerleader stereotype has been ingrained in American popular culture, as discussed throughout this book. These pervasive stereotypes minimize and misrepresent the lived reality of thousands of girls and women who work hard at their sport. Tumbling against a tidal wave of caricatures, they have pushed against the dominant culture to carve out a space for themselves, to force that culture to see them as they see themselves: strong, determined, athletic. The designation of cheerleading as a sport confers that longed-for status and legitimacy on their athletic identity. As a sanctioned sport, cheer would have the backing of a governing body—and the backing of the schools—confirming that, indeed, cheerleaders are athletes, what they do matters, and who they are brings value to the overall athletic program.

So, why does the cheerleading-as-sport debate matter outside the small world of cheer? Because the debate itself reveals much about gender roles and expectations, both in the past and in the present. As discussed earlier in the chapter, sports have long been a site where normative gendered expectations have played out. For the first seventy years of its existence, the

NCAA refused to include women as official athletes—a stance that received little pushback from female physical educators, coaches, professors, and administrators. As late as the 1950s, they promoted a model of sports that renounced traditional markers of masculinity, such as competition, aggression, and winning. But their rationale was steeped in conventional beliefs about gendered bodies. Early arguments suggested that sports would lead to infertility in women, that exercising during menstruation was harmful, and that women's bodies were fragile and needed to be protected from overexertion.[57] Later, female physical educators and administrators sought to protect women from the win-at-all-costs ethos so prevalent in men's intercollegiate sports. Their mantra "Every girl in a sport and a sport for every girl" touted the social and educational value of women's sports as superior to that of the ultracompetitive culture of men's sports.[58]

The passage of Title IX and changing social and cultural views about women's role in society opened the doors for girls and women to compete in sports. It provided a route for the professionalization of sports and increased the status of female athletes. But women's place and presence in the sports world have always threatened the deeply entrenched dichotomy between masculine and feminine spheres and male and female roles in society. Thus, female athletes, even today, are plagued by what Birgit Palzkill and Angela Fisher call "the inner strife between gymshoes and high heels," or what Pat Griffin calls "the heterosexy athlete."[59] They are continuously reminded that on the court, they can play the game and be as tough and athletic as they want, but off the court, they need to present an appropriate dose of heterosexual femininity. Many female athletes over the years have complied with these rules, quickly showering and applying makeup before speaking in a postgame press conference. Queer athletes have been forced to remain closeted, fearful that revelations of their sexual identity may result in being kicked off the team or losing corporate sponsorships. In the era of NIL deals, a host of female athletes, such as the college gymnast Livvy Dunne, have leaned into the "heterosexy" athlete image to secure lucrative endorsements and millions of social media followers. But other athletes, such as Caitlin Clark, Megan Rapinoe, Sue Bird, Candace Parker, Brittney Griner, and Elena Delle Donne (to name just a few), have resisted these normative gendered expectations, adopting less gender-conforming physical appearances and speaking out publicly about wage discrimination, anti-trans legislation, and the full inclusion of LGBTQ+ athletes. In 2021, the entire Norwegian women's beach handball team was fined for refusing to wear the required bikini bottoms at a tournament. Their activism eventually led to a wholesale policy change when the International Handball Federation announced that bikinis were no longer part of the required uniform.

Unlike female athletes in more traditional sports, female cheerleaders have never seriously threatened the status quo. Cheerleading began for the sole purpose of supporting male athletes on the field. Even as it changed to a more athletic endeavor, cheer continued to demand a certain performance of femininity that aligned with traditional gendered beliefs and expectations. Female cheerleaders were expected to be pretty and thin and presumed to be straight. As the two previous chapters illustrate, the evolution of cheerleading over its 160-plus years demonstrates that cheerleading is not a static entity. It continues to evolve. The introduction of two new forms of cheer, acro and STUNT, are intentional moves to disentangle the sport from its close association with hyperfemininity. Thousands of cheerleaders opt to cheer on All Star teams for the sole purpose of competition, rather than to support other athletes. As discussed in chapter 11, they do not see themselves as popular, pretty girls who entertain fans. Rather, they are serious athletes who love their sport and want to win, just like any other athlete. Cheer competitions have adopted new rules to discourage overly sexual moves, excessive makeup, and skimpy uniforms. Most All Star competitions have eliminated any reference to appearance in their scoring. High school, collegiate, and All Star cheerleaders are quick to distance themselves from professional cheerleaders, whom they often blame for the persistent stereotype of cheerleaders as sex objects. Some queer cheerleaders, such as the comedian and actor Hannah Einbinder, have touted the inclusiveness of their tight-knit cheer communities where the collective identity of the team supersedes the individual identities of the athletes.[60]

Cheer's ambiguity as a complicated American cultural icon will not be resolved simply by declaring it a sport; however, its place in the sociocultural history of sport warrants recognition. The story of cheerleading and its fight for sports legitimacy reveals the elasticity and rigidity of gender norms and roles in American culture and enriches our knowledge of both sports and society.

## Notes

1. Susan Cahn, *Coming on Strong: Gender and Sexuality in Twentieth-Century Women's Sports* (Harvard University Press, 1994); Richard Mandell, *Sport: A*

*Cultural History* (Columbia University Press, 1984); George Sage, *Power and Ideology in American Sport: A Critical Perspective* (Human Kinetics, 1990); Eric A. Moyen and John R. Thelin, *College Sports: A History* (Johns Hopkins University Press, 2024).

2. For a more thorough discussion of this role, see Cahn, *Coming on Strong*; and Pamela Grundy, *Learning to Win: Sports, Education, and Social Change in Twentieth-Century North Carolina* (University of North Carolina Press, 2001).

3. Richard C. Bell, "A History of Women in Sport Prior to Title IX," *Sport Journal* 10, no. 2 (2007), https://thesportjournal.org/article/a-history-of-women-in-sport-prior-to-title-ix/. For a description of a typical "women's play day," see Moyen and Thelin, *College Sports*, 217–218.

4. John Sayle Watterson, *College Football: History, Spectacle, Controversy* (Johns Hopkins University Press, 2000).

5. Quoted in Mary Jo Festle, *Playing Nice: Politics and Apologies in Women's Sports* (Columbia University Press, 1996), 13.

6. "U.S. Female Participation in the Olympics and Paralympics," US Olympic and Paralympic Museum, accessed October 30, 2025, https://usopm.org/a-quick-look-at-u-s-female-participation-in-the-olympics-and-paralympics/.

7. Louise Weisiger, "The Status of Interscholastic Athletics in Secondary School for Girls," *School Activities* 22 (February 1951): 184–187.

8. Sheryl Marie Szady, "The History of Intercollegiate Athletics for Women at the University of Michigan" (PhD diss., University of Michigan, 1987).

9. Moyen and Thelin, *College Sports*, 240.

10. For a thorough discussion of the history of the AIAW and its battles with the NCAA, see Ying Wu, "Early NCAA Attempts at the Governance of Women's Intercollegiate Athletes, 1968–1972," *Journal of Sports History* 26, no. 3 (1999): 585–601; Hollis Elkins, "Time for a Change: Women's Athletics and the Women's Movement," *Frontiers* 3, no. 1 (1978): 22–25.

11. Bell, "History of Women in Sport."

12. Wu, "Early NCAA Attempts."

13. *National Collegiate Athletic Association v. Califano*, 444 F. Supp. 425 (D. Kan. 1978). For a detailed discussion of the case, see Kevin A. Nelson, "Title IX: Women's Collegiate Athletics in Limbo," *Washington and Lee Law Review* 40, no. 1 (1983): 297–312.

14. Mark Bechtel, "AIAW vs. NCAA: When Women's College Basketball Had to Choose," *Sports Illustrated*, June 14, 2022, https://www.si.com/college/2022/06/14/aiaw-ncaa-womens-college-basketball-league-title-ix-daily-cover.

15. G. Ann Uhlir, "Athletics and the University: The Post-Woman's Era," *Academe* 73, no. 4 (1987): 25–29.

16. R. Vivian Acosta and Linda Jean Carpenter, "Women in Intercollegiate Sport: A Longitudinal, National Study; Thirty-Five Year Update, 1977–2012," 2012, https://files.eric.ed.gov/fulltext/ED570883.pdf.

17. Steve Megargee, "Study: Most Women's NCAA Teams Are Still Coached

by Men," *Associated Press*, March 22, 2023, https://apnews.com/article/diversity-ncaa-coaches-30958ab74d4b61efc0d54eee361dafef.

18. Corbin McGuire, "Celebrating Progress: Women's Representation in NCAA Sports, Leadership Roles," NCAA, March 1, 2025, https://www.ncaa.org/news/2025/3/1/media-center-celebrating-progress-womens-representation-in-ncaa-sports-leadership-roles.aspx.

19. "Quick Facts About Title IX and Athletics," National Women's Law Center, June 21, 2022, https://nwlc.org/resource/quick-facts-about-title-ix-and-athletics/.

20. Rachel Axon and Lindsay Schnell, "50 Years After Title IX Passed, Most Top Colleges Deprive Female Athletes of Equal Opportunities," *USA Today*, June 3, 2022, https://www.usatoday.com/in-depth/news/investigations/2022/06/03/title-ix-failures-50-years-colleges-women-lack-representation/9664260002.

21. "Letter to Chief State School Officers, Title IX Obligations in Athletics," Office for Civil Rights, US Department of Education, September 1975.

22. Laura Grindstaff, "Hold That (Gender) Line! Cheerleading on ESPN," *Contexts* 4, no. 3 (2005): 72, https://doi.org/10.1525/ctx.2005.4.3.71.

23. Jim Suhr, "Cheerleading Ban Has Coach Upset," *Herald-Tribune*, March 8, 2006, https://www.heraldtribune.com/story/news/2006/03/09/cheerleading-ban-has-coach-upset/28465910007/; Laurie Schreier, "Byrne Bans Cheerleaders' Stunts," *Daily Nebraskan*, March 12, 2002, https://www.dailynebraskan.com/byrne-bans-cheerleaders-stunts/article_0a4fea3b-fea4-5e32-b0d6-29dbd720ec21.html.

24. "Catastrophic Injury Research, 38th Annual Report," National Center for Catastrophic Sport Injury Research, Fall 1982–Spring 2020, https://nccsir.unc.edu/wp-content/uploads/sites/5614/2022/05/2020-Catastrophic-ReportAS-38th-AY2019-2020-FINAL-public.pdf.

25. "Catastrophic Injury Research, 38th Annual Report."

26. Council on Sports Medicine and Fitness, "Cheerleading Injuries: Epidemiology and Recommendations for Prevention," *Pediatrics* 130, no. 5 (2012): 966–971, https://publications.aap.org/pediatrics/article/130/5/966/32509/Cheerleading-InjuriesEpidemiology-and.

27. Brenda Shields, Soledad Fernandez, and Gary Smith, "Epidemiology of Cheerleading Stunt-Related Injuries in the United States," *Journal of Athletic Training* 44, no. 6 (2009): 586–594.

28. "Cheerleading Safety Data and Research," USA Cheer, 2025, https://usacheer.org/safety/research.

29. Dustin Currie, Sarah Fields, Michael Patterson, and R. Dawn Comstock, "Cheerleading Injuries in United States High Schools," *Pediatrics* 137, no. 1 (2016): 15.

30. Quoted in Alyssa Roenigk, "Sorry, Cheerleading Is Not a Sport," ESPN, June 24, 2014, https://www.espn.com/espnw/news-commentary/story/_/id/11128302/espnw-formercollege-cheerleader-says-sorry-cheerleading-not-sport.

31. "2018–2019 High School Athletics Participation Survey," National Federation of State High School Associations, 2019, https://www.nfhs.org/media/1020412/2018-19_participation_survey.pdf.

32. Lee Green, "Impact of Competitive Cheer Laws, Regulations on Title IX Compliance," National Federation of State High School Associations, April 16, 2019, https://www.nfhs.org/articles/impact-of-competitive-cheer-laws-regulations-on-title-ix-compliance.

33. James J. Hefferan Jr., "A Sporting Chance: *Biediger v. Quinnipiac University* and What Constitutes a Sport for Purposes of Title IX," *Marquette Sports Law Review* 26, no. 2 (2016): 583–671; Jacqueline R. Liguori, "Sticking the Landing: How the Second Circuit's Decision in *Biediger v. Quinnipiac Univ.* Can Help Competitive Cheerleading Achieve 'Sport' Status Under Title IX," *Jeffrey S. Moorad Sports Law Journal* 21, no. 4 (2014): 153–183.

34. *Biediger v. Quinnipiac University*, 728 F. Supp. 2d 62 (D. Conn. 2010).

35. *Biediger v. Quinnipiac University*, 691 F.3d 85 (2d Cir. 2012).

36. Hefferan, "Sporting Chance"; Liguori, "Sticking the Landing."

37. *Biediger v. Quinnipiac University*, 728 F. Supp. 2d 62 (D. Conn. 2010).

38. Leif Reigstad, "Varsity Brands Owns Cheerleading and Fights to Keep It from Becoming an Official Sport," *Houston Press*, July 21, 2015, https://www.houstonpress.com/news/varsity-brands-owns-cheerleading-and-fights-to-keep-it-from-becoming-an-official-sport-7606297.

39. Jaime Schultz, "Cheerleading's Peculiar Path to Potential Olympic Sport," *The Conversation*, February 1, 2017, https://theconversation.com/cheerleadings-peculiar-path-to-potential-olympic-sport-70386.

40. For a discussion of the contradictory stance Varsity has espoused about cheerleading as a sport, see Daniel Libit, "A Tangled Jeff Webb Weaves Cheerleading's Olympic Dream," *Sportico*, September 16, 2021, https://www.sportico.com/personalities/executives/2021/cheerleading-varsity-brands-webb-1234638714/.

41. Rebecca Ruiz, "Cheerleading and Muay Thai Given Provisional Olympic Status," *New York Times*, December 6, 2016, https://www.nytimes.com/2016/12/06/sports/olympics/cheerleading-muay-thai-provisional-olympic-status.html.

42. "Cheerleading Earns Full Recognition by International Olympic Committee," Varsity Spirit, July 20, 2021, https://www.varsity.com/about/press/cheerleading-earns-full-recognition-by-international-olympic-committee/; "IOC Executive Board Proposes Full Recognition of Six International Federations," International Olympic Committee, June 10, 2021, https://olympics.com/ioc/news/ioc-executive-board-proposes-full-recognition-of-six-international-federations.

43. "How Are Sports Chosen for the Olympics?," *Encyclopedia Britannica*, revised August 8, 2025, https://www.britannica.com/story/how-are-sports-chosen-for-the-olympics.

44. "Meeting of the General Assembly of the International Cheer Union," International Cheer Union, April 23, 2019, https://cheerunion.org/wp-content/uploads/2023/09/ICU_GeneralAssembly_MeetingMinutes_2019.pdf.

45. Lauri Harris, interview with Amy Moritz, June 6, 2024.

46. "STUNT Receives Emerging Sport Recommendation from the NCAA's

Committee on Women's Athletics," USA Cheer, May 12, 2020, https://usacheer.org/stunt-receives-emerging-sport-recommendation-from-the-ncaas-committee-on-womens-athletics; Michelle Brutlag Hosick, "Acrobatics and Tumbling, Women's Wrestling Added to NCAA Emerging Sports for Women Program," NCAA, June 17, 2020, https://www.ncaa.org/news/2020/6/17/acrobatics-and-tumbling-women-s-wrestling-added-to-ncaa-emerging-sports-for-women-program.aspx.

47. "Emerging Sports for Women," NCAA, 2016, https://www.ncaa.org/sports/2016/3/2/emerging-sports-for-women.aspx.

48. Maggie Vanoni, "A Sport of Their Own: How Acrobatics and Tumbling Is Fighting for NCAA Recognition," *Daily Emerald*, April 22, 2019, https://dailyemerald.com/76735/sports/a-sport-of-their-own-how-acrobatics-and-tumbling-is-fighting-for-ncaa-recognition/; Hannah Blair, "A Decade of Growth: The Path to Emerging Sport Status," National Collegiate Acrobatics and Tumbling Association, August 1, 2020, https://thencata.org/news/2020/8/1/acrobatics-tumbling-a-decade-of-growth.aspx; Katie Thomas, "Born on the Sideline: Cheering Clamors to Be a Sport," *New York Times*, May 23, 2011.

49. Nancy L. Malcolm, Christina Gipson, Kristen S. Pirie, and Rachel Miller Wood, "The Creation of Stunt Cheer: A Story of Innovation, Cheerleading and Gender Politics of Sport," in *Social Innovation in Sport*, ed. Anne Tjønndal (Palgrave Macmillan, 2021), 245–264; "Cheering Could Become NCAA Sport," ESPN, September 8, 2010, https://www.espn.com/college-sports/news/story?id=5546963.

50. Sean Gregory, "Cheer Factor," *Time*, April 23, 2012, 54–57.

51. Mary Helen Sprecher, "Two Emerging Sports on the Grow: STUNT and Acrobatics & Tumbling," *Sports Destination Management*, June 3, 2022, https://www.sportsdestinations.com/sports/cheer-dance/two-emerging-sports-grow-stunt-and-acrobatics-30306.

52. "Administrator's Guide," High School STUNT Association, https://www.usacheer.org/wp-content/uploads/2016/05/2014Administrator_Guide_HS.pdf.

53. "Meet Format," National Collegiate Acrobatics and Tumbling Association, 2019, https://thencata.org/sports/2019/8/26/information-Meet-Format.aspx.

54. College Stunt Association, "2018 STUNT Handbook," USA Cheer, 2018, https://www.usacheer.org/wp-content/uploads/2017/10/2018-College-STUNT-Rule-Book-10-13-17.pdf.

55. Kiley Bouchard, "Why Clemson Cheer Feels Overlooked by Community and Athletics," *The Tiger*, October 5, 2023, https://thetigercu.com/14803/sports/why-clemson-cheer-feels-overlooked-by-community-and-athletics/.

56. "UA Cheerleaders Disappointed They Won't Get Championship Rings After Winning Nationals," AL.com, January 29, 2011, https://www.al.com/sports/2011/01/ua_cheerleaders_disappointed_t.html.

57. Martha H. Verbrugge, "Gender, Science & Fitness: Perspectives on Women's Exercise in the United States," *Health and History* 4, no. 1 (2002): 52–53.

58. Joan Hult, "The Story of Women's Athletics: Manipulating a Dream, 1890–1985," in *Women and Sport: Interdisciplinary Perspectives*, ed. D. Margaret Costa and Sharon R. Guthrie (Human Kinetics, 1994), 83–107.

59. Birgit Palzkill and Angela Fisher, "Between Gymshoes and High-Heels: The Development of a Lesbian Identity and Existence in Top Class Sports," *International Review for the Sociology of Sport* 25, no. 3 (1990): 226; Pat Griffin, "Changing the Game: Homophobia, Sexism, and Lesbians in Sport," *Quest* 44, no. 2 (1992): 251–265.

60. Terry Gross, host, "Comic Hannah Einbinder on 'Hacks,' Cheerleading and Laughs as a Love Language," *Fresh Air*, NPR, June 17, 2024, https://www.npr.org/transcripts/nx-s1-5006044.

CHEER NOTE #3

# Cheer Lingo

Cheerleading has a subculture all its own, complete with rituals, traditions, and a specialized vocabulary. How cheer literate are you? Match the term with its correct definition.

| | |
|---|---|
| 1. base | A. location of the annual NCA collegiate championship |
| 2. flyer | B. form of cheerleading whose sole purpose is competition |
| 3. stumbler | C. cheerleader who capitalizes financially on their social media presence |
| 4. Daytona | D. cheerleader on the top of the pyramid and/or tossed in the air |
| 5. full out | E. to perform a skill successfully |
| 6. hit | F. cheerleader who supports the flyer by holding, lifting, or tossing them |
| 7. make mat | G. flawless routine with no mistakes or deductions |
| 8. mat talk | H. international championship for competitive / All Star cheerleaders |
| 9. no zero routine | I. encouraging words cheerleaders give to each other |
| 10. on mat | J. cheerleader who tumbles and stunts |
| 11. spotter | K. cheerleaders who perform in front of judges at a competition |
| 12. Worlds | L. competitive selection process to determine who will perform in front of judges |
| 13. Nationals | M. cheerleader standing in the back, responsible for protecting flyer from injury |
| 14. All Star | N. National Cheerleaders Association's premier national collegiate championship |
| 15. cheerlebrity | O. when a team performs its entire routine from start to finish in preparation for competition |

(Answers found on page 283.)

CHAPTER 4

# Between Legitimacy and Femininity

## CHEERLEADING AND THE POLITICS OF GENDER IN SPORT

*Emily West and Laura Grindstaff*

Other athletes lift weights. Cheerleaders lift athletes.

Popular cheer T-shirt

As the previous chapter outlined, cheerleading's status as a sport is very much contested. The sport debate reflects the origins of cheerleading as a sideline activity—meant to support and promote school spirit for sports at the heart of collegiate and high school life—and its subsequent transformation into an athletic activity in its own right, complete with competitions, judges, titles, and even injuries, due to the intensive acrobatics at the most elite levels of cheerleading.

But we can't fully understand why the sport debate exists, and why it matters, separately from the politics of gender in cheerleading. By gender politics, we mean the unequal expectations, demands, and rewards for cheerleading relative to other sports because of its long-standing association with girls, women, and femininity. We also mean the gender politics *within* cheerleading, in terms of the unequal expectations, demands, and rewards for cheerleaders based on their gender identity and expression.

We learned about both types of gender politics through our years of ethnographic fieldwork with college cheerleading teams, spanning ten years from the late 1990s to the late 2000s.[1] Both together and separately, we did long-term observations of three college teams on the East and West Coasts of the United States: two focused primarily on sideline cheerleading and one that combined sideline obligations with participation in high-level collegiate competitions. In addition, we attended a dozen college camps and fifteen cheerleading competitions, including All Star competitions featuring cheerleading teams that train in private gyms, unconnected to any school and therefore free of sideline obligations. Drawing from the teams we observed regularly, people we met at camps and competitions, and cheer executives and coaches whom we reached out to, we interviewed more than 150 people about cheerleading. The sport debate and the gender politics of cheerleading came up readily in these conversations, often before we could broach these issues ourselves, as they shape the very meaning of cheerleading and lie at the heart of its struggle for respect.

Our analysis of the gender politics of cheerleading is shaped by our theoretical understanding of gender as an organizing category of social life. This sociological understanding denaturalizes gender as something simply assumed or taken for granted. Rather, we recognize the social expectations for gender performance and expression that we are all subject to, and the ways that we are then called upon in our social environments to "do" gender in a manner consistent with the gender assigned to us, typically in alignment with our sex characteristics.[2] In Judith Butler's terms, "gender is an identity tenuously constituted in time, instituted in an exterior space through a stylized repetition of acts."[3] In other words, gender is not merely an individual attribute that one has; it is something enacted, produced in interaction with others, "an emergent property of social situations,"[4] a "constructed identity," and "a performative accomplishment."[5]

Likewise, people do not simply import their already gendered selves into neutral institutions; rather, institutions are themselves gendered and invite us to perform gender in particular ways or, conversely, discourage or sanction particular performances of gender.[6] The military, for example, is a male-dominated institution with a relatively narrow range of options for "doing" masculinity. Cheerleading, too, is a gendered institution and is an especially interesting case because its gender expectations have changed over time depending on whether it has been male or female dominated. Once a paragon of elite masculinity in all-male American colleges, cheerleading transformed into a feminized sideline activity by the mid-twentieth century, particularly popular in high schools.[7] Then, in the late twentieth century, as it became more athletic and organized in the hands of professional cheerleading associations, it became more appealing to men once again. Male participation did not so much revive the all-male origins of cheerleading as spur the rise of coed squads, both in college and All Star settings.

Indeed, at the highest levels of cheerleading competition, it is the coed teams, with both men and women competing, who are most revered. Our interviewees generally attributed this to the spectacular nature of the pyramids and stunts these teams can execute, especially when the male stunters are large and the female flyers are petite. "Big guys, little girls" was a common phrase used by cheerleaders to reference the preferred gender dynamic in coed cheer. At the same time, we can't rule out the legitimizing function of the mere presence of men on coed teams, given the historic association of men with sport and a broader patriarchal context that grants men more power and prestige than women.

The greater prestige and visibility for coed teams is apparent on a number of fronts: their placement in competition programs, typically with the last and most well-attended performances reserved for their finals; the attention given to them in mainstream media, as in the hit Netflix series *Cheer*; and the teams that reportedly offer the biggest scholarships—coed programs like the University of Kentucky, the University of Florida, and the University of Alabama. It's not unusual, for example, for a university's coed squad to cheer at the varsity men's football and basketball games, while the all-girl squad is required to cheer at junior varsity games.

Here we see a hierarchy between coed and all-girl cheer squads that points to two key observations from our research. First, that visibility is a valued reward, both in the culture in general and in the cheer world particularly. And second, that the historic association of cheerleading with women, girls, and femininity is not only key to its distinctiveness and appeal (for participants as well as audiences) but also a liability when it comes to garnering legitimacy. The stakes are high, with resources on the line that may include gym time, money, coaching support, access to facilities and college scholarships, and respect from peers, institutions, and the culture at large. In the end, we concluded that the issue of whether or not cheerleading is a "real" sport is a proxy for the issue of respect.

Considering these tensions between the rewards for feminized performances of visibility and the threat to legitimacy that such feminized performances pose, we describe how participants in the cheer world understand the ways they are called upon to "do" gender in this environment, and how they ultimately choose to inhabit their cheerleader role and perform gender within it.

## The Gender Politics of Cheerleading and Sport

Scholars generally agree that organized athletics, like the military, have been central to the construction of what R. W. Connell calls "hegemonic masculinity," meaning a traditional or idealized masculinity that helps to socialize men into business, politics, and war.[8] In the perennial debate about whether cheerleading is a sport—or at least whether it should be taken seriously as a sport, even if not officially designated so in a particular school—the way that people imagine sport itself as a masculine, and therefore legitimized, category revealed itself over and over. The default sport against which our interviewees compared cheerleading was invariably football, played primarily by men and boys. In these conversations it was assumed that people take football seriously, while cheerleading is constantly on the back foot, defending itself and making a bid for recognition. For all the participants in our study, the term "sport" signified high status; cheerleaders knew that playing sports was more prestigious than cheerleading, especially for men, and they complained about being disrespected by the collegiate athletes for whom they cheered. One college cheerleader was quite blunt about this, saying, "I want it to be considered a sport so people can't trash it."

Despite cheerleading's all-male origins, cheerleading has long been associated with women and girls, who are still the vast majority of its participants, especially when taking high school cheer into account.[9] Our interviewees saw this association as a major obstacle to full public acceptance. A male cheerleader on one of the college teams we observed, who also served as captain, insisted that assigning the label "sport" would make little difference unless people also stopped thinking of cheerleading as "just a bunch of ditzy girls on the sidelines who jump around and entertain the crowd." A woman cheering on the same squad reinforced this point, saying, "People take us more seriously when guys are involved [in cheerleading]." Her male teammate agreed, noting that the presence of "big guys" in cheerleading was crucial to the successful transition to sport, but that public acceptance was being undermined by the predominance of girls. "As long as that's around," he said, "I think it's going to be hard to classify ourselves as a sport. . . . It's got the stigma of an all-girl thing still."

Of course, girls and women do play sports, and more prominently and successfully as the years go by, thanks in large measure to the passage of Title IX in 1972.[10] But within sport there is a persistent gender hierarchy in terms of pay for professional athletes,[11] media coverage,[12] resources and facilities,[13] and societal recognition. Women may participate at higher levels than decades ago, but that doesn't mean sport is no longer a male-dominated and male-privileging institution. Even in traditional sports in which women have made significant inroads, such as soccer and basketball, women struggle for parity with men; the gender equity complaints of the hugely successful US Women's World Cup soccer team is a case in point.[14] Cheerleading, by contrast, resembles "gender-appropriate" sports historically associated with women, such as figure skating and gymnastics, where the basis of competition includes aesthetic and performance considerations in combination with strength, flexibility, and skill.[15] These aesthetic and performative elements, in combination with the predominance of women's participation, are seen as obstacles to legitimacy, even by many cheerleaders themselves.

During competitions no less than on the sidelines, cheerleaders are expected to entertain and pump up the crowd through ritualized displays of spirit intended to encourage audience participation. These performance expectations stem from the legacy of sideline cheering, combined with styles of feminized performance informed by popular music and dance. Thus cheerleading, for women, embodies what sociologists have called "emphasized femininity"[16]—or, more commonly, stereotypical feminine behavior. This embodiment includes never-ending smiles, positivity, and energy; bouncing; eye contact and "facials," which are exaggerated expressions of joy or surprise; and uniforms for female cheerleaders that combine girlishness and sex appeal, with short skirts, tight crop tops, and long hair (typically if not universally) worn in high ponytails adorned with bows (figs. 4.1 and 4.2 illustrate a number of these types of embodiment). As we'll see, the degree to which the feminized performance of spirit is exaggerated—and the degree to which male cheerleaders are expected to embrace it—varies depending on the type of cheerleading (collegiate vs. All Star) and the governing professional association.

The cheerleaders we interviewed recognized the performance demands of cheerleading as part of what made its qualification as a sport, and therefore as a fully respected activity, more complicated. According to one cheerleader, the physical training "is similar to what other sports teams do . . . but [cheerleading] is hard to define because, at the same time, you're performing." Another invoked the same opposition when she compared cheerleading to gymnastics; whereas the latter was "certainly a sport" in her view, she hesitated to characterize cheerleading in the same way

FIGURE 4.1. *Jacksonville University cheerleader performing collegiate-style facials, February 23, 2009. Photo by DeusX-Florida, https://openverse.org/image/72437919-f7d1-4e95-8b3c-fd761345178b?q=JU+cheerleaders&p=2.*

FIGURE 4.2. *Isabelle Bennington (author of chapter 11) demonstrates All Star–style facials while performing at the COA Midwest Nationals in February 2021. Photo used with permission from Isabelle Bennington.*

because "cheerleading is a spectacle, which is like more performance than sport."[17] A third cheerleader remarked disdainfully that "a game face for a cheerleader is a big smile," and connected this to the subjectivity involved in judging the aesthetics of cheerleaders' performances, which in his view removed cheerleading from the center of the category of sport, and therefore from full legitimacy.

## The Gender Politics Within Cheerleading

The gender politics of cheerleading also express themselves within cheerleading, in terms of how men and women relate to the activity, and what expectations they confront when tasked with the performance of spirit. Across our interviews and observations at practices, camps, games, and competitions, we observed and heard about the ways male cheerleaders felt they must navigate the stigma of femininity in cheerleading. They strove both to manage perceptions of their involvement in an activity culturally coded as feminine and to negotiate how, and/or how much, they would participate in the aspects of cheerleading associated with feminized performance. For example, while coaches of coed teams would constantly remind the women to smile and perform facials, they prompted the men less, requiring instead a more muted smile or set of expressions. While the women shake poms and do spirit fingers on the sidelines or during the sideline portion of a competition routine (required by some cheerleading associations), men wield placards and megaphones.

On some teams, the different expectations and pressures experienced by male versus female cheerleaders to perform enthusiasm were designed to keep the activity appealing to men and to protect their masculine image and identity. On coed teams, men, and particularly men with the strength to base difficult stunts, can be a scarce resource, so coaches and cheer programs are inclined to allow more leeway over how they perform in order to retain them. At some schools, we learned that male cheerleaders are released from sideline obligations altogether; the women must put in hours performing the traditional spirit function of cheer (a time-consuming and sometimes thankless task), but their male teammates only attend practices and competitions.

In some settings it was the male cheerleaders themselves setting the terms of performance in negotiation with coaches, while in others the school, coach, or, even more powerfully, the cheer association overseeing a team's camps and competitions determined the gendered division of performative labor on the team. The three largest cheerleading associations at the time of our research—the Universal Cheerleaders Association (UCA), the National Cheerleaders Association (NCA), and the United Spirit Association (USA) (all owned by Varsity Brands)—offered a range of gendered styles of cheer. The UCA's brand was the most "collegiate" (i.e., traditional), a reputation confirmed by our interviewees. At UCA competitions, men typically did not dance (especially since it wasn't part of the official scoring), and they didn't participate in the specialized jumps that the women executed in unison. On NCA-affiliated teams, male cheerleaders did dance and execute jumps, but in a so-called masculine way that differentiated them from their female teammates: no twirls, spins, or leaps, no bumping or grinding, "nothing suggestive," was how the coach of an NCA-affiliated squad put it.

And finally, the USA aligned with a style that more closely resembled All Star cheer, characterized by big facials and frenetic dance moves ranging from sassy to suggestive. Designed to communicate attitude, this style was more show business than collegiate, with tighter uniforms, shorter skirts, brighter colors, more sparkles, and heavier makeup (the stylistic contrast between collegiate-style cheerleading and All Star cheerleading is illustrated by figs. 4.1 and 4.2). In USA competitions, we saw the least division of labor across male and female cheerleaders, with men fully participating and sometimes disproportionately featured and celebrated for their dancing, jumping, and emoting. And then there is All Star cheer, widely recognized as the most show business–like of all ("over the top" was a common descriptor). With no connection to scholastic settings or audiences interested in anything other than cheerleading itself, All Star cheer is relatively free from the pressures to meet public expectations of appropriate gender display. Performances were uninhibited and unapologetically flashy for men and women alike.

Despite the variation in cheerleading styles, or perhaps because of them, the aesthetic and emotional aspects of the cheerleading performance were deemed natural expectations for women who cheer, but potentially disconfirming or even threatening to hegemonic masculinity, a version of masculinity meant to communicate power, stoicism, and heterosexuality.[18] In just about every setting, people mentioned or recognized something one of our male cheerleaders called the "gay cheerleader syndrome": the assumption on the part of viewers that men who participate in feminized activities and fail to communicate hegemonic masculinity must be gay. Gender and sexuality are conflated in our culture, such that the "wrong" (gay) sexual orientation is automatically assumed based on the "wrong" (feminized) gender performance for men. Plenty of male cheerleaders are gay, of course. But the point is not whether male cheerleaders are "really" gay; the point is what impression or performance of masculinity is defined as acceptable to convey to audiences by a team, school, or cheer association. Cheerleading can be, and often is, a welcoming and inclusive space for gay men; it can also be a space where the public performance of masculinity is policed even as offstage expressions of gayness are embraced. This may stem from pressures from school administrators, spectators at games where squads cheer, and competition judges. It is also no doubt due to the legitimation that a certain *version* of male participation affords.

The experiences of male cheerleaders navigating the so-called gay cheerleader syndrome are the inverse of those long experienced by women playing sports historically associated with masculinity.[19] Women playing sports like basketball, soccer, and hockey have historically and are still today stigmatized as insufficiently feminine in appearance and bodily comportment, again because of the conflation of gender performance and sexuality and a culture of "compulsory heterosexuality."[20]

Although a fully intersectional analysis of the gender politics of cheerleading is beyond the scope of this chapter, it bears mentioning that performances of hegemonic masculinity within cheerleading appeared to vary by racial identity.[21] Black men, for example, more frequently showed off their dance skills at competitions and summer training camps, and they were more likely than white or Latino men to express facial "attitude" during routines. Their efforts, typically celebrated by audiences and rewarded by judges, were interpreted as consistent with a performance of straight masculinity in those contexts. This is likely because of the historic association of African Americans with music and dance, and their continued visibility as leaders and innovators in the realm of popular entertainment—in part a function of their historic and ongoing exclusion from business and politics. But Black men also spoke of strong resistance to the performative elements of cheer because of their overrepresentation in "real" sports (e.g., football and basketball) and the pressure to uphold a tough guy image. Latino men reported the same thing, sometimes using the stereotypical term "macho." This illustrates that understandings of hegemonic masculinity are culturally and contextually specific, and the latitude afforded different men for achieving or performing it may vary with dimensions of social identity other than gender.

Coed teams highlight the gender politics of cheerleading because the relational nature of masculinity and femininity plays out side by side. But the gender politics of cheerleading are just as powerful for women in so-called all-girl settings. Women, regardless of racial identity, were granted much less flexibility regarding the aesthetic and performance demands of cheerleading—how they look and act. The performance of spirit, with its compulsory smiling, unfailing supportiveness, and bubbly enthusiasm, naturalizes the connection between femininity and the emotional support of others, as well as the notion that affective performance itself is somehow inherent to femininity.[22] This understanding has been forged within a white, middle-class, heterosexual framework of feminized emotional expression that communicates deference even in the face of increased skill and athleticism: deference to those being supported and to the social norms that dictate the terms of acceptable feminine expressiveness. Regardless of a female cheerleader's actual racial, sexual, or class identity, all were expected to embrace a feminized performance of spirit.

Interviewees had quite mixed opinions about the emotional and feminized demands of the activity. Many merely tolerated them as part of the job: "You just have to suck it up and do it," as one college cheerleader put it. Another acknowledged matter-of-factly that the smiles and other expressions of spirit were inauthentic: "A lot of it's fake. Sometimes you're having fun," she said, but much of the time putting on a smile is "like putting on makeup," just part of "getting ready for the game." Some cheerleaders of color similarly raised the issue of authenticity but in cultural rather than individual terms. A Black woman on the West Coast squad we observed said she was frequently accused of "acting white" by coethnic peers, and we heard similar reports from Black female cheerleaders at summer camps and competitions, even those belonging to all-Black teams. An Asian American college cheerleader reported parental objections to cheerleading—less because of performing spirit per se and more because of the skimpy uniforms and the highly visible nature of the performance. As the daughter of first-generation immigrants, she was told good Asian girls don't call attention to themselves like that in public. A Latina college cheerleader reported, in contrast, that her immigrant parents encouraged cheerleading in high school as a vehicle for assimilation into "all-American" girlhood.

Other women fully embraced the spirit dimension of cheerleading on its own terms. A veteran college cheerleader on a Florida college team insisted that the high school cheerleaders she coached "exist first to be ambassadors of the school, second to promote school spirit and bring people to the games, third to support their teams—every team, not just the football team, not just the basketball team, but every team—and then finally to compete." Here, like women in caretaking roles in the labor force and in the home, cheerleaders are supposed to demonstrate selflessness by putting the needs and desires of others before their own while also insisting (often unsuccessfully) on the cultural value of doing so.[23]

Many interviewees who didn't necessarily see their performance of spirit as authentic nevertheless embraced the "girly" parts of the performance as pleasurable and as a form of play that they understood to be separate from "real life." They accepted the feminine accoutrements of cheerleading such as short skirts, makeup, and hair bows as "just part of the show," "just for entertainment," and "necessary to please the crowd"—in other words, a taken-for-granted necessity in an activity focused on entertainment and bodily display. This comment is illustrative: "I think it's fun, quite honestly. As a girl I like to do my makeup kind of fun and sparkly and get out there. . . . I like wearing ribbons in my hair. It's a girly feminine thing and I think it's something that shouldn't be lost." A teammate of this cheerleader pointed out the continuities between the performance of femininity in cheerleading and the rest of American culture, saying, "It's the same with being on TV, like, or being a singer. You want them to be cute, you're watching them, you know. . . . If you gotta wear the short skirts to make people look at you, then I guess that's what you gotta do."

We see this cheerleader articulate the way that cheerleading institutionalizes the demands and rewards for women, especially young women, in American culture of being visible in ways consistent with an emphasized femininity rooted in white, middle-class heteronormativity. If you want people to look at you, and to reap the rewards of positive attention, you must understand the expectations for a certain kind of feminine display. This is conditional visibility, hinging on being attractive for an imagined heterosexual gaze, being positive and peppy and taking responsibility for other people's emotions, doing hard things but making them look easy, and never being seen breaking a sweat.

## The Meaning of Performance in a Gendered World

In our research, the performance demands of cheerleading were a constant thread of conversation that sat uneasily with assumptions about what constitutes "real" sports such as football. In football, as in most other male-dominated sports, aesthetics are considered incidental rather than carefully rehearsed and executed (elaborate touchdown and goal-scoring celebrations notwithstanding). Ironically, performance is simultaneously what makes cheerleading appealing to many participants and popular with audiences *and* what marks it as "less than" in gendered cultural hierarchies.

In our research, the category of performance itself was conflated with women and femininity (regardless of gender), and secondarily, if partially, with Black masculinity. Female cheerleaders either embraced or reluctantly tolerated the performance elements demanded of them to receive attention and to be rewarded for meeting cultural expectations. Men, particularly those invested in appearing straight, were more likely to view these demands as a disagreeable aspect of cheerleading that had to be actively managed to maintain an acceptable image of masculinity.

Our point is not that performance is bad, or fake, or that it should be stigmatized. Rather, we note that its association with femininity reinforces restrictive gender norms and a gendered hierarchy of what is considered serious or legitimate. For it to be a naturalized expectation of women but not of men is limiting for women and can undermine their accomplishments and worth. Why should women have to execute death-defying acrobatics with a smile, take responsibility for making others feel good, or make sex appeal part of the entertainment? Likewise, for men to be excluded from the opportunity to perform in these ways, or to do so only at the expense of their own gender or sexual identity, is also limiting. Performance is a powerful form of play, and as such would ideally be open to all, but not compulsory.

The dissatisfaction that we heard from some young women in our research about the performative dimensions of cheerleading has prompted an institutional response in the form of acro and STUNT,[24] discussed in the previous chapter. As the development of these new forms of cheering shows, cheerleading is constantly evolving. Relative to the period in which we conducted this research, ideas about gender itself are changing, with greater openness and awareness that gender is neither fixed nor something that can be defined by a binary between "man" and "woman." We have also seen greater visibility and acceptance of lesbian, gay, bisexual, trans, and queer identities in society, especially among young people, so the pressures on cheerleaders to conform to idealized images of masculinity and femininity as conflated with opposite-sex attraction may be shifting or dissipating. At the same time, to continue dismissing the "traditional" cheerleading of girls and women as trivial, unserious, and unimportant compared to "real" sports is to continue reinforcing the stigma of femininity that has marginalized women in "real" sports and contributed to the definition of what "real" sports even are. The goal, in our view, is not to enforce gendered mandates but to have options and possibilities across all social institutions.

## Notes

1. See Laura Grindstaff and Emily West, "Cheerleading and the Gendered Politics of Sport," *Social Problems* 53, no. 4 (2006): 500–518; Laura Grindstaff and Emily West, "Hands on Hips, Smiles on Lips! Gender, Race, and the Performance of Spirit in Cheerleading," *Text and Performance Quarterly* 30, no. 2 (2010): 143–162; Laura Grindstaff and Emily West, "Hegemonic Masculinity on the Sidelines of Sport," *Sociology Compass* 5, no. 10 (2011): 859–881.

2. Candace West and Sarah Fenstermaker, "Doing Difference," *Gender and Society* 9, no. 1 (1995): 8–37.

3. Judith Butler, *Gender Trouble: Feminism and the Subversion of Identity* (University of Minnesota Press, 2006), 191.

4. West and Fenstermaker, "Doing Difference," 9.

5. Butler, *Gender Trouble*, 192.

6. Joan Acker, "Hierarchies, Jobs, Bodies: A Theory of Gendered Organizations," *Gender and Society* 4, no. 2 (1990): 139–158; R. W. Connell, *Gender and Power* (Stanford University Press, 1987); Michael Messner, *Taking the Field: Women, Men, and Sports* (University of Minnesota Press, 2022).

7. For more, see chapter 1 of this volume.

8. Connell, *Gender and Power*.

9. The Sports and Fitness Industry Association estimated in 2018 that out of all cheerleaders, 21.8 percent were boys and men. See Cameron Schofner, "The Diversity and Challenges of the Rising Sport of Competitive Cheerleading," *Insight by Balance Now*, January 27, 2022, https://insight.balancenow.co/competitive-cheerleading-the-diversity-challenges-of-the-rising-sport/.

10. Title IX is a federal law prohibiting gender discrimination in educational institutions that receive federal funds. The law prohibits high schools and colleges that receive federal funds from discriminating on the basis of gender in the provision of any educational activity, including athletics.

11. Taylor Kennedy Gersch, "The Gender Pay Gap: Seeking Fairness for Women in Professional Sports," *Oregon Review of International Law* 22 (2021): 147; Nicole Zerunyan, "Time's Up: Addressing Gender-Based Wage Discrimination in Professional Sports," *Loyola of Los Angeles International Law Review* 38 (2017): 229.

12. Janet S. Fink, "Female Athletes, Women's Sport, and the Sport Media Commercial Complex: Have We Really 'Come a Long Way, Baby'?," *Sport Management Review* 18, no. 3 (2015): 331–342; Cheryl Cooky, LaToya D. Council, Maria A. Mears, and Michael A. Messner, "One and Done: The Long Eclipse of Women's Televised Sports, 1989–2019," *Communication and Sport* 9, no. 3 (2021): 347–371.

13. Ellen J. Staurowsky, Courtney L. Flowers, Erin Buzuvis, Lindsay Darvin, and Natalie Welch, "The Women's Sports Foundation, 50 Years of Title IX: We're Not Done Yet; Executive Summary and Policy Recommendations," *Women in Sport and Physical Activity Journal* 30, no. 2 (2022): 71–84, https://www.choice360.org/wp-content/uploads/2023/08/The_Women_s_Sports_Foundation_50_Years_o.pdf.

14. Henry Bushnell, "The USWNT on Equal Pay: The Women's Soccer World Is Still Fighting," *Yahoo! Sports*, July 18, 2023, https://sports.yahoo.com/the-uswnt-won-equal-pay-the-womens-soccer-world-is-still-fighting-150005810.html; Andrew Das, "US Soccer and Women's Players Agree to Settle Equal Pay Lawsuit," *New York Times*, February 22, 2022, https://www.nytimes.com/2022/02/22/sports/soccer/us-womens-soccer-equal-pay.html.

15. Nathalie Koivula, "Perceives Characteristics of Sports Categorized as Gender-Neutral, Feminine and Masculine," *Journal of Sport Behavior* 24, no. 4 (2001): 377–393; Mary Louise Adams, "From Mixed-Sex Sport to Sport for Girls: The Feminization of Figure Skating," in *Women in Sports History*, ed. Carol Osborne and Fiona Skillen (Routledge, 2014), 29–52.

16. Connell, *Gender and Power*.

17. At the same time, some women's gymnastics disciplines, particularly floor and beam, award points for performance elements such as dance movements and grace.

18. Connell, *Gender and Power*; R. W. Connell and James W. Messerschmidt, "Hegemonic Masculinity: Rethinking the Concept," *Gender and Society* 19, no. 6 (2005): 829–859.

19. Susan K. Cahn, *Coming On Strong: Gender and Sexuality in Women's Sport* (University of Illinois Press, 2015); Helen Jefferson Lenskyj, *Out of Bounds: Women, Sport and Sexuality* (Women's Press, 1986).

20. Butler, *Gender Trouble*, 24.

21. The concept of intersectionality originates from the critical legal scholar Kimberlé Crenshaw's 1989 article "Demarginalizing the Intersection of Race and Sex: A Black Feminist Critique of Antidiscrimination Doctrine," *University of Chicago Legal Forum* 1 (1989): 139–168. It has gone on to inspire a wide variety of scholarship and activism that recognizes the ways oppression and discrimination operate differently for people at different intersections of marginalized identities, rooted in Crenshaw's original argument that discrimination against women as a class is qualitatively different than the discrimination experienced by Black women specifically. The concept of intersectionality is also central to Judith Butler's analysis of gender as a category: "If one 'is' a woman, that is surely not all one is." This is because "gender is not always constituted coherently or consistently in different historical contexts, and because gender intersects with racial, class, ethnic, sexual, and regional modalities of discursively constituted identities. As a result, it becomes impossible to separate out 'gender' from the political and cultural intersections in which it is invariably produced and maintained." Butler, *Gender Trouble*, 4–5.

22. Arlie Russell Hochschild, *The Managed Heart: Commercialization of Human Feeling* (University of California Press, 1983).

23. Jennifer L. Pierce, *Gender Trials: Emotional Lives in Contemporary Law Firms* (University of California Press, 1996); Christine L. Williams, *Still a Man's World: Men Who Do Women's Work* (University of California Press, 1995).

24. STUNT is capitalized in reference to this new sport to distinguish it from the activity of stunting, which is one of the sport's component skills.

PART II

# The Other Cheerleaders

## SEX, WORK, AND PROTEST

CHAPTER 5

# Dallas Cowboys Cheerleaders

## MAKING AMERICA'S SWEETHEARTS

*Lauren R. Nowosatka*

Often imitated, never equaled.

Dallas Cowboys Cheerleaders tagline

I remember watching *Dallas Cowboys Cheerleaders: Making the Team* on Country Music Television when I was a tween-aged girl. At the time, I was a high-level competitive gymnast, so watching potential Dallas Cowboys Cheerleaders vying for their spot on the coveted thirty-six-member kick line, enduring strict training regimes under merciless, tyrannical authority, was familiar to me. I related to the women on the screen, presuming everything they faced was customary for high-level athletes.

I came back to *Making the Team* as a young adult, having randomly scrolled past the show as I desperately tried to find something to watch during COVID-19 lockdowns, eager to put it on and recalling my youthful fascination with it. Watching what would have been at that time the most recent season, I was shocked by what I saw. Though, when I thought back to when I had watched the show as a young gymnast, it made sense why I had found the show so appealing at that point in my life. Returning to the show as a young adult, having just started my first semester of graduate school in physical cultural studies, I still found the show wildly appealing, but this time for an entirely different reason. I no longer related to the women. Rather, I was bewildered by them.

In the opening episode of season 13 (what I refer to as the #MeToo season), Dallas Cowboys Cheerleaders director and alumna Kelli McGonagill Finglass proudly declares that the squad "empowers women."[1] But what I saw over the course of the season's thirteen episodes seemed very disempowering as I watched these cheerleader-hopefuls try to transform their natural appearance and physical attributes to align with the unrealistic beauty standards of a human Barbie doll. During weigh-ins in the rehearsal studio or the locker room, Finglass and choreographer Judy Trammell frequently discuss the women in terms of their body parts.[2] Their criticism is often harsh, and the disappointment of the hopefuls who don't make the team is heartbreaking as the girls pack up and leave. For the interview part of the tryouts, the candidates appear in front of a panel consisting, in part, of powerful men who applaud and chuckle at their coquettish behavior. It seemed that the more hyperfeminine and sexualized they presented themselves, the greater their chances of becoming one of "America's Sweethearts." What was empowering about this?

The Dallas Cowboys Cheerleaders became the topic of my first graduate-level, physical cultural studies–focused manuscript. I was keen to dive into the cheerleaders as a subject of critique. Learning for the first time about gendered (bio)hegemonies, sporting neoliberalism, and sport governance, I saw each of those institutionally embedded within the squad. As I wrote and researched, I was surprised at the dearth of scholarly research about the Dallas Cowboys Cheerleaders or professional cheerleading. Learning and writing more that first semester, I was convinced I had struck gold, and I practically jump-splitted for joy when my advisor thought an analysis of the reality TV show would make a suitable master's thesis topic.[3] Over the following year and a half, I watched enough *Making the Team* to make the team myself. I knew everything they were looking for like the back of my pom-pom-less hand: high kicks, a beaming white smile, bouncy and voluminous long hair, formal technical dance training, a curvy yet mannequin-like thin physique, coy manners and a seductive allure, and utter submission to authority. None of which, I might add, I was willing—or interested, for that matter—to consent to. What perplexed me most was how many women were so ready to acquiesce, so willing to do whatever it took to wear the uniform now archived in the Smithsonian.[4]

In this chapter, I dive into the world of the Dallas Cowboys Cheerleaders (the matriarch of professional cheerleading)—their origins, their evolution, and their representation on two popular series: *Dallas Cowboys Cheerleaders: Making the Team* and *America's Sweethearts: Dallas Cowboys Cheerleaders*. I examine why the Dallas Cowboys Cheerleaders matter—not only to the hundreds of women who audition every year for a coveted spot on the thirty-six-member team but also for understanding how key feminist narratives (in particular, empowerment and choice) are appropriated to perpetuate patriarchal norms.[5] To conclude, I present a quandary that questions how the Dallas Cowboys Cheerleaders, and professional cheerleaders at large, are made "to feel like they're valued, that they're special," within the context of a rather disempowering or faux empowering environment.[6]

But first, some Dallas Cowboys Cheerleaders history.

## The Making of America's Sweethearts

Despite early cheerleading's roots in the masculine, "elite confines" of late nineteenth- and early twentieth-century collegiate life,[7] professional cheerleading in America did not take shape, albeit loosely, until the 1950s. Early professional sports teams, namely the National Football League's Baltimore and Washington teams, recruited cheerleaders from local high schools to support and promote their franchises in the mid-1950s. Throughout the 1960s, the volunteer cheerleaders primarily accompanied marching bands during halftime shows and performed pom-pom-style dances on the sidelines, emulating collegiate dance squads and drill teams. From 1961 to 1969, Dallas Cowboys fans were entertained at halftime shows by a group of high school students, consisting of both girls and boys, called the Belles and their Beaux. In 1969, the boys were dropped from the squad, as was the name Beaux, and young women were deployed as ambassadors to sell the team, making public appearances while also "look[ing] sexy."[8]

The exact origin story of the current iteration of the Dallas Cowboys Cheerleaders and their iconic uniform is a bit harder to pin down. One story goes like this: At the 1967 Cotton Bowl game between the Dallas Cowboys and the Atlanta Falcons, Bubbles Cash, a local burlesque performer, paraded down the stadium steps wearing a leopard microminiskirt and blowing kisses while carrying two hot-pink cotton candies. Her performance created quite a stir among the fans and gained the attention of Tex Schramm, the Dallas Cowboys general manager. He had an idea, one that he put in place several years later when he hired local dance studio owner Texie Waterman to create flashier dance routines for an older, more glamorous, all-female squad.[9] Schramm's vision imagined a squad that would look more like Bubbles Cash than a group of chaste high school girls. He also hired a local fashion designer named Paula Van Wagoner to design a new uniform for a spicier cheerleading look. Voilà—the Dallas Cowboys Cheerleaders and their iconic sexy outfits were born.[10]

Dee Brock, whom Schramm hired in the 1960s as the director of the Belles and Beaux, tells a different story to Sarah Hepola on the podcast *America's Girls*.[11] Brock takes credit for being the brains behind the world's most famous cheerleading squad. She relates, "Tex Schramm had nothing to do with starting [the Dallas Cowboys Cheerleaders] except to finally give his permission." She insists that the franchise had needed a new look, with adult women, racier uniforms, and flashier dance routines. "I've never heard of Bubbles Cash," the ninety-one-year-old Brock tells Hepola. Brock initiated the hiring of Texie Waterman, a Dallas-native New York choreographer and an old friend. Brock also claims that she first sketched a rough outline of the iconic uniform. Paula Van Wagoner, on the other hand, remembers it differently. She recalls showing Schramm and Brock two sketches she had drawn of potential uniforms. One had a Western-style, cowgirlish fringe skirt. Schramm and Brock opted for the second sketch: white, hip-hugging hot pants; a royal-blue, cleavage-baring bolero top tied just below the chest; white go-go boots; a tiny, white, fringed vest; and a star-studded belt. This became the iconic Dallas Cowboys Cheerleader uniform that has changed little in the last forty years.[12]

While the origins of the team and the uniform are debatable, two facts are undisputable: First, although Dee Brock and Paula Van Wagoner were instrumental in the creation of the Dallas Cowboys Cheerleaders brand and uniform, neither has been given much credit for her contributions, and neither has profited financially for her role in creating the iconic team. And second, the Dallas Cowboys Cheerleaders capitalized on an existing male voyeuristic fantasy of "making it" with the popular, pretty girl, and in doing so, birthed an entire professional cheerleading industry. Just four years later, when network television producers at Super Bowl X captured an amorous Dallas Cowboys Cheerleader winking directly at the cameras, the squad became a national sensation.[13]

Suzanne Mitchell, the director of the Dallas Cowboys Cheerleaders from 1976 to 1989, was highly protective of the individual women on the squad as well as the image of the collective and of the Cowboys franchise.[14] She instituted a strict image policy with stringent weight requirements for team members and a lengthy list of rules to ensure that the cheerleaders were viewed as classy women with high moral standards: no wearing jeans in public, no jewelry, no smoking or drinking in uniform, no gum chewing, no cursing, no appearing at events where alcohol was served, and most definitely no fraternizing in any way with the football players. Initially, she insisted on hiring only women who were either full-time students, mothers and/or wives, or full-time workers. Being physically attractive was a given, but Mitchell also wanted the cheerleaders to be seen as independent, professional, and capable women who keenly desired to be ambassadors for the franchise, despite and in addition to their other impressive achievements and responsibilities.[15] Before every game, Mitchell and her cheerleaders locked pinkies and recited the Lord's Prayer.[16] Mitchell may not have created the Dallas Cowboys Cheerleader brand, but she strategically nurtured it throughout her tenure.

The rules discussed above were implemented to protect the squad members from tawdry insults and critique by projecting an image of polished, professional, and virtuous women. At the same time, however, the Dallas Cowboys Cheerleaders were unmistakably erotic, as evident in their iconic uniform, provocative dances, sultry smiles, winks, moves, and sexy look with lots of cleavage, hair, and makeup. As Hepola notes, Mitchell's militarized rule book sought to "keep the cheerleaders safe while presenting them as endlessly available."[17] That is, they were meant to convey, on one hand, the all-American good girl while, on the other, oozing sexuality. As three former Dallas Cowboys Cheerleaders explain:

> How do you tap into the paradox of the sexy, wholesome girl[,] the girl you'd like to take home to mother but make love to on the way over there? Well, take Miss America and dress her in hot pants and a halter top. Then put her out on a football field grinding out a lot of provocative dances, but the whole time keep telling the fans that these are good girls, wholesome girls.[18]

It was under Mitchell's leadership that the Dallas Cowboys Cheerleaders became America's Sweethearts, and their popularity skyrocketed in the late 1970s. Their 1977 poster was purportedly the most popular poster of the day, selling more than one million copies. With fame came threats to their personal safety and criticism. Alumnae have recalled being chased and grabbed at on their way out of an out-of-town performance, repeatedly called late at night by strange men, and one even woke up in the middle of the night to find an unknown, older man looming over her. Some of the harshest critics of the Dallas Cowboys Cheerleaders were feminists, who were fighting in the 1970s for the end of the sexual objectification of women, as well as political and social rights such as workplace equality and equal pay. They saw cheerleaders as the antithesis of feminism and publicly declared the Dallas Cowboys Cheerleaders in particular as "demeaning to women."[19] In 1982, when the cheerleaders visited California State University, Fresno, protestors threw rocks at them and barraged them with slurs.

Feminist criticism did not deter the growth of professional cheerleading in the 1970s and early 1980s. Other teams took notice of the success of the Dallas Cowboys Cheerleaders and began their own similar squads. When the Atlanta Hawks began looking for cheerleaders for their National Basketball Association team, their promotions director made no pretense of hiding their intent: "We're gonna put them in the skimpiest uniforms possible that won't be obscene and won't get us arrested."[20] By 1978, professional cheerleaders had become so popular that John Madden, coach of the Oakland Raiders, half-jokingly predicted that professional cheerleaders would attract a larger audience on Sunday afternoon than the game being played on the field. "After the girls have competed, the football players will come out at halftime for their exhibition," Madden told *Sports Illustrated*, "but the press won't notice because they'll be too busy watching replays of the cheerleaders."[21]

Since professional cheerleaders first high-kicked onto the 50-yard line, individual women and their respective squads have been subject to a great deal of controversy. Upon the rise of professional cheerleading's popularity in the late 1970s, which correlated with that of televised sports broadcasting, critics asserted that cheerleaders posed a threat to football by distracting audiences inundated with footage of the "honey shot."[22] A journalist writing in *Sports Illustrated* in 1978 quipped, "Goodness knows, the only thing anybody talks about anymore is S-E-X and the Dallas Cowboy Cheerleaders."[23] That same year, several cheerleaders across the National Football League were featured in the "NFL Bares All" issue of *Playboy* magazine.[24] Though no Dallas Cowboys Cheerleaders were pictured in the issue, five former squad members—who had left the squad "fed up with the rules, worn down by the demanding schedule and low pay"[25]—were printed in a similar, "Texas Cowgirls" *Playboy* spread, also published in 1978, parodying the iconic Dallas Cowboys Cheerleader poster created just one year prior.[26] Ironically, the "sex sells" mantra that initially sashayed professional cheerleaders into fame did not leap the women into further fortune, presumably because of *Playboy*'s X-rated depiction of the cheerleaders, eradicating any sense of the girl-next-door facade of innocence.

As Suzanne Mitchell and current team director Kelli Finglass have discovered, crafting a public image built around sexuality (good girl / bad girl) and empowerment, individualism and professionalism is difficult.[27] Finglass works as tenaciously as her predecessor to ensure that the cheerleaders are viewed as role models, not sex objects. "The Dallas Cowboys Cheerleaders are high-achievers and powerful, educated, thoughtful, kind and successful women," Finglass told CMT News. "They're role models—an inspiration for those eager to know the balancing act of family, a career, and a wild, all-American dream."[28] But as already discussed here, and more thoroughly in the next chapter, many Dallas Cowboys Cheerleaders have begun speaking up about the contradiction inherent in the franchise's attempts to brand them as professional and empowered women while continuing to pay them abysmally low wages and subject them to toxic work conditions.

In September 2015, four Dallas Cowboys Cheerleaders pursued legal action for voyeurism committed by former Dallas Cowboys personnel, who reportedly accessed the cheerleaders' private locker room by hiding around a corner with a phone extended in the direction of the cheerleaders as they changed out of their uniforms.[29] They settled for $2.4 million in May 2016, several months after the incident initially took place and following the same four cheerleaders' attempt to file complaints internally within the Cowboys organization. The conditions of the settlement mandated that the cheerleaders could speak no further of the incident. The public relations and communications vice president responsible for the misconduct quietly retired in February of 2022, just two short weeks before Don Van Natta's report of the matter was published by ESPN.[30] In 2018, former cheerleader Erica Wilkins sued the Cowboys organization for lost wages. During her first year, which included mandatory attendance at game days, rehearsals, and additional inner-squad "show group" appearances and performances, she only earned $4,500.[31] In 2024, former cheerleader Victoria Kalina, a breakout star of *America's Sweethearts*, revealed that she took a gap year between her third and fourth seasons because of mental health issues manifesting in disordered eating. As revealed on the show, Victoria's weight had been an issue the first time she tried out for the team in 2018, when the "eleven pounds creep[ing] up on [her]" and her inability to shed the weight in two weeks' time resulted in Finglass removing her from training camp with the justification that Victoria was "immature" and "lacked professionalism."[32]

By the end of the 1970s, the Dallas Cowboys Cheerleaders had forever revolutionized sporting entertainment, significantly influencing the formation and style of professional cheerleading squads to come—the Chicago Honey Bears, the San Diego Chargettes, the Cincinnati Ben-Gals, the Buffalo Jills, the Los Angeles Rams Embraceable Ewes, and the Oakland Raiderettes. They set the standard for what type of woman and what form of American femininity was valued in professional cheerleading. She was thin yet curvy, white, blond, and looked good in cleavage-revealing and butt-showing uniforms. This look is, of course, impossible to achieve for most women, while for others it can only be realized conditionally and temporarily. As evident in the two TV series about the Dallas Cowboys Cheerleaders team, there seems to be a singularity to what an America's Sweetheart should look like, how she should carry herself, as well as the regulated, long-established practices to achieve that status. And the body work required to make the team seems in direct contradiction to a discourse of empowerment, leaving most women, not just the cheerleaders and the squad hopefuls, on the margins of idealized American Sweetheart femininity.

## Inside America's Sweethearts: Dallas Cowboys Cheerleaders in the Media

*Dallas Cowboys Cheerleaders: Making the Team* premiered in 2006. The show chronicles the annual Dallas Cowboys Cheerleader auditions and highlights many of the team's rituals—one of the most important being the fitting for the classic, patented uniform. Yes, the women must be interviewed by a panel of judges, and yes, they are tested on their knowledge of the Dallas Cowboys history and players. But ultimately, being beautiful with a gorgeous body is more important than intellectual acuity, professional achievement, and even dancing ability. A big part of the show, particularly in the early seasons, focuses on the behind-the-scenes comments made by team director Kelli Finglass and choreographer Judy Trammell, both former Dallas Cowboys Cheerleaders. Viewers are privy to frank discussions about weight, jiggles, cellulite, sagging breasts, chunky legs, wide hips, and dimply thighs. You learn quickly that a very narrow image of the desirable cheerleader body exists in Finglass's office. The series ran on CMT for sixteen seasons until it was canceled in 2022.[33]

Two years later, America's Sweethearts reappeared onscreen, this time on the Netflix docuseries and global phenom *America's Sweethearts: Dallas Cowboys Cheerleaders*. Since Netflix's release of the initial series in June

2024 and the second season in June 2025, Dallas Cowboys Cheerleaders past and present, Cowboys and their fans, the dance community, reality TV fiends, and the average Netflix subscriber alike have all been, for lack of a better term, thunderstruck. In the weeks after the show's initial release, I witnessed social media feeds, popular press outlets, and media broadcasts become enthralled once more by the Dallas Cowboys Cheerleaders. Popular media resurfaced the squad's signature choreography, the personal narratives of individual candidates featured on the show, and longstanding narratives about professional cheerleaders (e.g., wage discrepancies, harsh rule books, and the prevalence of mental health issues among professional cheerleaders). TikTok was taken over by users attempting the famous game-commencing "Thunderstruck" dance choreography.[34] In July 2024, Netflix reset their marquee billboard overlooking Sunset Boulevard in Los Angeles with "Please stretch before attempting Thunderstruck."[35] On the other hand, many Twitter users expressed alarm about the squad's ghastly working conditions and advocated for them to form a union. They expressed shock at the cheerleaders' low pay, which, according to team alumna Katherine Puryear, is equivalent to that of a substitute teacher or a Chick-fil-A worker.[36]

Making the team, as highlighted in both of these series, is not as easy as "one-two-three D-C-C." Greg Whiteley, director of the Netflix hit, notes that there is a "heartbreaking authenticity" to Dallas Cowboys Cheerleaders performances. He emphasizes, "All of them have to sort of set aside their troubles and try and put on this game face to go perform."[37] In her analysis of the Miss America pageant, Sarah Banet-Weiser notes that the pageant industry is built around "produc[ing] . . . appropriate representative[s] of the national body."[38] The same is true of the Dallas Cowboys Cheerleaders and other similar professional cheerleading teams. What is readily apparent in these inside views of making the team is the franchise's deft deployment of a seeming assimilation-of-difference narrative to construct a thirty-six-member squad that looks remarkably the same. Watching both series, we discover that the Dallas Cowboys Cheerleaders organization has a very narrow definition of the "national body" of an American Sweetheart. If you want to become one, you must assimilate to the restrictive tenets of emphasized femininity,[39] and to neoliberalism's self- and faux empowering ideologies.[40] Squad hopefuls and members are required by the director, choreographer, stylists, photographers, media personnel, and Dallas Cowboys executives to alter their personal appearances, abide by strict fitness regimes, and surveil their behavior at all times. As former Dallas Cowboys Cheerleader Caroline Sundvold notes in *America's Sweethearts*, "You don't make the cheerleading team for being yourself."[41]

In *Making the Team*, viewers are privy to a behind-the-scenes look at the auditioning process, in which rookies and returning veterans try to mold themselves into a "national body" steeped in a thin-idealizing discourse and sexually objectifying practices. Following the initial three-day auditions, rookie candidates who qualify for the ten-week summer training camp are required to undergo the annual rookie makeovers. During the makeover sessions, blond and brunette candidates receive highlights to give them a "dose of glamour"; a candidate with violet-hued red hair gets it stripped so it is not too "severe for this kind of bouquet we call the Dallas Cowboys Cheerleaders"; and Black candidates undergo hair-straightening treatments, conforming to Eurocentric, white-dominant cultural beauty standards.[42] Though these hair treatments are presented under the guise of enhancing individual beauty, Finglass states, "If someone doesn't look *right* in the uniform, it could be a contributing factor to a final decision if they make this team." Seemingly trivial concerns about appearance become the sole criteria for "making those tough decisions."[43] Clearly, the organization restricts self-expression and reinforces gender-, race-, culture-, and sexuality-based discrimination and disadvantages.[44] Making the team is not about accentuating the diversity of bodies in the national body politic. It's about conforming to a standardized look in which individuality fades and a corporate, collective image takes over—all in the name of women being empowered to make the choice, on their own, to engage in these practices.

Like the rookie candidates, veterans, too, are not immune from weight-based critiques; however, veterans' weight is more typically noted to be a concern during preliminary auditions, often justifying why they are not invited back into training camp. On season 13 of *Making the Team*, veteran candidate Selina Flores was cut for weighing "fourteen pounds heavier than last year's audition."[45] On *America's Sweethearts*, returning veteran candidate Kayla H. was cut following preliminary auditions after judges noted, "There was a little more weight in her face"—showcasing how both candidates' weight and their body shape can be used arbitrarily to assess whether or not candidates possess the right look for the squad.[46] Finally, the "very form-fitting . . . definitely not one-size-fits-all" uniform demands strict conformity to the thin ideal. Even for the final thirty-six women who do make the team, "once [they're] fitted for that uniform, that size is the size [they] get. [They] don't get to go up."[47] This requires Dallas Cowboys

Cheerleaders to maintain the exact same bodily dimensions, and therefore weight, throughout the nearly five-month NFL season.

As previously discussed, central to the Dallas Cowboys Cheerleaders brand is a type of playful and suggestive but innocent provocativeness. This form of coquettish behavior is not an inherent attribute of women; it certainly does not come naturally to most of us. Thus, the team hopefuls must be taught how to achieve this look of sexy piety. Throughout *Making the Team*, candidates are given sultry-focused criticism on their dance performances from their head choreographer—for example, "[You're] supposed to serve it from the back," and "You need to be sexier. . . . it looks robotic right now."[48] These sentiments are repeated again on *America's Sweethearts*—"Watch Kelcey. . . . She uses her curves a lot and makes the step look . . . sexier"—exemplifying the ways in which sensuality is embedded within the Dallas Cowboys Cheerleaders' signature professional-cheerleading (dance) style.[49]

Outside the studio, candidates receive similar instruction, as featured during the squad's veteran swimsuit calendar photoshoot in season 13 of *Making the Team*. Crawling through the white-sand beaches of Bimini, Bahamas, on all fours, sprawled across a reflective tile floor, or practicing pursed lips among peers, the cheerleaders are encouraged to pose provocatively. Per one photographer's directives, "Just kick your booty out a little bit, boom," "Let's go back there, love buckets," and "Find your sexy, lick your lips"—all of which are delivered as the posing cheerleaders are constantly referred to as "babe" and "baby."[50] Interestingly, this case is juxtaposed with an incident in season 1 of *America's Sweethearts*, when a veteran cheerleader reports a photographer for inappropriately touching her while she is dancing on the sidelines at AT&T Stadium in the middle of a Cowboys game.[51]

The thin ideal upheld by squad authorities is maintained by the locker room weigh-ins, the ridiculing of candidates whose bodies do not obtain—or retain, in some cases—the right look or weight, and the construction of the official squad uniform. This constant pressure to remake one's body to fit the Dallas Cowboys Cheerleaders mold is situated within the context of an organization that touts its membership as the embodiment of today's empowered woman: strong, independent, confident, career oriented, and unafraid to be beautiful, sexy, and the object of the gaze. On *Making the Team*, Finglass asserts that being a Dallas Cowboys Cheerleader is "more than just about performing. It's making lifelong friends, empowering women, and growing in a safe environment."[52] The series constantly reminds viewers that being a Dallas Cowboys Cheerleader is a highly sought after title that only the few, the select, can achieve. Whatever decisions individual women make to achieve the squad's requisite look is their choice. And shouldn't we all, in a postfeminist world, celebrate a woman's right to choose? And if we judge them for their decisions, aren't we the ones being anti-feminist? This is the central tenet of what Angela McRobbie calls the "undoing of feminism."[53]

On the first season of *America's Sweethearts*, Charlotte Jones (daughter of team owner Jerry Jones), the president of the Dallas Cowboys Cheerleaders and chief brand officer for the Cowboys, responds to questions about the historically low wages the cheerleaders receive: "They actually don't come here for the money. . . . They have a chance to feel like they're valued, that they're special."[54] What we, the viewers, discover is that a group of veteran cheerleaders featured on the series (including Jada McLean, Megan McElaney, Armani Latimer, and others) took their wage concerns directly to Dallas Cowboys executives, thereby circumventing the internal squad management. Initially, they were met with resistance, and some of them suffered for their demands by no longer receiving assignments for squad appearances and other miscellaneous performances. But redemption occurs in the final episode of season 2. Finglass proudly announces the cheerleaders' newly increased wages with the description "sixty-plus-years-long overdue."[55] *The New York Times* followed up with the headline "The Dallas Cowboys Cheerleaders Get a 400 Percent Pay Raise."[56] Despite this landmark victory for the Dallas Cowboys Cheerleaders—and its presumed eventual applicability to other professional cheerleaders in the United States—the noted 400 percent increase in pay did not satisfy many of the squad members, who still consider themselves woefully underpaid, given all their time commitments and job responsibilities. "Hoping for one day to make 75K," commented veteran group leader Megan McElaney on a 2025 TikTok touting the salary increase.[57]

The rigid restrictions on weight, physical appearance, and the presentation of a certain form of femininity, even as the franchise boasts of a significant increase in pay for the cheerleaders' hard work, rightly leads many to ask: Can sexual objectification and empowerment coexist? Can professional cheerleaders be empowered, be valued, and feel good about themselves within a franchise and a sporting culture that offers them a (sidelines) platform and insists they adhere to a particular mold of American femininity that does not come naturally to most women?

**Professional Cheerleading: Making a Postfeminist Ambassador**

The Dallas Cowboys Cheerleaders were "international icons and the first pinups of modern sports, the sizzle on the steak that established the Cowboys as America's team as much as the players on the field."[58] As Natalie Adams and Pamela Bettis note, the close link between the Dallas Cowboys Cheerleaders, patriotism, and the military hearkens back to an earlier era in which women were used to boost the spirits of our troops overseas. During World War II, pinups were one of white American womanhood's most recognized contributions to the war effort: that of uplifting the morale of US troops.[59] Pinups provided a sense of community for all (straight) men, officer or enlisted, as they ogled beautiful, yet far-away, American women while enduring the harsh conditions of war. Pinups also reminded them why they were fighting: to protect what was waiting for them at home.[60]

The Dallas Cowboys Cheerleaders branded themselves as America's Sweethearts and cultivated this patriotic connection with star-spangled, blue-and-white uniforms and frequent trips to perform for US troops overseas. The first trip began in 1979. The Department of Defense asked Tex Schramm if some of the Dallas Cowboys players could visit troops stationed in Korea over the Christmas holidays. Schramm replied that the players were in the middle of the football season—but what about some cheerleaders? Acting as ambassadors for the Cowboys, Texas, and by extension the United States, twelve Dallas Cowboys Cheerleaders made that first trip, and the team has continued to market itself not only as America's Sweethearts but as important international ambassadors.

The role of ambassadors allows the squad's management to downplay the physical attributes of the cheerleaders and instead to emphasize the high-status position these women hold as the public face of the Cowboys franchise and of the United States. This emphasis on a very small part of the cheerleaders' job responsibilities is evident in the prominent placement of their role as international ambassadors on the official website:

> The [Dallas Cowboys Cheerleaders] have dazzled stages across the globe. To date, they have made over 85 United Service Organizations (USO) tours, spanning over 40 countries, including Japan, South Korea, Iraq, Afghanistan, Bosnia, Iceland, Greenland and Cuba. For their continuous commitment and dedication to entertaining US troops, the Cheerleaders were the first recipients of the first-ever USO Spirit of Hope Award and have been honored with

> the Veterans of Foreign Wars Hall of Fame Award. They have also earned the American Legion's Distinguished Service Medal.[61]

Interestingly, *Making the Team* and *America's Sweethearts* focus very minimally on the cheerleaders' role as ambassadors; both shows feature short segments of the squad at community and charitable events, but for whatever reason, the producers of both series did not find that aspect of the organization conducive to making a hit series about one of America's most titillating icons.

The current Dallas Cowboys Cheerleaders management speak frequently about the public-speaking skills, poise, confidence, and emotional acuity of their cheerleaders—criteria, they suggest, imperative for being a successful ambassador and for making the team. Finglass states, "It is important that these ladies speak intelligently and be quick on their feet because a lot of times they're in live interview situations and if they're not likable, at some point you don't really care how well they dance."[62] Similarly, Charlotte Jones notes that "the pursuit of excellence is a standard at the Dallas Cowboys, and when it comes to the Dallas Cowboys Cheerleaders, they are no exception. How you present yourself off the field is every bit as important as how you present yourself on the field."[63] Although these statements emphasize important ambassadorial traits, they can also be read as exercising strict control over the cheerleaders' behavior so they will not "tarnish the Star"[64]—the Star being both the logo of the Cowboys franchise and a metaphor for the United States. Emphasizing the importance of ambassadorship also allows the franchise to dictate the women's public appearance and behaviors to ensure that they communicate the approved franchise script, thus denying them much autonomy to speak as individuals with their own ideas and perspectives.

While this chapter has focused on the Dallas Cowboys Cheerleaders, it is important to note that other professional cheer squads also emphasize that their cheerleaders are first and foremost ambassadors. As illustrated in the following excerpts, taken from footage of other professional cheerleading squads' auditions, this focus on ambassadorship seeks to emphasize that being a good role model and franchise representative is paramount to making the team:

> We do important work. We are great role models. We are out in the community, so we need candidates that are going to be able to

> articulate what our brand is all about, and just really set a strong example for youth everywhere.[65]
>
> Rebecca Smoker, Detroit Lions director of entertainment

> Really our job is to find the best representatives of the Patriots and the organization, because ultimately these are going to be ambassadors for this team and they're going to be out in the community, on the sidelines entertaining fans, and we want to make sure we find the best people for the role.[66]
>
> Jennifer Sullivan, New England Patriots Cheerleaders manager

> I think the Raiderettes are important to our community, as they are one of the first faces, sometimes the only face, that a fan may ever meet or see.[67]
>
> Stephanie Hardy, Las Vegas Raiderettes manager

> They are the ambassador to the organization, and so that interview will carry about 50 percent of their total score overall.[68]
>
> Keely Fimbres, Los Angeles Rams Cheerleaders director

So, how do we make sense of the Dallas Cowboys Cheerleaders in a postfeminist world? How do we reconcile the assimilating tactics employed by the squad's management, the emphasis on a narrow beauty ideal, the continued popularity of the team (as evident in the hundreds of women who flock to Arlington, Texas, every year to try out for the team), the franchise's appropriation of the feminist discourse of empowerment, and the political groundings of the feminist movement itself? A close look at the Dallas Cowboys Cheerleaders reveals how the empowerment discourse has metamorphosed into practices antithetical to feminism, which emphasizes equality for women, safe and productive opportunities for growth, and respect for women's value in all spheres of society.[69] Angela McRobbie refers to this as the "undoing" or "disarticulation" of feminism,[70] wherein

> the various political issues associated with feminism are understood to be now widely recognised and responded to . . . with the effect that there is no longer any place for feminism in contemporary political culture. But this disavowal permits the subtle renewal of

> gender injustices, while vengeful patriarchal norms are also re-instated. . . . Gender retrenchment is secured, paradoxically, through the wide dissemination of discourses of female freedom.[71]

McRobbie argues that in the twenty-first century, many view feminism as an issue of the past: Feminism's concerns (e.g., equal pay for equal work) have been seemingly resolved, and thus there is no need for feminist activism. She posits, "Young women are able to come forward on the condition that feminism fades away."[72]

The undoing of feminism is achieved through a watered-down feminism (e.g., women are empowered to choose to wear skimpy halter tops for public consumption) palatable to a media-saturated culture. The old rules denouncing the sexual objectification of women are tired, antiquated tropes in a postfeminist world. This, of course, is predicated on young women's participation in a contemporary consumer culture built around technologies of self. According to McRobbie, "It becomes increasingly difficult to function as a female subject without subjecting oneself to those technologies of self that are constitutive of the spectacularly feminine. There are new norms of appearance and self-presentation expected not just in leisure and in everyday life but also in the workplace."[73] This conditional empowerment is the epitome of the sidelined positioning, ostensible celebration, and concerted sexualization of the Dallas Cowboys Cheerleaders. They are "empowered" through an official (albeit secondary and woefully underpaid) position within the patriarchal structure of an NFL franchise while having few of the rights and responsibilities and little of the status and respect of the men who control the NFL or the individual players who profit significantly from their contributions to the multi-billion-dollar professional football enterprise.[74]

This analysis of the Dallas Cowboys Cheerleaders reflects the conundrum of the way "empowerment" has been used seemingly to elevate women by suggesting that hypersexualization and feminization are not disempowering since women profit from their empowerment in many ways.[75] McRobbie's postfeminist logic illustrates the problematic and dubious contentions between Finglass's proclamation that the Dallas Cowboys Cheerleaders are about "empowering women" and Jones's assertion that the cheerleaders "feel like they're valued." The squad operates within an institutional structure that does not pay them what they are worth, demands that they "choose" bodily manipulation and surveillance, and then tells them that if they suffer any repercussions for their choices (e.g., disordered eating, mental health challenges, and physical injuries), it is simply the price one pays to be one of America's Sweethearts. As they are often reminded, "there are a million other women ready to take [their] place."[76]

The Dallas Cowboys Cheerleaders claim to be "often imitated, never equaled." As many franchises high-kick themselves away from the Cowboys model of professional cheer squads (e.g., the Detroit Lions Cheerleaders, the New England Patriots Cheerleaders, the Las Vegas Raiderettes, and the Los Angeles Rams Cheerleaders), many wonder if in the future, the Dallas Cowboys Cheerleaders will be the last professional cheerleaders still kicking. With the addition of male-presenting cheerleaders and trans cheerleaders on professional squads in the last few years, will the Dallas Cowboys Cheerleaders seem antiquated in a new gender regime in which gender, sexuality, and gendered expectations are more fluid? Given that professional cheerleaders' demands for higher wages and safer work environments preceded the #MeToo movement, perhaps this move to a different form of empowerment and value has already begun to occur, with cheerleaders finding their own voice and practicing their own form of feminist protest and politics, as discussed in the next chapter.

## Notes

1. *Dallas Cowboys Cheerleaders: Making the Team*, season 13, episode 1, 2018, CMT.

2. Over the course of sixteen seasons, *Making the Team* has regularly featured training camp candidates being weighed in the rehearsal studio and locker room, although this practice is shown more consistently in earlier seasons. Despite later seasons eliminating the weigh-in as an on-camera feature, it is evident that the custom of weighing the young women remains consistent, as squad management is shown frequently calling in candidates for private office visits to discuss their weight gain. As referenced in the Netflix docuseries *America's Sweethearts: Dallas Cowboys Cheerleaders*, this particular standard—among others—has resulted in cheerleaders struggling with body image issues, disordered eating, and other mental health challenges.

3. Lauren Nowosatka, "America's Sweethearts? A Feminist Discourse Analysis of *Dallas Cowboys Cheerleaders: Making the Team*" (master's thesis, University of Maryland, 2022), https://doi.org/10.13016/upid-1tyr.

4. "Dallas Cowboys Cheerleaders Donate Artifacts to National Museum of American History," Smithsonian Institution, February 26, 2018, https://www.si.edu/newsdesk/releases/dallas-cowboys-cheerleaders-donate-artifacts-national-museum-american-history.

5. Angela McRobbie, *The Aftermath of Feminism: Gender, Culture and Social Change* (Sage, 2008).

6. *America's Sweethearts: Dallas Cowboys Cheerleaders*, season 1, episode 1, 2024, Netflix.

7. Mary Ellen Hanson, *Go! Fight! Win! Cheerleading in American Culture* (Bowling Green State University Popular Press, 1995).

8. Hanson, *Go! Fight! Win!*, 52.

9. Hanson, *Go! Fight! Win!*, 52.

10. Natalie G. Adams and Pamela J. Bettis, *Cheerleader! An American Icon* (Palgrave Macmillan, 2003), 74–77.

11. Sarah Hepola, host, *America's Girls*, episode 4, *Texas Monthly* podcasts, December 21, 2021.

12. Hepola, *America's Girls*, episode 4.

13. The exact date of the "wink that went around the world" is also disputable. In episode 4 of the podcast *America's Girls*, Sarah Hepola notes that the event actually occurred a couple of months before the Super Bowl.

14. Robert Draper, "Remembering Suzanne Mitchell, the Longtime Director of the Dallas Cowboys Cheerleaders," *Texas Monthly*, September 29, 2016, https://www.texasmonthly.com/the-daily-post/remembering-suzanne-mitchell-longtime-director-dallas-cowboys-cheerleaders/.

15. Kavitha A. Davidson, "A Look at the Untold Story of the Dallas Cowboys Cheerleaders," ESPN, March 16, 2018, https://www.espn.com/espnw/culture/feature/story/_/id/22792423/a-look-untold-story-dallas-cowboys-cheerleaders.

16. Ken Belson, "No Sweatpants in Public: Inside the Rule Books for N.F.L. Cheerleaders," *New York Times*, April 2, 2018, https://www.nytimes.com/2018/04/02/sports/nfl-cheerleaders.html.

17. Sarah Hepola, "Sex, Scandal, and Sisterhood: Fifty Years of the Dallas Cowboys Cheerleaders," *Texas Monthly*, September 2022, https://www.texasmonthly.com/arts-entertainment/fifty-years-of-dallas-cowboys-cheerleaders/.

18. Suzette Scholz, Stephanie Scholz, and Sheri Scholz, *Deep in the Heart of Texas: Reflections of Former Dallas Cowboys Cheerleaders* (St. Martin's Press, 1991), 146.

19. Hepola, "Sex, Scandal, and Sisterhood."

20. Diane Shar, Stephen Gayle, and Mary Lord, "Sis-Boom-Bah!," *Newsweek*, November 7, 1977, 87–89.

21. Bruce Newman, "Gimme an S," *Sports Illustrated*, May 22, 1978, 19.

22. Hanson, *Go! Fight! Win!*, 53.

23. Newman, "Gimme an S," 18.

24. Sarah Hepola, "In Search of the Dallas Cowboys Cheerleaders Who Posed for Playboy," *Texas Monthly*, December 15, 2021, https://www.texasmonthly.com/arts-entertainment/search-dallas-cowboys-cheerleaders-posed-playboy/.

25. Hepola, "Sex, Scandal, and Sisterhood."

26. Stanley Jenkins, "Iconic 1977 Dallas Cowboys Cheerleaders Poster Will Hang in the Smithsonian," *Dallas Morning News*, February 24, 2018, https://www.dallasnews.com/opinion/commentary/2018/02/24/iconic-1977-dallas

-cowboys-cheerleaders-poster-will-hang-in-the-smithsonian/; Hepola, "Sex, Scandal, and Sisterhood"; Hepola, "In Search of the Dallas Cowboys Cheerleaders."

27. In 1989, when Jerry Jones bought the Cowboys franchise, Suzanne Mitchell resigned, and fourteen Dallas Cowboys Cheerleaders quit after hearing that the cheerleaders might be asked to appear in a beer commercial wearing an even skimpier uniform. Jones held a press conference to reassure the nation he had no intention of changing the cheerleaders: "My intent is absolutely to have our cheerleaders hold their heads up high and be as important for moms and dads and their children in the future that there ever has been." See Marie Saavedra, "1989: The Year 14 Dallas Cowboys Cheerleaders Quit," WFAA, September 25, 2107, https://www.wfaa.com/article/sports/nfl/cowboys/1989-the-year-14-dallas-cowboys-cheerleaders-quit/287-478566806.

28. Samantha Stephens, "Kelli Finglass Follows Her Heart All the Way to the Dallas Cowboys Cheerleaders," CMT News, October 24, 2019, http://www.cmt.com/news/1813689/kelli-finglass-follows-her-heart-all-the-way-to-the-dallas-cowboys-cheerleaders/.

29. Don Van Natta Jr., "Cowboys Paid $2.4 Million to Settle Cheerleaders' Voyeurism Allegations Against Senior Team Executive," ESPN, February 16, 2022, https://www.espn.com/nfl/story/_/id/33231841/dallas-cowboys-paid-24-million-settle-cheerleaders-voyeurism-allegations.

30. Van Natta, "Cowboys Paid $2.4 Million."

31. Cheryl Kast, "Dallas Cowboys Cheerleader Reveals Why She's Suing the Team," *New York Post*, February 2, 2019, https://nypost.com/2018/06/17/dallas-cowboys-cheerleader-reveals-why-shes-suing-the-team/.

32. *Making the Team*, season 13, episode 8.

33. Sarah Hepola, "The Dallas Cowboys Cheerleaders Reality Show Ends Its Run on CMT," *Texas Monthly*, March 31, 2022, https://www.texasmonthly.com/arts-entertainment/dallas-cowboys-cheerleaders-reality-show-ends/.

34. Samantha Thornfelt, "Dallas Cowboys Cheerleaders' Thunderstruck Routine Takes Over TikTok," *Dallas Observer*, July 12, 2024, https://www.dallasobserver.com/arts/dallas-cowboys-cheerleaders-routine-takes-off-on-tiktok-19845017.

35. Tara Bitran, "Netflix's New Billboard on Sunset Boulevard Features a List of Its Most Popular Shows," *Tudum*, August 1, 2023, https://www.netflix.com/tudum/articles/netflix-billboard-sunset-boulevard-list.

36. *America's Sweethearts*, season 1, episode 1.

37. Angelique Jackson, "Inside Netflix's Dallas Cowboys Cheerleaders Docuseries: What 'Cheer' and 'Last Chance U' Director Greg Whiteley Learned from Following 'America's Sweethearts' for a Season," *Variety*, June 28, 2024, https://variety.com/2024/tv/news/netflix-dallas-cowboys-cheerleaders-docuseries-greg-whiteley-1236049689/.

38. Sarah Banet-Weiser, *The Most Beautiful Girl in the World: Beauty Pageants and National Identity* (University of California Press, 1999).

39. R. W. Connell, *Gender and Power: Society, the Person, and Sexual Politics* (Polity, 1987).

40. Sarah Banet-Weiser and Laura Portwood-Stacer, "'I Just Want to Be Me Again!': Beauty Pageants, Reality Television and Post-Feminism," *Feminist Theory* 7, no. 2 (2006): 255–272, https://doi.org/10.1177/1464700106064423; Hester Eisenstein, "Hegemonic Feminism, Neoliberalism and Womenomics: 'Empowerment' Instead of Liberation?," *New Formations* 91 (2017): 35–49, https://www.muse.jhu.edu/article/671949.

41. *America's Sweethearts*, season 1, episode 1.

42. Tracey Owens Patton, "Hey Girl, Am I More Than My Hair? African American Women and Their Struggles with Beauty, Body Image, and Hair," *NWSA Journal* 18, no. 2 (2006): 24–51; Cheryl Thompson, "Black Women, Beauty, and Hair as a Matter of Being," *Women's Studies* 38, no. 8 (2009): 831–856, https://doi.org/10.1080/00497870903238463.

43. *Making the Team*, season 13, episode 5.

44. Deborah L. Rhode, *The Beauty Bias: The Injustice of Appearance in Life and Law* (Oxford University Press, 2010).

45. *Making the Team*, season 13, episode 3.

46. *America's Sweethearts*, season 1, episode 1.

47. *America's Sweethearts*, season 1, episode 7.

48. *Making the Team*, season 13, episode 9.

49. *America's Sweethearts*, season 1, episode 6.

50. *Making the Team*, season 13, episode 4.

51. *America's Sweethearts*, season 1, episode 6.

52. *Making the Team*, season 13, episode 1.

53. McRobbie, *Aftermath of Feminism*.

54. *America's Sweethearts*, season 1, episode 1.

55. *America's Sweethearts*, season 2, episode 7.

56. Alisha Haridasani and Katie Van Syckle, "The Dallas Cowboys Cheerleaders Get a 400 Percent Pay Raise," *New York Times*, June 18, 2025, https://www.nytimes.com/2025/06/18/style/dallas-cowboys-cheerleaders-salary-americas-sweethearts.html.

57. Mehera Bonner, "Dallas Cowboys Cheerleader Confirms New Salary with 400% Raise and It's Less Than You'd Think," *Cosmopolitan*, June 20, 2025, https://www.cosmopolitan.com/entertainment/celebs/a65122985/dallas-cowboys-cheerleaders-exact-new-salary-confirmed/.

58. Joe Nick Patoski, "Dallas Cowboy Cheerleaders," *Texas Monthly*, September 2001, 124.

59. Adams and Bettis, *Cheerleader!*, 75.

60. For a more in-depth discussion of the role of pinups in World War II, see John Costello, *Love, Sex and War: Changing Values, 1939–1945* (Collins, 1985); Philomona Goodman, *Women, Sexuality and War* (Palgrave Macmillan, 2002); Charles Martignette and Louis Meisel, *The Great American Pin-Up* (Taschen, 1996).

61. "History," Dallas Cowboys Cheerleaders, accessed July 25, 2015, https://dallascowboyscheerleaders.com/history/.

62. *Making the Team*, season 13, episode 3.

63. *Making the Team*, season 13, episode 3.

64. Hepola, "Sex, Scandal, and Sisterhood."

65. "Detroit Lions Cheerleaders: Making the Squad," posted June 23, 2023, by Detroit Lions, YouTube, https://www.youtube.com/watch?v=xsVjabSVPrE.

66. "Making the Squad: 2021 New England Patriots Cheerleaders," posted October 6, 2021, by New England Patriots, YouTube, https://www.youtube.com/watch?v=kpKbTG1g8x8.

67. "The Making of the 2023 Raiderettes: The Chase Begins (Ep. 1) | Las Vegas Raiders | NFL," posted July 27, 2023, by Raiders, YouTube, https://www.youtube.com/watch?v=N4XHLyLvbfs; "The Making of the 2023 Raiderettes: Sink or Swim (Ep. 2) | Las Vegas Raiders | NFL," posted August 2, 2023, by Raiders, YouTube, https://www.youtube.com/watch?v=EJ83WE7dMvc.

68. "Making the Squad Ep. 1: Preliminary Auditions | LA Rams Cheerleaders," posted August 18, 2023, by Los Angeles Rams, YouTube, https://www.youtube.com/watch?v=JGoeXDt7V5w; "Making the Squad Ep. 2: The Blood, Sweat & Tears of Semi-Finals | LA Rams Cheerleaders," posted August 25, 2023, by Los Angeles Rams, YouTube, https://www.youtube.com/watch?v=6XrTe9pphXE; "Making the Squad Ep. 3: Final Auditions & Announcing the Team | LA Rams Cheerleaders," posted September 2, 2023, by Los Angeles Rams, YouTube, https://www.youtube.com/watch?v=51JdNqhylBQ.

69. Cheryl Cooky, "What's New About Sporting Femininities? Female Athletes and the Sport-Media Industrial Complex," in *New Sporting Femininities: Embodied Politics in Postfeminist Times*, ed. Kim Toffoletti, Holly Thorpe, and Jessica Francombe-Webb (Palgrave Macmillan, 2018), 23–41; Rosalind Gill, *Gender and the Media* (Polity, 2007); Rosalind Gill, "Post-Postfeminism? New Feminist Visibilities in Postfeminist Times," *Feminist Media Studies* 16, no. 4 (2016): 610–630, https://doi.org/10.1080/14680777.2016.1193293.

70. Angela McRobbie, "Post-Feminism and Popular Culture," *Feminist Media Studies* 4, no. 3 (2007): 255–264, https://doi.org/10.1080/1468077042000309937; McRobbie, *Aftermath of Feminism*.

71. McRobbie, *Aftermath of Feminism*, 55.

72. McRobbie, *Aftermath of Feminism*, 56.

73. McRobbie, *Aftermath of Feminism*, 60.

74. Eisenstein, "Hegemonic Feminism, Neoliberalism and Womenomics."

75. McRobbie, "Post-Feminism and Popular Culture."

76. *America's Sweethearts*, season 2, episode 1.

CHEER NOTE #4

# Cheer Stunts: Speaking the Language

Cheerleading stunts are at the heart of the exciting sport of cheer. How well do you know your cheer stunts? Match the stunt with its correct description.

| | |
|---|---|
| 1. cupie | A. a stunt in which the flyer is held in a horizontal position and thrown, twisting parallel to the ground, and recaught in a horizontal position |
| 2. elevator or prep | B. a stunt in which the flyer starts standing on one leg and then switches to the other |
| 3. squish, sponge, smush, or load | C. an extended stunt position in which the flyer is standing on two feet and they are together |
| 4. bow and arrow | D. a stunt in which the flyer starts standing on the ground and backflips up to the top of the stunt |
| 5. scorpion | E. a stunt position in which the flyer is standing on two feet at the base's chest level |
| 6. scale | F. a variation of the scorpion in which the leg behind the head is completely straight |
| 7. needle | G. a type of inversion stunt in which the flyer balances with their hands in the base's hands with toes pointed to the sky |
| 8. rewind | H. a stunt in which the flyer is held in a sitting straddle position |
| 9. tic toc | I. a body position in which the flyer holds their leg behind them with one hand, with the other free, usually in a high V |
| 10. barrel or log roll | J. a body position in which the flyer holds their foot and leg behind their head |
| 11. teddy bear | K. a prep for a half-, full-, or double-up stunt in which the flyer's heels are together with toes pointed out in the load |
| 12. ruby slipper | L. a variation of the heel stretch where the flyer holds their foot with the opposite hand, with the free arm held out straight in front of the leg |
| 13. hand in hand | M. a position where the flyer holds themself with straight arms on the base's shoulders with knees pulled up beneath them, used to transition in or out of stunts |

(Answers found on page 283.)

CHAPTER 6

# "Look Like a Supermodel but Perform Like an Athlete"

## PROFESSIONAL CHEERLEADING IN A POST-#METOO WORLD

*Lauren C. Hindman*

> From Dream Job to Nightmare: More Than a Dozen Women Allege Sexual Harassment and Verbal Abuse by Former Employees at Redskins Park
>
> *Washington Post* headline, July 16, 2020

> The Dallas Cowboys Cheerleaders Get a 400 Percent Pay Raise
>
> *New York Times* headline, June 18, 2025

A few weeks before the Kansas City Chiefs' appearance in Super Bowl LVIII in 2024, the official Instagram account of the Chiefs Cheerleaders featured a video highlighting members of its squad. The video shows clips of women at work and at school, with text on the screen identifying each woman by role: A civil engineer wearing a hard hat and a yellow-and-orange reflective vest over a Chiefs jersey, seated at an office cubicle. A law student in a sweatshirt and jeans, standing in an empty classroom with a textbook in her hand. A registered nurse wearing scrubs in a room with shelves full of medical supplies. A middle school English teacher in an oversized red-and-white varsity jacket and sneakers, in front of a classroom whiteboard and projector screen. The women each mark out a cheer routine as music plays over the video. The text overlay at the top reads, "POV: You're at work but you're also an NFL cheerleader and have practice tonight."[1]

Nine months later, the video has nearly eight hundred thousand likes. But most user comments express surprise or outrage at the cheerleaders' multiple jobs. One comment reads, "Not me thinking being a cheerleader WAS their job," while another states, "Tell me you don't pay your employees a livable wage without telling me you don't pay your employees a livable wage." One user homed in on the gender disparity between the women on the cheerleading squad and the men they are cheering for: "Oh oh oh! This is fun! Do the football players next! What's their day job?!?"

Michael Messner has described the dichotomy between cheerleader and football player as emblematic of a hegemonic gender ideology, a worldview that presumes women are subordinate to men.[2] Thus, in sport, the "bare and vulnerable bodies of the cheerleaders" versus "the armored male bodies of the football players" serve as concrete evidence of men's purported superiority over women.[3] In recent years, that same dichotomy has been used to highlight the gender inequities that women face in the National Football League (NFL), as well as in sport and society more broadly. Media coverage and lawsuits from the cheerleaders themselves have brought attention to the differences in cheerleader-versus-football-player pay and other employment conditions.[4] Even the Chiefs Cheerleaders' own caption of the above video seemed to express exasperation at the gender inequalities in their own organization. The phrase "Women in sports!" was punctuated by a telling emoji expressing annoyance or frustration.

Professional cheerleading in the twenty-first century is a contested site with multiple competing ideological discourses: (1) a hegemonic ideology in which cheerleaders represent glamour and sex appeal and are naturally subordinate to football players; (2) a postfeminist ideology in which inequality experienced by cheerleaders is attributed to their own choices; and (3) a feminist ideology in which cheerleaders are viewed as deserving of fair and equal treatment.[5] Over the past decade, NFL cheerleaders have spoken up to challenge their working conditions, securing some victories that have resulted in improved employment practices.[6] Yet NFL cheerleading remains a site that produces specific meanings of professionalism, gender, and race. This chapter explores those meanings and how they influence who gets to be a professional cheerleader.

### The "Professional" in Professional Cheerleading

In episode 6 of the 2024 Netflix docuseries *America's Sweethearts: Dallas Cowboys Cheerleaders*, Dolly Parton's "9 to 5" plays over a montage of the cheerleaders on game day. Cowboys sideline reporter Kristi Scales explains in a voice-over, "There's this huge misconception. 'Oh it's a part-time job, and oh they're pretty and they're good dancers.' But holy smokes. When they're in front of ninety-three thousand people—there's so much more to it than just three hours on game day."[7] In fact, even the "working nine to five" lyrics in Parton's song undervalue the time the cheerleaders put in for football games. Dallas Cowboys Cheerleaders director Kelli Finglass has stated that the squad works eleven hours on game days.[8] Add in hours-long evening practices and various performances throughout the week—this is what being a professional cheerleader in the NFL looks like.

The word "professional" has various meanings, many of which relate to competence or qualification within a particular activity. When used as an adjective before a noun, such as in "professional cheerleader," the word often suggests the receipt of compensation. The *Oxford English Dictionary*, for instance, provides one such definition: "a person engaged in a specified activity, especially a sport or branch of the performing arts, as a main paid occupation rather than as a pastime."[9] Within the sports industry, "professional" typically denotes participation for pay or as a full-time job.[10] For NFL cheerleaders, one might interpret "professional" to have multiple meanings. It could suggest a high level of skill compared to other types of cheerleaders, or it could convey that the cheerleaders are paid. It could also refer to the context in which these cheerleaders perform—much as college cheerleaders cheer for a college athletic program, professional cheerleaders cheer for a professional sports team.

The professional cheerleaders of the NFL are paid—though historically pay has been low, as many teams classified squad members as independent contractors not subject to state and federal minimum wage standards.[11] In fact, the Seattle Seahawks were the first team to pay their cheerleaders a minimum wage rate, in 1997.[12] On top of low pay and unpaid practice and preparation time, many NFL cheerleaders have had to pay to rent or buy their uniforms. They have also faced fines from their squads for violating team rules—for example, arriving to practice with the wrong poms. Meanwhile, they have been required to sell raffle tickets and swimsuit calendars to bring in revenue for the team.[13]

Christopher McLeod and Tarlan Chahardovali have found that low-paid athletes in the United States, particularly women, claim the label of "professional" to improve their working conditions.[14] In the past few decades, professional cheerleaders have done just that. First, in 1995, the Buffalo Jills (cheerleaders for the Buffalo Bills) became the first cheerleading squad to try to form a union, a move that was portrayed as betrayal by the squad's sponsor, Andrew Gerovac.[15] He stated that unions were for "hard workers," a classification that, in his mind, the cheerleaders did not meet: "To me, jumping around on the sidelines isn't really work. It isn't labor at all."[16] *Los Angeles Times* columnist Robin Abcarian noted in her satirical opinion piece that the Jills were unionizing for the "radical ideas" of receiving fair compensation and having input into their routines, uniforms, practice locations, and personal appearances.[17] Ultimately, the unionization attempt was unsuccessful. While members of the Jills overwhelmingly voted in favor of unionization, they failed to agree on a collective-bargaining agreement.[18] The business sponsoring the Jills dropped its sponsorship following the unionization, and another business agreed to sponsor the squad only if the union was dissolved. As then cocaptain Erin McCormack Oliver recalled to *Vanity Fair*, "Just being professional was a bridge too far for them."[19]

Then, in 2014, NFL cheerleaders filed a wave of lawsuits, with cheerleaders for the Buffalo Bills, Cincinnati Bengals, Oakland Raiders, and Tampa Bay Buccaneers all alleging their organizations paid squad members less than minimum wage.[20] While the Bills lawsuit ultimately led to the dissolution of that squad, the Bengals, Raiders, and Buccaneers Cheerleaders settled their lawsuits for more than $2.6 million combined and guaranteed pay rates of at least minimum wage.[21] A group of fifty-two cheerleaders for the New York Jets sued their team in 2016 and were awarded nearly $325,000 in a settlement.[22] Two years later, former cheerleaders filed lawsuits against four additional NFL teams, with allegations including gender and religious discrimination, harassment, and underpayment.[23] Former Houston Texans Cheerleaders alleged that while their hourly wage rate had been $7.25 (the federal minimum hourly wage), the team had failed to compensate them for all of the hours they worked, to the extent that they were paid "pennies for each hour worked."[24] The women ultimately dropped their lawsuit in favor of arbitration. A lawsuit by former Dallas Cowboys Cheerleader Erica Wilkins alleged that the Cowboys organization had also sometimes paid her less than minimum wage. Wilkins specifically called attention to the fact that the cheerleaders earned less than the Cowboys mascot, who was paid $60,000 a year. The Cowboys and Wilkins settled the dispute prior to arbitration, but reports noted that the Dallas Cowboys Cheerleaders' pay increased following Wilkins's suit: from an $8 to a $12 hourly wage and from a $200 to a $400 game day rate.[25] By 2020, cheerleaders from ten different NFL teams had filed lawsuits related to wages, workplace treatment, harassment, and discrimination.[26]

These lawsuits also brought attention to strict rules about appearance and behavior set by NFL cheerleading squads. In a 2021 documentary about the Raiders and Bills lawsuits, former Jills cheerleader Maria Pinzone described doing jumping jacks in front of squad director Stephanie Mateczun to see if "things were jiggling"—an infraction that could result in being benched for the upcoming game.[27] Cheerleading handbooks from other squads described regular weigh-ins and requirements to stay within three pounds of their "ideal body weight."[28] Some rules governed cheerleaders' behavior away from the job, including what they could not wear in public, how they could not interact with football players, and what they could not post on personal social media accounts.[29] It was this latter rule that led to the New Orleans Saints firing cheerleader Bailey Davis for posting a photo of herself wearing what the team deemed lingerie—and to Davis filing a complaint with the US Equal Employment Opportunity Commission, alleging gender discrimination because the football players were not subject to the same rules as the cheerleaders.[30] Leslie Levy, an attorney who represented some of the cheerleaders in their suits, expressed how such rules exceed the bounds of typical employer-employee relationships: "You see a disparate treatment between the cheerleaders, and the mascots and anyone else who works for the team. I can't think of another arena where employers exert this level of control, even when they are not at work."[31]

Amid these lawsuits, cheerleaders also spoke out about the sexual harassment they experienced on the job, with male fans leering at them and touching them inappropriately.[32] Perhaps the most egregious allegations were those of the cheerleaders for Washington's football team (now the Commanders). A 2018 *New York Times* story detailed how, during a 2013 trip to Costa Rica, the cheerleaders were made to pose topless for the squad's calendar photo shoot, while a group of men—sponsors and suite holders invited by the team—looked on. Later, the team director told nine of the cheerleaders that they had been selected by the men to be their "personal escorts" to a nightclub. Cheerleaders told the *Times* they felt the team was "pimping us out."[33] Stories such as this exemplify how, rather than being treated as professionals, NFL cheerleaders were frequently exploited as sex objects, pressured to accept low pay and mistreatment over fear of losing their jobs.[34]

Even with some improvements in pay following the lawsuits in the 2010s, professional cheerleading is still widely a low-paying, part-time gig. In a TikTok video, New England Patriots Cheerleader Taylor Yeley explains that "it's a part-time job, but a full-time commitment."[35] The Atlanta Falcons website for the team's 2024 cheerleader auditions noted that in order to try out, potential members "must have a part-time or full-time job or be a college student." The website described compensation for the job as a "nominal fee for home games and rehearsals," with additional paid appearances and performances available at "the discretion of the Director."[36] Despite the requirement to hold outside employment, working as a Falcons Cheerleader does not offer much in the way of flexibility. The squad's website describes two three-hour rehearsals per week—and if cheerleaders miss a rehearsal, they cannot perform in that week's game. Missing a single game can lead to removal from the team.[37]

NFL cheerleaders may have made inroads toward better pay and working conditions in the past decade, but their motivations for joining their teams are sometimes painted in a light that undermines their efforts to be seen as professional athletes worthy of fair compensation. Charlotte Jones, chief brand officer for the Dallas Cowboys, says of the Dallas Cowboys Cheerleaders, "They're not paid a lot. But the facts are that they don't actually come here for the money. They come here for something that's actually bigger than that to them. . . . When the women come here, they find their passion, and they find their purpose."[38] In this framing, NFL cheerleaders do not seek professional status to be paid for their skill in the way that other professional athletes do. Low pay is justifiable because the cheerleaders receive something else instead—a purpose and a fulfillment of passion.

Many former cheerleaders echoed this mindset in defense of their working conditions in 2018. For instance, former San Diego Chargers Cheerleader Flavia Berys points to the influence her time as a cheerleader had on her life, saying, "The training we had was all for a reason, and looking back, I think it was all for the right reasons."[39] Rather than NFL cheerleading being the pinnacle of an athletic career, it was a training ground for future experiences, putting "professional" cheerleading more on par with the work of amateurs.

Yet in 2025, the push for higher wages for NFL cheerleaders continued. Though the Cowboys' Charlotte Jones characterized Dallas Cowboys Cheerleaders members as motivated by passion rather than pay in the 2024 season of the Netflix docuseries, the show's 2025 season highlighted the cheerleaders' push for higher wages. Their efforts culminated in an announcement during the season's final episode: a 400 percent pay increase for the 2025 football season.[40] The impact this pay raise will have on the NFL's other cheerleading squads remains to be seen.

## Professional Cheerleading and Ideal Womanhood: Meanings of Gender and Race

Professional cheerleading discourse—the language we use and the images we present—creates meanings not only about what it means to be a cheerleader but also about what it means to be a woman.[41] If youth cheerleading represents ideal girlhood,[42] professional cheerleading constructs images of ideal womanhood. Although ten NFL cheerleading squads now include men, women embody the look of the prototypical NFL cheerleader, perhaps best represented by the Dallas Cowboys Cheerleaders, who use the nickname America's Sweethearts. Consider these quotes from Dallas Cowboys Cheerleaders in the first five minutes of the 2024 Netflix docuseries:

> You need to look like a supermodel but perform like an athlete.
>
> Beautiful. Bossy. Feminine. That is a little girl's dream.
>
> It's like prom queen times a hundred. Everything would be perfect if I were that woman.[43]

NFL cheerleaders, then, embody a modern hegemonic femininity that is "high powered, confident, and glamorous."[44] They are both beautiful and strong, and they present a level of perfection that is meant to be aspirational to women and appealing to men.

Peruse the twenty-five NFL cheer squad rosters and a consistent look of a professional cheerleader quickly emerges: thin, athletic, and curvy at once, with glamorous makeup and perfectly styled hair. This look is not by accident. For instance, on the FAQ page for the Miami Dolphins Cheerleaders auditions, personal appearance is first on a list of judging criteria, above dance technique, kicks, showmanship, personality, poise, and enthusiasm.[45] In Netflix's Dallas Cowboys Cheerleaders docuseries, team director Finglass and head choreographer Judy Trammell carefully select individuals who match the squad's aesthetic. As they view a photo of a white woman with blond hair auditioning for the squad, they note, "She's not a Thunderstruck girl" (referring to the team's signature dance routine).[46] Finglass and Trammell have long faced criticism for body-shaming current and would-be Dallas Cowboys Cheerleaders. For example, in a 2014 episode of *Dallas Cowboys Cheerleaders: Making the Team* on CMT, they cut team hopeful Meagan Pravden from auditions after commenting on her "stockier" build. Finglass explained that Pravden did not have the body for the Dallas Cowboys Cheerleader uniform because of her "thutt"—a term they coined to refer to the "thigh and butt running together."[47]

The NFL professional cheerleader aesthetic is also one of white, heterosexual femininity, with women of color—particularly Black women—often styled to conform to white beauty standards.[48] A 2018 analysis of media photos of NFL cheerleaders found that less than 10 percent of cheerleaders pictured appeared to be Black, with only one Black cheerleader photographed without her white teammates. Additionally, only three of the twenty-four Black women photographed sported natural hairstyles.[49] The construction of professional cheerleaders as white women can even be seen in doll form, as featured in the Netflix docuseries: As Finglass calls up women to present them with a Dallas Cowboys Cheerleader Barbie doll in honor of their selection to training camp, she asks, "You want blond or brunette? You pick," as the camera cuts to a shot of Anisha, a team hopeful of Indian descent.

Most 2024 NFL cheerleading squads consisted of between 15 and 30 percent women of color, with the Washington Commanders Command Force an outlier, with nearly half of the women appearing to be nonwhite. One-third of the Falcons Cheerleaders were people of color, despite the team's location in Atlanta, a city that is nearly 50 percent Black. The Command Force's diversity is intentional. They bill themselves as "one of the league's most diverse squads" and describe their aim "to bring to life the rich culture of DC's iconic dance scene through high-energy, industry hip hop-based choreography while also showcasing traditional pom style routines often seen in the NFL."[50] Notably, they call themselves an entertainment squad rather than a cheerleading team. The Commanders, then known as the Washington Football Team, replaced their previous cheerleading squad with this coed configuration in 2021.[51] The change came on the heels of the 2018 revelations about the Costa Rica trip (discussed above), the cheerleading photo shoot scandal, and 2020 reports of broader issues of gender discrimination and harassment in the team's front office, as well as amid the football team's rebranding from a formerly racist name.[52] Their success at building a more diverse group while distancing themselves from the cheerleading label brings into question professional cheerleading's compatibility with racial diversity.

But even the Command Force adheres to the NFL cheerleading aesthetic when it comes to the women's looks: sequined sports bra tops, glam makeup, and styled hair. And while it was more common to see Black NFL cheerleaders with natural curls in 2024 than it was in Lauren Hindman and Nefertiti Walker's earlier analysis, the favored hairstyle continues to be long locks with smooth, loose curls, regardless of race.[53]

In 2022, Justine Lindsay broke a barrier by becoming the NFL's first openly transgender cheerleader when she was hired by the Carolina Panthers TopCats.[54] Lindsay's inclusion on the team suggests there is room for growth beyond the heterosexual femininity that dominates the league, although it takes more than one person to become a trend. And while Lindsay's bald head sets her apart from her teammates, her glamorous style and confidence otherwise match the NFL cheerleader look.

Constructions of men as NFL cheerleaders are more varied. Men first joined two NFL cheer squads—the New Orleans Saints (Jesse Hernandez) and the Los Angeles Rams (Napoleon Jinnies and Quinton Peron)—in 2018.[55] These men, some of whom publicly identified as gay, were described as "fitting the bill," with their dance skill and aesthetic matching the existing women squad members.[56] By 2024, ten NFL cheer squads included one to twenty-one men, though the teams utilize men in different ways. Men with the Saints, Rams, Philadelphia Eagles, Atlanta Falcons, San Francisco 49ers, and Tampa Bay Buccaneers are presented as dancers on their teams. These men have slender physiques and don stretchy tops and pants that coordinate with the women's wear. On some of the teams (Buccaneers, Falcons, and 49ers), men carry poms just like the women. Such men cheerleaders perform the same version of femininity as the women, just with less revealing uniforms. Yet the recent brouhaha about the Minnesota Vikings squad's inclusion of two male-presenting cheerleaders on their 2025–2026 roster demonstrates how threatening the mere presence of a man dancing can be to those adhering to traditional notions of normative gender built on strict rules about separate spheres for men and women.[57]

Two other teams—the Washington Commanders and the Seattle Seahawks—present men squad members as dancers, but with a more masculine, hip-hop aesthetic that differentiates them from the women. Other teams feature men with muscular upper bodies who act as bases and spotters, lifting and throwing the women on their squads into the air. For these teams (which include the Rams, the Baltimore Ravens, and the Tennessee Titans), the cheer squads operate akin to a collegiate cheerleading team, with strong, muscular men lifting and throwing the smaller women. Such a configuration is suggestive of a hegemonic gender hierarchy that positions men as stronger and more powerful than women, who are in contrast weaker and submissive.[58]

Even with the growing inclusion of men on professional squads, the women (and their femininity) remain at the forefront of NFL cheerleading—either because the men dancers are consumed in the feminine aesthetic or because, as with the bases and spotters, their presence tends to blend into the background. Take the Baltimore Ravens squad, which was the most gender-balanced team in 2024, with twenty-one men and twenty-nine women. The men wore black T-shirts and pants and often blended into the background in game day photography behind the women in their brightly colored and sequined uniforms. In one cheerleading game day gallery of thirty-five photos, the men were the sole subject of just six photos. In multiple shots of women cheerleaders in the air, the men who threw them were cropped either completely or almost completely out of the photo, with just their arms visible.[59] Likewise, in a game day gallery of the Seahawks Dancers, only seven of thirty-seven photos included a man from the team in frame, and only one photo featured a man as the focus.[60]

Another difference between men and women NFL cheerleaders is their racial diversity. Of the men on the 2024 NFL squad rosters, more than 60 percent appeared to be men of color. On many of these teams, the racial diversity of the men far exceeded that of the women—for example, the Saints Cheer Krewe, which included over 80 percent men of color and under 33 percent women of color. These discrepancies raise the question of why NFL cheer teams are building more diversity among men, who are relative newcomers in professional cheerleading, compared to women. A possible answer is that while the participation of women of color in professional cheerleading is constrained by white hegemonic femininity, the men face no such constraint.

## Is Change Coming? The Future of Professional Cheer

NFL cheerleaders have made strides toward securing better pay and working conditions over the last decade. In the same time period, the internal diversity of squads has increased, particularly with the addition of men as well as a transgender woman. Some of these changes, including shifts to coed squads and more modest uniform styles, have been framed as progressive choices by teams. Yet the timing of such changes, on the heels of cheerleaders speaking out in the media and in lawsuits, suggests they resulted from public and legal pressures.[61]

While the cheerleaders' lawsuits did succeed in securing some improvements, they also led to unintended consequences: the disbanding of multiple NFL cheerleading squads. The Buffalo Jills disbanded in 2014 amid the lawsuit against the squad, while the Los Angeles Chargers dropped their squad in 2022, citing financial reasons.[62] The New York Jets have quietly gone without their Flight Crew cheerleading squad for the 2023 and 2024 seasons, with various online forums describing the squad as either disbanded or "on hiatus until 2024 as they undergo a rebranding initiative."[63] And as previously discussed, the Washington Commanders replaced their cheer squad with their Command Force entertainment squad in 2021.[64] The women who spoke out against their employers had hoped to secure better wages and treatment for themselves and future cheerleaders. But for some NFL teams, the solution was to get rid of the squads altogether, leaving dozens of women without their part-time jobs and opportunities to pursue the work they loved. For the Washington cheerleaders, the news of their job loss was delivered through an online meeting, scheduled with about thirty minutes' warning. The cheerleaders were informed that they were being released from their contracts early via Zoom webinar, which prevented them from speaking or asking questions.[65]

This treatment exemplifies how, even as NFL cheerleading has evolved, in many ways things have remained the same. Just as the cheerleaders' fight for better working conditions—a fight aligned with feminist work for equal treatment—has brought changes to NFL cheerleading, so too have hegemonic and postfeminist ideologies constrained it.[66] Hegemonic views about gender limit women's value and suggest that cheerleaders' role is to be appealing to men,[67] and so a white, heterosexual, hegemonic femininity continues to dominate the space. Such views also lead teams to treat cheerleaders as disposable or replaceable—a discourse that kept many of them silent about their mistreatment for so many years.[68] Postfeminist ideology, meanwhile, frames cheerleading as a choice: They agreed to work for these wages and to wear these uniforms; therefore, there is no reason for conditions to change.[69]

And even as the cheerleaders' stories aligned with the #MeToo movement of women speaking out about workplace harassment and assaults, some feminists seemed reticent to include cheerleaders in larger fights for gender equality. For instance, *The Boston Globe* published an opinion piece titled "It's Time to Say Goodbye to the NFL Cheerleaders," arguing that the squads are sexist and outdated, just months before the wave of 2018 cheerleading lawsuits began.[70] From this perspective, NFL cheerleaders, with their perfectly done hair and makeup, dancing in revealing uniforms for an audience of mostly men, are the antithesis of the feminist movement. While feminists might call out their working conditions as exploitive, they also see their very existence as problematic. An online comment, read by former Jills cheerleader Maria Pinzone in the 2021 film documenting her lawsuit, summed up this viewpoint: "I don't feel sorry for them at all. I have no respect for these women."[71]

Ultimately, constructions of professionalism, gender, and race in NFL cheerleading are not just about NFL cheerleaders. They reflect larger concerns around both workers and women in society. For instance, California Assemblywoman Lorena Gonzalez connected the cheerleaders' labor plight to that of other workers in the United States: "There's some things that are just American. And football and cheerleading, those top the list, right? I mean, nothing's more American than that. Well unfortunately, you know, nothing's more American than cheating workers out of an honest day's pay too."[72] In particular, the low pay of cheerleaders mirrors the low pay of other feminized professions and the gender wage gap in the United States.[73] As Darci Burrell, a lawyer representing cheerleaders in the Oakland Raiders lawsuit, said, "As a society, there's an unconscious devaluing of women."[74] Further, from a gender and racial perspective, NFL cheerleaders are cultural icons that produce meanings of idealized femininity for all women.[75] In this framing, efforts to evolve professional cheerleading are about the worth of all workers and all women—to have safe working conditions and fair pay; to be valued for their talents and not just their looks. As was seen following lawsuits from cheerleaders in the 2010s, change is possible.[76] But it will require continued attention and pressure on NFL organizations to happen.

## Notes

1. Chiefs Cheer (@chiefscheer), "Women in sports! [face exhaling emoji]," Instagram, January 20, 2024, https://www.instagram.com/reel/C2WDdx6uOGf/.

2. Michael Messner, "When Bodies Are Weapons: Masculinity and Violence in Sport," *International Review for the Sociology of Sport* 25, no. 3 (1990): 203–220; R. W. Connell and James Messerschmidt, "Hegemonic Masculinity: Rethinking the Concept," *Gender and Society* 19, no. 6 (2005): 829–859.

3. Messner, "When Bodies Are Weapons," 213.

4. Ken Belson, "How an Instagram Post Led to an N.F.L. Cheerleader's Discrimination Case," *New York Times*, March 25, 2018, https://www.nytimes.com/2018/03/25/sports/saints-cheerleader.html.

5. Lauren Hindman and Nefertiti A. Walker, "Feminine and Sexy: A Feminist Critical Discourse Analysis of Gender Ideology and Professional Cheerleading," *Journal of Sport Management* 36, no. 2 (2022): 130–144.

6. Eric Johnson, "Cheerleaders Reach $1.25 Million Settlement in Lawsuit Against Raiders," Reuters, September 4, 2014, https://www.reuters.com/article/world/us/raiders-agree-to-pay-125-million-to-cheerleaders-suing-over-unfair-pay-idUSKBN0H002R/; Tierney Sneed, "String of Cheerleader Lawsuits the Next Headache for the NFL," *U.S. News and World Report*, April 25, 2014, https://www.usnews.com/news/articles/2014/04/25/buffalo-bills-suspend-cheerleading-squad-after-lawsuit-third-of-its-kind.

7. *America's Sweethearts: Dallas Cowboys Cheerleaders*, season 1, episode 6, 2024, Netflix.

8. *America's Sweethearts*, season 1, episode 6.

9. *Oxford English Dictionary*, "professional," accessed September 21, 2024, https://www.oed.com/dictionary/professional_adj.

10. John Beech and Simon Chadwick, *The Business of Sport Management* (Pearson Education, 2004); Neil Wigglesworth, *The Story of Sport in England* (Routledge, 2007).

11. Nily Rozic and Lorena Gonzalez, "Cheerleaders, Until They See Their N.F.L. Paychecks," *New York Times*, September 11, 2015, https://www.nytimes.com/2015/09/12/opinion/cheerleaders-until-they-see-their-nfl-paychecks.html.

12. Laura Vikmanis and Amy Sohn, "Little to Cheer About," *New York Times*, April 12, 2018, https://www.nytimes.com/2018/04/12/opinion/cheerleading-nfl-gender-discrimination.html.

13. Ken Belson, "No Sweatpants in Public: Inside the Rule Books for N.F.L. Cheerleaders," *New York Times*, April 2, 2018, https://www.nytimes.com/2018/04/02/sports/nfl-cheerleaders.html; Rozic and Gonzalez, "Cheerleaders"; Vikmanis and Sohn, "Little to Cheer About."

14. Christopher M. McLeod and Tarlan Chahardovali, "How Do Low-Paid Athletes in the United States Understand the Meaning of the Word 'Professional' in 'Professional Athlete,'" *Sport in Society* 27, no. 1 (2024): 142–161.

15. Katie Thornton, "NFL Cheerleaders Have Spent Years Fighting for Justice;

Why Don't We Take Them Seriously?," *The Guardian*, February 10, 2023, https://www.theguardian.com/sport/2023/feb/09/nfl-cheerleaders-super-bowl-justice.

16. Robin Abcarian, "C'mon, Girls—This Is How It Goes: You Cheer, They Think," *Los Angeles Times*, March 12, 1995, https://www.latimes.com/archives/la-xpm-1995-03-12-ls-41682-story.html.

17. Abcarian, "C'mon, Girls."

18. Yu Gu, director, *A Woman's Work: The NFL's Cheerleader Problem*, 2019, aired on PBS in 2021.

19. Michelle Ruiz, "Sex on the Sidelines: How the N.F.L. Made a Game of Exploiting Cheerleaders," *Vanity Fair*, October 4, 2018, https://www.vanityfair.com/style/2018/10/nfl-cheerleaders-history-scandal.

20. Johnson, "Cheerleaders Reach $1.25 Million Settlement"; Lucy Mangan, "Three Cheers for the Cheerleader Suing the Cincinnati Bengals," *The Guardian*, February 14, 2014, https://www.theguardian.com/lifeandstyle/womens-blog/2014/feb/14/cheerleader-cincinnati-bengals-alexa-brenneman; Tony Marrero, "Bucs Settle Lawsuit Over Cheerleaders' Pay," *Tampa Bay Times*, March 7, 2015, https://www.tampabay.com/news/courts/civil/bucs-settle-lawsuit-over-cheerleaders-pay/2220433/; Sneed, "String of Cheerleader Lawsuits."

21. Josh Peter, "NFL Cheerleaders Scoring Victories in Labor Lawsuits," *USA Today*, February 4, 2016, https://www.usatoday.com/story/sports/nfl/2016/02/04/nfl-cheerleaders-scoring-victories-labor-lawsuits/79821670/.

22. CBS New York, "Jets to Pay $324K to Settle Cheerleaders' Wage Lawsuit," CBS News, January 27, 2016, https://www.cbsnews.com/newyork/news/new-york-jets-jets-flight-crew-lawsuit/.

23. Belson, "How an Instagram Post Led to Discrimination Case"; A. J. Perez, "Ex-Cowboys Cheerleader Claims in Lawsuit She Was Paid Fraction of What Mascot Earned," *USA Today*, June 13, 2018, https://www.usatoday.com/story/sports/nfl/cowboys/2018/06/12/ex-cowboys-cheerleader-lawsuit/696998002/; A. J. Perez, "Former Houston Texans Cheerleaders Allege Harassment, Physical Assault in Federal Lawsuit," *USA Today*, May 22, 2018, https://www.usatoday.com/story/sports/nfl/2018/05/22/former-houston-texans-cheerleaders-allege-harassment-physical-assault/633490002/; Alysha Tsuji, "Former Dolphins Cheerleader Talks About Mistreatment She Experienced," *USA Today*, May 10, 2018, https://ftw.usatoday.com/story/sports/nfl/2018/05/10/former-dolphins-nfl-cheerleaders-kristan-ann-ware-mistreatment-emotional-video-change/81758126007/.

24. Michael McCann, "NFL Teams Previously Have Settled in Cheerleader Lawsuits; Will Texans' Ex-Cheerleaders Set Different Precedent?," *Sports Illustrated*, June 25, 2018, https://www.si.com/nfl/2018/06/26/houston-texans-cheerleaders-sued-lawsuit-nfl.

25. Jason Whiteley and Mark Smith, "Cowboys Settle Cheerleader Pay Dispute, Entire Squad Gets Pay Boost," WFAA, September 9, 2018, https://www.wfaa.com/article/sports/nfl/cowboys/287-7dc7f6a3-8d36-44bf-8a5c-466cff75c3de.

26. Thornton, "NFL Cheerleaders Have Spent Years Fighting."

27. Gu, *A Woman's Work*.

28. Belson, "No Sweatpants in Public."

29. Belson, "How an Instagram Post Led to Discrimination Case"; Belson, "No Sweatpants in Public"; Vikmanis and Sohn, "Little to Cheer About."

30. Belson, "How an Instagram Post Led to Discrimination Case."

31. Belson, "How an Instagram Post Led to Discrimination Case."

32. Vikmanis and Sohn, "Little to Cheer About."

33. Ken Belson and Juliet Macur, "Washington Football Team Will Replace Cheerleaders with a Coed Dance Team," *New York Times*, March 3, 2021, https://www.nytimes.com/2021/03/03/sports/football/washington-football-team-cheerleaders.html.

34. Juliet Macur, "Washington Redskins Cheerleaders Describe Topless Photo Shoot and Uneasy Night Out," *New York Times*, May 2, 2018, https://www.nytimes.com/2018/05/02/sports/redskins-cheerleaders-nfl.html; Ruiz, "Sex on the Sidelines."

35. Taylor Yeley (@tayloryeley), "Part time job Full time commitment #nflcheerleader," TikTok, June 13, 2023, https://www.tiktok.com/@talesfromtay/video/7244209831832325419.

36. "2024 Atlanta Falcons Cheerleaders Auditions: Information and Frequently Asked Questions," Atlanta Falcons, 2024, https://www.atlantafalcons.com/cheerleaders/auditions-info-guide.

37. "2024 Atlanta Falcons Cheerleaders Auditions."

38. *America's Sweethearts*, season 1, episode 1.

39. Belson, "No Sweatpants in Public."

40. Alisha Haridasani Gupta and Katie Van Syckle, "The Dallas Cowboys Cheerleaders Get a 400 Percent Pay Raise," *New York Times*, June 18, 2025, https://www.nytimes.com/2021/03/03/sports/football/washington-football-team-cheerleaders.html.

41. Hindman and Walker, "Feminine and Sexy."

42. Natalie G. Adams and Pamela J. Bettis, "Commanding the Room in Short Skirts: Cheering as the Embodiment of Ideal Girlhood," *Gender and Society* 17, no. 1 (2003): 73–91.

43. *America's Sweethearts*, season 1, episode 1.

44. Shelley Budgeon, "The Dynamics of Gender Hegemony: Femininities, Masculinities and Social Change," *Sociology* 48, no. 2 (2014): 317–334.

45. "Miami Dolphins Cheerleading Auditions FAQs," Miami Dolphins, 2024, https://www.miamidolphins.com/cheerleaders/auditions/faq.

46. *America's Sweethearts*, season 1, episode 1.

47. Paige Skinner, "Former Dallas Cowboys Cheerleader Hopeful Reflects on Body Shaming on Reality TV Show," *Dallas Observer*, August 24, 2020, https://www.dallasobserver.com/arts/meagan-pravden-reflects-on-body-shaming-from-cmts-dallas-cowboys-cheerleaders-making-the-team-11921926.

48. Kathy Deliovsky, "Normative White Femininity: Race, Gender and the Politics of Beauty," *Atlantis* 33, no. 1 (2008): 49–59; Hindman and Walker, "Feminine and Sexy."

49. Hindman and Walker, "Feminine and Sexy."

50. "General FAQs," Washington Commanders Command Force, 2024, https://www.commanders.com/command-force/faqs.

51. Belson and Macur, "Washington Football Team Will Replace Cheerleaders."

52. Will Hobson and Liz Clarke, "From Dream Job to Nightmare," *Washington Post*, July 16, 2020, https://www.washingtonpost.com/sports/2020/07/16/redskins-sexual-harassment-larry-michael-alex-santos/; Macur, "Cheerleaders Describe Topless Photo Shoot."

53. Hindman and Walker, "Feminine and Sexy."

54. Jim Businski, "Carolina Panthers Hire NFL's First Transgender Cheerleader," *OutSports*, June 6, 2022, https://www.outsports.com/2022/6/6/23157111/carolina-panthers-transgender-cheerleader-justine-lindsay/.

55. Christina Cauterucci, "Bro Boom Bah," *Slate*, August 8, 2018, https://slate.com/culture/2018/08/the-real-reason-teams-are-bringing-men-on-to-their-squads.html.

56. Hindman and Walker, "Feminine and Sexy"; Daniel Villarreal, "These Openly Gay Men Just Made History by Becoming the NFL's First-Ever Male Cheerleaders," *Hornet*, March 28, 2018, https://hornet.com/stories/male-cheerleaders-nfl/.

57. Natalie Stechyson, "Male Cheerleaders Aren't New; So Why Are People Mad About the Minnesota Vikings," *CBC News*, August 21, 2025, https://www.cbc.ca/news/world/nfl-male-cheerleaders-minnesota-vikings-1.7614479.

58. Connell and Messerschmidt, "Hegemonic Masculinity"; Laura Grindstaff and Emily West, "Hegemonic Masculinity on the Sidelines of Sport," *Sociology Compass* 5, no. 10 (2011): 859–881.

59. "Cheerleaders: Ravens vs. Bills, Week 4," Baltimore Ravens, 2024, https://www.baltimoreravens.com/photos/cheerleaders-ravens-vs-bills-week-3.

60. "Photos: Seahawks Dancers During Week 3 vs. the Miami Dolphins," Seattle Seahawks, 2024, https://www.seahawks.com/photos/photos-seahawks-dancers-during-week-3-vs-the-miami-dolphins.

61. Belson and Macur, "Washington Football Team Will Replace Cheerleaders"; Chad Calder, "The Story Behind Major Changes to New Orleans Sainsations' 2018 Uniforms," NOLA.com, January 12, 2019, https://www.nola.com/news/the-story-behind-major-changes-to-new-orleans-saintsations-2018-uniforms/article_7c5aaae1-21b4-5ddb-8b38-b9795d866094.html; Hindman and Walker, "Feminine and Sexy."

62. Thornton, "NFL Cheerleaders Have Spent Years Fighting."

63. Wikipedia, "Jets Flight Crew," accessed November 27, 2024, https://en.wikipedia.org/wiki/Jets_Flight_Crew.

64. Belson and Macur, "Washington Football Team Will Replace Cheerleaders."

65. Emily Leibert, "The Washington Football Team Rebranded; Why Did It Get Rid of Its Cheerleaders Over Zoom?," *Refinery 29*, August 2, 2021, https://www.refinery29.com/en-us/2021/08/10532592/washington-football-team-cheerleaders.

66. Hindman and Walker, "Feminine and Sexy."

67. Ruiz, "Sex on the Sidelines."

68. Belson, "No Sweatpants in Public."

69. Kayce Smith, "A Dallas Cowboys Cheerleader Is Suing the Organization and, Hear Me Out, It's Something We Should Get Behind," *Barstool Sports*, June 18, 2018, https://www.barstoolsports.com/blog/1020203/a-dallas-cowboys-cheerleader-is-suing-the-organization-and-its-something-we-should-get-behind.

70. Margery Eagan, "It's Time to Say Goodbye to the NFL Cheerleaders," *Boston Globe*, January 22, 2018, https://www.bostonglobe.com/opinion/2018/01/22/time-say-goodbye-nfl-cheerleaders/0jt8QbTA0MquvgCPiuGzZJ/story.html.

71. Gu, *A Woman's Work*.

72. Gu, *A Woman's Work*.

73. Carolina Aragão, "Gender Pay Gap in U.S. Hasn't Changed Much in Two Decades," Pew Research Center, March 1, 2023, https://www.pewresearch.org/short-reads/2023/03/01/gender-pay-gap-facts/; Felix Busch, "Occupational Devaluation Due to Feminization? Causal Mechanics, Effect Heterogeneity, and Evidence from the United States, 1960 to 2010," *Social Forces* 96, no. 3 (2018): 1351–1376.

74. Gu, *A Woman's Work*.

75. Hindman and Walker, "Feminine and Sexy."

76. Hindman and Walker, "Feminine and Sexy."

CHAPTER 7

# We're Here, We're Queer, Get Used to It

## LGBTQ+ ADULT PERFORMANCE TEAMS IN THE UNITED STATES

*Laura Grindstaff*

CHEER for Life!

Fundraising slogan of CHEER San Francisco

Despite the conventional image of cheerleading in US culture—as dominated by young, sexy-fit, white women cheering for male athletes at school sporting events—in reality the activity is, and has been, far more diverse. As chapters in this volume attest, cheerleading can be a supportive sideline activity in schools, a competitive sport seeking Olympic recognition, an opportunity for protesting racial segregation, the basis for a lucrative business empire, and a springboard for media celebrity. Whereas cheerleading was once all male and exclusively white, then mostly white and female, today it's more gender inclusive (particularly in the context of collegiate competition), as well as racially and ethnically diverse.

Yet even this broad picture misses an important face of cheerleading as it has been taken up by distinct groups and communities in the United States. Over a decade spanning the 2000s, when I was conducting ethnographic research on college-level cheer (much of it with my colleague Emily West, as discussed in chapter 4), I came across three alternative forms of cheerleading I hadn't known existed. The first type is senior citizen cheerleading—sometimes called elderly cheerleading, or simply eldercheer—which features squads of women fifty-five and older, often living in retirement communities. They defy stereotypes about aging and vitality by performing simple choreographed routines, complete with sparkly poms and color-coordinated activewear, at various civic and charitable events.[1] I witnessed one such squad at a ribbon-cutting ceremony in the Villages retirement community just outside of Orlando, Florida (I was there visiting a relative after attending the Cheerleading Worlds All Star competition). The second type is a nationwide network of queer-friendly adult performance teams affiliated with the nonprofit Pride Cheerleading Association. PCA member teams perform high-level cheer routines in spaces that celebrate LGBTQ+ diversity and raise funds for charitable causes.[2] The oldest and largest of the PCA teams is CHEER San Francisco. Early on in my fieldwork, I joined Sacramento Spirit (later renamed Cheer Sacramento)—not officially a PCA team but welcomed at the same events. The third type is radical cheerleading, a form of performance-based political activism popular during the late 1990s through the mid-2000s. It uses the trappings and techniques of cheerleading to protest social injustice, in the process infusing "boring, male-dominated demonstrations" with a queer, riot grrrl sensibility.[3] A graduate student participant introduced me to, and subsequently helped me interview, roughly thirty radical cheerleaders from different squads across the United States and Canada.

All three groups broaden our understanding of cheerleading by challenging our assumptions about who cheerleaders are and what cheerleading is for. At the same time, to be recognizable as cheerleaders, the groups must reproduce or appropriate key elements of cheerleading, which necessarily shapes how "alternative" they can be. This chapter focuses on one of those groups, the PCA and its early member teams, to explore how and why they embrace cheerleading, and the affordances and limitations of that embrace in accomplishing their goals. In the next chapter, I explore the case of radical cheerleading.

### Queering Cheer: CHEER San Francisco and the Pride Cheerleading Association

The PCA was founded in 2004 by a coalition of charitable cheerleading squads. Such squads were multiplying in the late 1990s and early 2000s—not coincidentally the same period when traditional cheerleading itself was experiencing a renaissance—and sought a common organizational structure to support, promote, and coordinate their philanthropic mission. CHEER San Francisco (CHEER SF) is considered the grande dame of the fourteen affiliated teams, today sporting roughly fifty participants of diverse ages, genders, ethnicities, and body types. Their website details aspects of their history and mission.[4]

My firsthand knowledge of CHEER SF comes from volunteering at their performances, interviewing the founder and other key participants, and performing alongside them at San Francisco and Sacramento Pride events, first as a member of Sacramento Spirit and then as a member of Cheer Sacramento. This chapter therefore has autobiographical as well as ethnographic elements, in that I use my own experience, alongside the experiences of others, to make sense of the PCA phenomenon.[5] Centering the scholar's experience in ethnographic analysis is captured in the distinction between the term "observant participation" and the more traditional "participant observation"; while the former emphasizes the "emic" (subjective) concept of participation, the latter emphasizes the "etic" (objective/scientific) concept of observation, with accompanying differences in writing style, often characterized as descriptive versus analytic.[6] Yet, as Clifford Geertz has argued in his classic essay "Thick Description," observing, participating, and writing are all part of the ethnographic enterprise; when description is "thick" enough, as I hope it is in this chapter, analysis is already happening.[7]

CHEER SF began in 1980 as a small, all-male, all-gay dance and pom squad called the Hayward Raw Rahs under the stewardship of Guy Andrade, a young gay man originally from Hawaii who, in his interview with me, identified as Hawaiian and Portuguese. Initially consisting of a half dozen participants performing mostly at local bars and street fairs, the squad got rebranded as the Bay Area Raw Rahs as its membership and geographical reach expanded. In 1993, the Bay Area Raw Rahs partnered with the Jon Sims Center for the Performing Arts in San Francisco, which gave their fundraising efforts nonprofit status, and in 1996, under new leadership, the team became CHEER SF. In 2004, the same year in which the PCA was formed, CHEER SF established its own nonprofit, the CHEER for Life Foundation. Each year, CHEER SF selects several local or national organizations as beneficiaries of the team's fundraising efforts that year. The website currently lists fifty-five different beneficiaries, ranging from the AIDS Health Project and the Transgender Law Center to Foster a Dream and Hospice by the Bay. The events at which CHEER SF performs vary but tend to fall into two camps: civic events (e.g., Pride parades and street festivals), and public or corporate events (e.g., walk-a-thons and fun runs). Occasionally the group is hired to perform at private corporate events such as company picnics or conference kickoffs, for which they are paid a flat fee. More commonly, CHEER SF cheerleaders gather cash for beneficiaries in spirit buckets—bright-red plastic buckets emblazoned with the CHEER for Life logo, placed around the perimeter of the performance area and passed among spectators. More times than I can count, I helped circulate these buckets at CHEER SF performances, entreating people to dig deep to support the designated beneficiary. The team also sells merchandise (shirts, bags, stickers, phone cases, etc.) both at performance sites and online.

CHEER SF welcomes opportunities to showcase its athletes and promote LGBTQ+ visibility to broader publics even outside of fundraising opportunities (although one could argue, and CHEER SF members do, that visibility helps with, and is not separate from, fundraising). In addition to appearing on national television on ABC's *Good Morning America* and NBC's *America's Got Talent*, the team has performed at halftime shows for the Golden State Warriors (NBA), in victory parades for the San Francisco Giants (MLB), and at notable international venues such as the Sydney Opera House and the Royal Palace in Amsterdam. CHEER SF is the only PCA member team to have performed at every Gay Games since 1982.

Although I was not an official part of CHEER SF, I share the brief history above to contextualize my own experience on an adult performance team that was starting from scratch and looked up to CHEER SF for guidance and moral support. It was from CHEER SF that I learned about a new sister squad forming in Sacramento—Sacramento Spirit.

### Sacramento Spirit / Cheer Sacramento

There were six other people on Sacramento Spirit when I joined: five straight women and one gay man, Gary.[8] Only three had any prior cheerleading experience; I was not one of them, but Gary was, as was our founder and coach, Rachel. Rachel had cheered on all-girl squads in high school and junior college, while Gary had high school and All Star experience. Barely twenty, Rachel had always wanted to be a flyer but was a base on her previous teams. I myself was forty at the time, newly tenured and the mother of a two-year-old, while the others were in their twenties or early thirties. One teammate was Asian American and one was Latina; the rest of us were white. Within the first month, however, two Black women in their mid-thirties—close friends Kira and Kelsey—joined, bringing our number up to nine.

Reasons for participating varied. Some were looking for performance-oriented community engagement; others loved cheer but found few opportunities after graduation aside from All Star, which was expensive and, at the upper age ranges, highly competitive. I was in it for the research first, and for the LGBTQ+ allyship second. We were a ragtag bunch. Initially we practiced outdoors at a local park under the blazing sun with no mats or equipment, and then in an old, uninsulated toy warehouse on the outskirts of the city, still with no mats. Our performance uniforms were gaudy and ill fitting. Gary and I were the only members I would characterize as really fit. That I—with no experience, a fear of heights, and zero flexibility—became a flyer speaks volumes about our capabilities. Privately, I thought of us as the Bad News Bears of adult cheerleading, in reference to the 1976 film about a losing boys' baseball team whose star player is a girl (the star in our case being Gary). We couldn't have been further afield from CHEER SF.

Nevertheless, CHEER SF was unflaggingly supportive. They insisted we join them at San Francisco Pride; we weren't good enough to execute a routine on the main stage along with CHEER SF and the other PCA teams, but we took part in the street parade. Closer to home, we performed at Sacramento Pride and the Sacramento Rainbow Festival, and we cheered at walk-a-thons, raising money for breast cancer research and domestic violence prevention. Our first-ever public appearance was on the local TV show *Good Day Sacramento*—a simple pom and dance routine set to Britney Spears's hit single *Toxic*. We also participated in the annual Christmas parade in an adjacent town in near-freezing temperatures, where drunk men along the parade route catcalled us and loudly called Gary a slur.

But the most memorable event that first year was a four-day college summer camp at the University of California, Riverside, hosted by the Universal Cheerleaders Association (UCA). CHEER SF was also there, seeking to hone their stunting skills, but the rest of the camp consisted of all-girl and coed college teams, two dozen in all, some of them highly ranked in the UCA competition structure. Summer camps are often the first formal team event after spring tryouts, and consequently they serve as bonding experiences as well as opportunities to build skills. I found the four days of camp tortuous. While other teams picked up cheers, fight songs, and dance routines with ease, we struggled to master even the most rudimentary moves. Stunting was worse. Rachel insisted on flying despite being one of our larger members. Two of our bases suffered minor injuries that nevertheless sent them to the ER because of liability concerns. By day three, camp leaders began avoiding us, understanding that we needed remedial instruction well beyond their capacity. Instead, one of the CHEER SF captains stuck close, giving pointers and offering assistance. At some point, I recall Kira and I talking about menopause for some reason. A slim, blond cheerleader went bouncing past us on the path, and Kira remarked, "I bet we're the only ones at cheer camp having a conversation about menopause!" I laughed, "Yeah, and that's not the only way we stand out." Indeed, we were out of place: a small group of mismatched adults amid a sea of perky ponytails, sassy backflips, flexing biceps, and thirty-foot basket tosses.

Our outsider status was cemented on the final day, when each team performs before the entire camp and is evaluated by the instructors. Someone had borrowed my poms and not returned them, so I went without, and Rachel was furious with me. Miserable, I went through the motions of the routine, trying to avoid eye contact with the other campers. Even so, I locked eyes with a cheerleader I recognized; she had been on a college team I was observing for my research but had transferred schools and was now with a new team. She recognized me too, her expression incredulous. She was embarrassed for me. So was I. I considered myself an athlete, good at most sports, and excelling at some. Cheerleading wasn't among them.

The camp experience underscored for me both the difficulty of cheerleading, which most outsiders don't appreciate, and the fact that if one is going to be respected as a nontraditional cheerleader (not young, not thin, not white, not heterosexual, not conventionally attractive) in a setting meant for serious, college-level participation, one had better be skilled. It's one thing to be welcomed into the fold by CHEER SF and the PCA; it's another to be welcomed by college teams highly invested in proving cheerleading a legitimate sport. We represented exactly the image of cheerleading they had worked all their lives to dispel.

After that first year we lost some members, including Kira and Kelsey, but gained others, along with a new coach, Misty. She soon rebranded us as Cheer Sacramento (fig. 7.1), ordered new, athletic-looking uniforms, and secured a gym for our practices, which we shared with a karate club, who lent us their mats. Misty also successfully recruited several men (all strong, all good dancers, all gay, none white), enabling us to improve our stunting. She was a better flyer than I, as was another new member, so I began flying less and basing more. We got better and eventually did perform on the main stage of San Francisco Pride, although we were still the worst cheer team out there. Membership waxed and waned during the five years I participated, reaching a high of ten at one point but more typically

FIGURE 7.1. *Author Laura Grindstaff (center front) poses with her squad, Cheer Sacramento, 2007. Photo used with permission from Laura Grindstaff.*

hovering around eight. Misty was a good leader. There was a minimum of drama, and I enjoyed the company of my teammates. Today, nearly twenty years later, Sacramento finally has representation in the PCA in the form of Sacramento Cheer Elite, the association's newest member team.[9]

**CHEER SF: The Same, But Different**

The PCA and its affiliated teams are alternative, but within limits. Compared to conventional cheer teams, they have greater age and gender diversity, embracing cisgender and transgender men and women as well as nonbinary individuals of all ages eighteen-plus. At the time of my research, the oldest member of CHEER SF was forty-five, and today there is a skilled flyer in his fifties. Body types are also more diverse than college teams, as participants unable to tumble, execute jumps, or fly can contribute through basing and dancing. Moreover, there is no gendered division of labor when it comes to stunting and dancing: Small people fly and heavier people base regardless of gender identity or expression, and everyone dances. Today, this gender-neutral approach is not uncommon on All Star teams and even characterizes some collegiate coed teams, perhaps thanks to the rise and influence of LGBTQ+ adult cheerleading. Indeed, many members of PCA teams with elite skills come from All Star cheer, where they have either aged out or begun employment that precludes a rigorous practice schedule. Whereas All Star teams practice daily or near daily, CHEER SF practices once a week, albeit for two and a half or three hours. Of course, another way in which PCA teams are distinct is their fundraising mission and nonprofit status. Their cheering is not in support of high school or college sports teams, nor is it for a competition trophy. The main payoff for cheering is to increase the visibility of LGBTQ+ cheerleaders through tax-deductible philanthropy, and in the process to entertain audiences and expand the cheerleading landscape.

On the other hand, PCA teams embrace key elements of conventional cheerleading. They prize skill, precision, energy, and enthusiasm. They epitomize the concept of spirit and can outpep the peppiest squad. Despite being multigenerational, they replicate the structure of conventional cheer routines with stunts, jumps, tumbling, and dancing, all expertly choreographed and set to blaring, upbeat music. They get fitted and buy their uniforms from Varsity Brands. Although they practice less regularly than scholastic or All Star teams, they have a similar organizational structure, with a coach, one or more captains, governing bylaws, and a handbook outlining requirements and expectations.

At the time of my research, members of CHEER SF were adamant that they were *not* engaged in political activism via cheerleading, although other PCA teams may have felt differently. CHEER SF members insisted that their mission was to fundraise while promoting diversity and inclusivity for LGBTQ+ communities and beyond. For them, this was not political so much as civic-minded; they were ambassadors, not provocateurs. Indeed, they expressly strove to counter the image of the strident, in-your-face activist of the AIDS era, when the guerilla tactics of ACT UP and other groups captured media headlines. They appreciated such efforts, but they had different goals, which included mainstream acceptance. As Stan, one of the CHEER SF captains, explained during our interview, "That's what's a real thrill for me, to get into the mainstream environment, the straight environment, and show 'em that we're okay. And then, if we can do that, the world's gonna be a better place. So in fact, yes, we are creating societal change. We're out there doing it." For Stan, change can happen without activism per se.

The PCA squads also demonstrate aspects of gender conformity. As in the culture in the 2000s, gay men on CHEER SF were the public face of LGBTQ+ visibility, outnumbering women by a significant margin—roughly three to one. This was no doubt a function of the team's all-male origins, and it is telling that the decision to admit women was controversial. According to Stan, those opposed had felt that it would compromise their unique status as an all-male gay squad and had wanted to maintain the tradition. Those in favor had felt that excluding women was discriminatory, especially when inclusivity was an explicit goal. Those in favor prevailed, and the first woman joined in 1997. She was the only woman for two years before others gradually joined. Although women remained a minority for many years, today the team roster shows that roughly half the participants on CHEER SF are women or female appearing. Based on my own experience and conversations with my interviewees, most of these participants are straight identifying, further rendering invisible lesbian or otherwise nonheterosexual women even in the LGBTQ+ context. At the time of our interview in 2003, Stan estimated that in his thirteen years on CHEER SF, only a dozen or so of the women participants had identified as lesbian or bisexual. Conversations with members of Cheer New York, Cheer LA, and the Chicago Spirit Brigade confirmed this same pattern. The gay male–straight female combination characterizes All Star cheer as well, from which the PCA teams draw. To the degree that cheerleading is considered a feminine activity, and both straight women and gay men are associated with femininity, the pattern conforms to gender expectations.

The long tail of the all-male origins of CHEER SF manifests in team leadership, with the coach and captain positions filled by men, typically older members with deep roots in the gay male community. Cheer New York, founded in 2001, had male and female cocaptains, with the guy, Vince, serving as recruiter and visionary ("I'm the idea person," he told me) and the woman handling the details and logistics of booking performances—another conventionally gendered arrangement. By contrast, Cheer Seattle had a female (and queer-identified) founder and coach, but like Cheer Sacramento, they were a small (six participants), fledgling squad not yet affiliated with the PCA.

For me personally, the most interesting aspect of conformity to "regular" cheerleading on the part of CHEER SF pertained to appearance: uniforms, hair ribbons, makeup, poms. Although men could fly and women could base, uniforms adhered to convention: pants for men and male-appearing individuals, skirts for women and female-appearing individuals. Nonbinary participants presumably had to choose uniforms from one or the other side of the binary. Men could wear minimal makeup (foundation, a few sparkles), whereas women were expected to be in full face and to sport bows and ribbons (upward of 90 percent of the women I saw on PCA teams had long hair).

Poms were another gendered signifier to be managed. For example, in 2002 when CHEER SF traveled to Singapore for an exhibition performance after participating in the Gay Games that year in Australia, the big debate, according to Stan, was over poms: "Do we bring the pom-poms or don't we bring the pom-poms?" Unsure of their reception in a foreign country, the team worried that poms had the potential to deliver the wrong message about the US LGBTQ+ community. More generally, the decision to use poms or not hinges on whether the routine itself calls for them. The way Stan explained it, if the team is at cheer camp competing in the "fight song division" against Sacramento State (an elite coed college team), that occasion warrants poms: "Those guys are throwing all those little girls in the air, okay, we gotta do something here! We gotta pull out our secret weapon, we gotta pull our shiny Mylar! Bring the pom-poms!" But when performing a serious, formal stunt routine in public, the poms typically stay at home. You can see examples of CHEER SF's stunt routines on YouTube, in videos from various Pride main stage performances,[10] or the 2019 halftime performance for the Golden State Warriors.[11]

I queried the CHEER SF captains about their stance toward uniforms, thinking it antithetical to LGBTQ+ inclusivity. They explained the need to maintain a "professional" appearance, given their mission as well as their mixed audiences. Men in skirts and makeup would be entirely appropriate at a drag show, a gay bar, or the Castro Street Fair in San Francisco, but to be taken seriously as "real" cheerleaders, to be recognizable as "real" cheerleaders, certain gendered standards of appearance had to be upheld. They wanted recognition not for bending gender norms per se but for their love of cheerleading and their commitment to philanthropy. For them, gender bending could only go so far before it overshadowed the main purpose of the team. There was also the desire, in forbidding skirts for men, to avoid amplifying extant gay male stereotypes. As Vince of Cheer New York told me, "We will draw the line if a guy wants to wear a skirt. . . . We want to project a collegiate-style athletic squad. And get away from the whole stereotyping of us being a bunch of girls sitting in skirts and pom-poms."

At first blush, the PCA stance on gendered norms of appearance might appear to confirm sociologist R. W. Connell's concept of "the straight gay"—gay men who embrace conventional masculinity and eschew effeminacy in order to maintain the gender order and their place of male privilege within it.[12] But CHEER SF and other PCA teams do not reject femininity for men; rather, they differentiate between performance and everyday life, as well as between performances meant for insider audiences versus those meant for broader publics. With charitable cheerleading, they thread the needle between LGBTQ+ visibility or advocacy and gendered expectations of cheerleaders in the broader culture.

Concerns about amplifying stereotypes are not unfounded. When Guy Andrade started the Hayward Raw Rahs with his pom and dance routine in 1980, he was swimming against the tide of a macho gay male scene at the dawn of the AIDS epidemic. According to Andrade, his routines were just as likely to face jeers and catcalls as cheers and applause from other gay men. Even decades later, for PCA teams to be accepted as "legitimate" cheerleaders, they walk a fine line between confirming and challenging gender boundaries. When interviewing the rep of a mainstream cheerleading association, I learned that parents had complained when CHEER SF performed an exhibition routine at the association's annual competition: Parents, specifically dads, objected to the "inappropriate" message being conveyed about masculinity to the young boys in the audience, presumably because of the men flying and dancing. This is consistent with the research of the sociologist Emily Kane, who found that parents tolerated gender nonconformity more readily in young daughters than in sons, and that fathers were especially intolerant of sons' nonconformity because they feared it signaled future homosexuality and therefore a "failure" of masculinity. Masculinity is more rigidly defined and hotly defended than femininity to preserve its greater value in the gender hierarchy.[13]

In everyday life, pants for women are less controversial than skirts for men, yet CHEER SF opted to enforce "gender appropriate" uniforms for the women too. I don't know whether other PCA teams did, or do, the same, but at the time of this writing, there are no women or female-appearing individuals wearing a uniform with pants in any of the photos on team websites. Cheer New York did have a flexible approach when it came to tops for female cheerleaders, however. According to Vince, "We give [women] the option, 'cause there are some women who are larger and if they are uncomfortable with the half top, then they are more than welcome to wear the guys' shirts." I opted to wear a men's uniform one year when Sacramento Spirit attended San Francisco Pride in support of the PCA. Coach Misty had no objection, since we were not ourselves performing in the parade or onstage, only among the milling crowds. Interestingly, knowing me well, no one on my own team remarked on it, but half a dozen male

CHEER SF participants did, admonishing me that I had a cute body—why was I trying to hide it beneath baggy pants? I did not seize this opportunity to deliver a feminist lecture on the value of gender nonconformity regardless of gender identity or physical appearance.

### Closure: A Balancing Act

CHEER SF and other PCA member teams demonstrate both the capaciousness and the limitations of cheerleading for communicating alternative meanings about gender. To be legible as "real" cheer athletes who command respect for their high-level skills as well as their philanthropic spirit, they must toe the line between tradition and change, deciding where to breach and where to protect gendered cultural boundaries. What emerges is a picture of ongoing negotiation rather than resolution of these tensions. The squads appear to be actively working to create new models of what cheerleading can be, while still maintaining enough connection to traditional cheerleading to be recognized and taken seriously as cheerleaders. This requires careful navigation of gender presentation, stereotypes, and athletic expectations. My participant observation and interviews suggest that teams challenge gender stereotypes not through outright rejection of all traditional elements but through their strategic reformation to be more inclusive and equitable. The bottom line is a balancing act: societal inclusion for LGBTQ+ folks while also fundraising for compatible charitable causes. I close with words from Sunshine, the founder of Cheer Seattle, who told me, "I want their money. So, yes, we do some unconventional things but they're kind of minor, because I'm trying to evoke the 1950s stereotype back when everything was 'pure.'" The goal is to "get through to some woman in Bellevue [a wealthy Seattle suburb] who loves the idea of helping out her community by donating to the squad because, look, they're all good cheerleaders."

### Notes

1. See Sabrina Sanchez, "'It Gave Me a Purpose': Sacramento Senior Spirit Squad Proves You're Never Too Old to Cheer," ABC 10, December 18, 2024, https://www.abc10.com/article/news/local/sacramento-senior-spirit-squad-never-too-old-to-cheer/103-af9b0ab6-1e8d-45e7-b90f-e608dba308aa; Nance Ebert,

"Senior Cheerleading Squads Delight Audiences in Three Communities and Beyond," *Fifty Plus Advocate*, April 9, 2024, https://www.fiftyplusadvocate.com/2024/04/09/senior-cheerleading-squads-delight-audiences-in-three-communities-and-beyond/.

2. "About Us," Pride Cheerleading Association, accessed November 1, 2025, https://www.pridecheerleadingassociation.org/v2-about-us.

3. Jeanne Vaccaro, "Give Me an F: Radical Cheerleading and Feminist Performance," *Women and Performance* 14, no. 2 (2005): 43–50.

4. Home page, CHEER San Francisco, https://www.cheersf.org.

5. Although I do not consider my work to be autoethnographic, the blend of autobiography and ethnography is certainly one characteristic of autoethnography as a distinct genre of ethnographic practice. In autoethnography, the self becomes the prime vehicle for analyzing, either implicitly or explicitly, the social world. More personal, introspective, and evocative than traditional ethnographies, autoethnographies are often literary in style, making heavy use of metaphor and other literary devices. Contemporary practitioners in my own disciplines of sociology and communications include Carolyn Ellis, Arthur P. Bochner, Laurel Richardson, Norman K. Denzin, and Patricia Clough. For a good overview, see Norman K. Denzin, *Interpretive Autoethnography*, 2nd ed. (Sage, 2014); Carolyn Ellis, Tony E. Adams, and Arthur P. Bochner, "Autoethnography: An Overview," *Historical Social Research* 36, no. 4 (2011): 273–290. In 2006, the *Journal of Contemporary Ethnography* devoted a special issue to the topic.

6. See Brian Moeran, "From Participant Observation to Observant Participation: Anthropology, Fieldwork, and Organizational Ethnography," Copenhagen Business School, July 2007, 2–25.

7. Clifford Geertz, "Thick Description: Toward an Interpretive Theory of Culture," in *The Interpretation of Culture: Selected Essays* (Basic Books, 1973), 3–30.

8. With the exception of Guy Andrade, all names from my fieldwork are pseudonyms.

9. Home page, Sacramento Cheer Elite, https://www.sacramentocheerelite.org.

10. "CHEER SF - Debut of 2015 Stunt Routine @ Sacramento Pride Festival," posted June 12, 2015, by CHEERSF, YouTube, https://www.youtube.com/watch?v=QN51YFXTKOE; "CHEER SF - 'Ode to Cheer' Stunt Routine @ 2015 San Francisco Pride Celebration Main Stage," posted July 9, 2015, by CHEERSF, YouTube, https://www.youtube.com/watch?v=Vhw1gsiKcuE; "CHEER SF- 'Remix' Stunt Routine - San Francisco Pride Main Stage 2017," posted July 5, 2017, by CheerSF Artistic, YouTube, https://www.youtube.com/watch?v=IGdeatXD3i8; "CHEER SF - 'Swing' Stunt Routine at SF Pride 2019," posted July 11, 2019, by CHEERSF, YouTube, https://www.youtube.com/watch?v=Od4I0A3uHPU.

11. See "Cheer San Francisco Warrior Halftime Show Performance 2019," posted November 4, 2019, by Mary Rose Yoga, YouTube, https://www.youtube.com/watch?v=JAGmwhqT-Ms.

12. R. W. Connell, "A Very Straight Gay: Masculinity, Homosexual Experience, and the Dynamics of Gender," *American Sociological Review* 57, no. 6 (1992): 735–751.

13. Emily Kane, *The Gender Trap: Parents and the Pitfalls of Raising Boys and Girls* (New York University Press, 2012). See also Judith Lorber, *Paradoxes of Gender* (Yale University Press, 1994); Judith Lorber, *The New Gender Paradox: Fragmentation and Persistence of the Binary* (Polity, 2022); C. J. Pascoe, *Dude, You're a Fag: Masculinity and Sexuality in High School* (University of California Press, 2007).

CHEER NOTE #5

# Cheerleaders as Social Activists

Cheering as a form of social protest isn't new. Cheerleaders have used their voices to protest the Vietnam War, Jim Crow, gender discrimination, police brutality, wage discrimination, and a host of other social ills. In 1968, Jeff Sokol, a long-haired hippie, ran for head cheerleader at the University of California, Berkeley, on an antiwar platform. He beat his opponent by 1,100 votes. His squad of fifty members consisted of "a boy with a cowboy hat, another long haired friend and two others who hadn't even shown up to try out."[1] Their cheers included antiwar songs and chants created by a local radical theatrical group. Their uniforms were Levi's jeans and blue sweaters with a gold peace sign on the front. Sokol hired Country Joe and the Fish, a psychedelic rock band, to perform at halftime. He led the fans in chants of "End the war" and "Ban the bomb." Sokol didn't last long as the head cheerleader. Members of the university's fraternities and sororities held a recall petition, and he was ousted after a few games. He was surprised at all the publicity he received, telling *Mademoiselle* magazine, "I thought it would be easy to ease the spectators' aggressions away from school spirit to more worthy causes, like the peace movement. Instead they've directed them toward me."[2]

After the Watts riots in 1965, a Black student named Eddie Anderson ran for head cheerleader at the University of California, Los Angeles, with the intention of using cheer to deliver antiracism and antiwar messages to a larger audience. He won. At one game he performed "Bomb Around the Clock," a parody of the Bill Haley and His Comets song "Rock Around the Clock." When his school played Duke in basketball, a Duke fan appeared visibly upset that Anderson was dancing with a white girl from the UCLA spirit squad. He stopped the dance, grabbed the microphone, and announced, "This woman is trying to be heard, but we can't hear what she's saying through her white sheet"—a reference to the Ku Klux Klan.[3]

In 1982, John Hawkins became the first Black cheerleader selected at the University of Mississippi. It was a long-standing tradition that the cheerleaders carried the Confederate flag during the game. Hawkins announced that he would not participate in that ritual, explaining, "In my household, I wasn't told to hate the flag, but I did have history classes and know what my ancestors went through and what the Rebel flag represents. It is my choice that I prefer not to wave one." Hawkins's refusal to carry the flag reignited long-standing racial tensions on the Ole Miss campus. Six months later, Chancellor Porter Fortune banned any official use of the Confederate flag at school-sanctioned events.[4]

## Notes

1. Carol Matzkin, "Peacenik in the Center Ring," *Mademoiselle*, May 1968, 45–55.
2. Matzkin, "Peacenik in the Center Ring."
3. Pat Ryan, "Once It Was Only Sis-Boom-Bah?," *Sports Illustrated*, January 6, 1969, 45–55.
4. Wendell Rawls Jr., "Black Cheerleader Balks at Waving the 'Rebel' Flag," *New York Times*, September 4, 1982, https://www.nytimes.com/1982/09/04/us/black-cheerleader-balks-at-waving-the-rebel-flag.html; W. Ralph Eubanks, "The Confederate Flag Finally Falls in Mississippi," *New Yorker*, July 1, 2020, https://www.newyorker.com/news/news-desk/the-confederate-flag-finally-falls-in-mississippi.

CHAPTER 8

# Engendering the Body Politic

## THE CASE OF RADICAL CHEERLEADERS

*Laura Grindstaff*

Riot, don't diet! Get up, get out, and try it!
Popular radical cheer

From the late 1990s through the 2000s, an international network of feminists used cheerleading as a form of political protest. These "radical" cheerleaders combined elements of cheerleading, protest culture, and street theater to queer the macho, male-dominated spaces of social movement activism and create communities of young feminists invested in multi-issue politics. The website Radical Cheerleaders characterizes radical cheerleading as "activism with pom poms and middle fingers extended. It's screaming FUCK CAPITALISM while doing a split."[1]

Radical cheerleaders continue a long feminist tradition. From suffragist newspapers to the feminist blogosphere, from street protests to poetry circles, participants across the various movements and waves of feminist activism have relied on expressive, performative practices to articulate grievances and press for change. Social movement theory, however, has tended to relegate such practices to the cultural rather than the political arena—as if the two can be wholly separated.[2] The reification of the political/cultural binary is problematic for feminist activists who take seriously the dictum that the personal is political. And nothing could be more personal than the body. For the young people involved in radical cheerleading who are protesting the myriad forms of inequality that persist in the everyday world, including the male-dominated spaces of social movement activism itself, the main vehicle of their critique is embodied performativity—their own bodies, in motion, cheering.

My research on radical cheerleaders is one part of a larger ethnographic study of cheerleading in the United States and Canada involving more than a decade of fieldwork in the 2000s and roughly 150 in-depth interviews, much of it conducted with my friend and colleague Emily West (see chapter 4). The work focused on radical cheerleading includes interviews with thirty radical cheerleaders, observation of select performances at street protests and Pride events, and various online sources of information both by and about radical cheerleaders. This chapter explores who radical cheerleaders are and what they hoped to accomplish through their activism. I highlight the challenges for a feminist politics of appropriating the iconography of cheerleading, the affordances (and limitations) of embodied performativity as a communicative tool, and the relatively short-lived nature of the phenomenon, in contrast to conventional cheerleading. Although remnants of radical cheerleading remain (primarily in performance art spaces), it is not currently a collective force in protest politics.[3]

## What Is Radical Cheerleading? Who Are Radical Cheerleaders?

Radical cheerleading was the brainchild of two sisters in Florida, Cara and Aimee Jennings, who grew tired of activist spaces in which it was always the boys who got the bullhorn. They sought to infuse boring, male-centric demonstrations with feminist energy by combining their junior high cheerleading skills with a riot grrrl sensibility.[4] Emerging from the US Pacific Northwest in the early 1990s, the riot grrrl movement challenged the sexism and misogyny of the male-dominated punk scene of the 1980s by creating its own music, zines, and art combining feminist politics with punk music.[5] According to my interviewees, the inspiration for the aesthetics of radical cheerleading was the music video for Nirvana's "Smells Like Teen Spirit," which features a punked-out cheerleader wearing a black shirt with a red anarchy symbol splashed on the front. The Jennings sisters began performing publicly and published the first *Radical Cheerbook* as an independent zine in 1997. They also staged workshops about radical cheerleading at key feminist gatherings, such as the Southern Girls Convention, held annually in different cities throughout the South. Very quickly, new squads cropped up, spreading from the South to New York City and eventually across the United States, as well as internationally. In addition to the

FIGURE 8.1. *Resistin' Radicatz squad, Washington, DC, October 17, 2004. Photo by Ben Schumin, CC BY-SA 2.5, https://www.flickr.com/photos/schuminweb/50076103397.*

United States, the countries named by my interviewees include Canada, the United Kingdom, Ireland, Sweden, Poland, and the Czech Republic.

Radical cheerleaders retain many of the trappings and techniques of conventional cheerleading but at the same time subvert them: poms made of plastic garbage bags or red caution tape, hair spiked or dyed, short skirts combined with combat boots, and lingerie worn on the outside rather than the inside. Red and black and pink and black are common color combinations. Piercings and tattoos—forbidden for conventional cheerleaders—are on full display. One interviewee described radical cheerleaders as "Pippi Longstocking meets Catholic-school-girl pirate." Routines are typically loosely choreographed, with simple dance moves and arm motions, along with the occasional pyramid, although the skill level of squads varies, with some—especially the original squads forming in the South—aiming for a more put-together look. At protests, one participant usually has a megaphone or bullhorn to lead cheers, but instead of cheering to solicit school spirit, they cheer to end social injustice (fig. 8.1).

The cheers themselves are DIY, tailored to specific issues, and shared online as well as through word of mouth. Most often they are rhyming chants ("Butch, femme, fag, dyke, be who you are, dress how you like!"), but occasionally they adopt a more narrative, storytelling style or replace the words of a familiar cheer, chant, or song (including the US national anthem) with an anarchist message (figs. 8.2 and 8.3). The now-archived website created by Tricky[6]—a close friend of the Jennings sisters, a founding member of the Memphis Dirty Southern Belles, and one of my interviewees—documents hundreds of cheers, organized under four main categories: girl positive, queer/sex positive, environmental, and anti-authority.[7] The website of the radical cheerleaders formerly active in Victoria, British Columbia, also archives cheers, in this case using eighteen different categories.[8]

Although the names of most squads are place based—for example, the NYC Radical Cheerleaders, the Chicago Radical Cheerleaders, the Winnipeg Radical Cheerleaders, the Memphis Dirty Southern Belles, and the Rocky Mountain Rebels—some are not, such as the Rowdy Racoons (Indiana) and the Lickety Splits (Chicago). Interviewees consistently named the feminist punk subculture inspired by the riot grrrls (prior to its co-optation by mainstream media) as an important cultural touchstone. The feminist label is actively embraced, although radical cheerleaders are not united by a single issue, nor under the broader umbrella of women's rights; rather, informed by a more intersectional politics, they use cheerleading in the service of protesting a wide variety of issues. These include workers' wage struggles, immigrants' rights, animal rights, global warming, police brutality, media consolidation, and rising income inequality. Radical cheerleaders perform at pro-choice and take-back-the-night rallies, Pride parades, college teach-ins, antiwar protests, and a host of anti-globalization mobilizations. They show up at the local mall on Buy Nothing Day (aka Black Friday) to protest consumerism and at fast-food restaurants to demand better working conditions. They bring their energy to more celebratory occasions too, such as feminist art shows, feminist film and music festivals, and performances of *The Vagina Monologues*. Different groups of cheerleaders, and individuals within groups, are drawn to some issues more than others. What unites them is the vehicle of expression. Said a participant from Oakland, California, "Radical cheerleading is the most joyful expression of my rage that I've found."

Most of my interviewees formed squads on their college campuses with like-minded student peers, which helps explain the young and primarily white, middle-class demographics of radical cheerleaders more generally,

FIGURE 8.2. *Cover of* Radical Cheerbook, *published by the Sprout Anarchist Collective, circa 2000. The fourteen-page cheerbook was uploaded to the Internet Archive in 2014 after being "rescued from a dusty filing cabinet in 2012." Archived online at https://archive.org/details/RadicalCheerbook.*

FIGURE 8.3. *Sample page from* Radical Cheerbook, *circa 2000.*

in combination with the overall white profile of American social movement activists who espouse anarchist politics. Both my sample and the estimates given by interviewees about their own squads suggest that the ratio is about 80 percent white, 20 percent people of color. Almost everyone in my sample identified as lesbian, queer, bisexual, pansexual, and/or gender nonconforming. One of my interviewees joked that the greatest need for diversity was getting straight girls to join. Men are involved in small numbers, and a few of my interviewees were somewhat older women in their late twenties and early thirties who found radical cheerleading through marches and other protest activities outside of college. Roughly 20 percent came from poor or working-class backgrounds. A handful were currently engaged in sex work. At least half reported feeling marginal or on the fringes in high school, part of the punk or alternative music scene. In the words of one radical cheerleader from Chicago, "I spent most of my high school time in the projects taking acid and other drugs, dodging creepy guys who were known to sexually assault girls right on school grounds, and shaving my hair into different colored Mohawks."

At the same time, an almost equal number had more positive experiences of high school, and a handful were even former cheerleaders. Most reported coming from feminist households, or from families that were otherwise politically progressive. One interviewee spoke of accompanying her mother to Planned Parenthood clinics for defense actions in the face of the antiabortion group Operation Rescue, the mother wearing a bulletproof vest. Often, individuals belonged to a broader network of student or community activism, such that radical cheerleading was one rather than the only mode for expressing their political views, and in this sense, participation was, as one interviewee put it, "a process and not an endgame."

## Radical Cheerleaders in Action

I first saw radical cheerleaders for myself (outside of an interview setting) during a Pride event in San Francisco in June 2003, where I was performing as a member of Cheer Sacramento, a queer-allied adult performance team (see chapter 7). The cheerleaders were taking part in the parade, and I caught sight of them afterward among the crowd. Some months later I got to meet some of them at an antiwar protest in the city, alerted to the event by a graduate student in my own department, Maggie, who moved in the same activist circles. There were six or seven cheerleaders at the protest, from two different squads in the San Francisco Bay Area. The decision to show up had been spontaneous, and they were unapologetically disorganized, with no attempt to coordinate outfits in advance or to synchronize movements during the march. The cheer I recall hearing most was "Resist"—"Resist, resist, raise up your fist! Resist, resist, show 'em that you're pissed!"—and there were others mocking then-President Bush, condemning sweatshops, and praising masturbation. When belting out a spoof of the national anthem, they couldn't stay in tune and surrounding marchers were cracking up. It struck me that learning all the words to enough cheers to last an entire protest event was no small feat.

Not long afterward, I witnessed a more polished performance at the semiannual FemSex Extravaganza at the University of California, Berkeley, an end-of-semester event organized by graduating gender studies majors. I will describe it in some detail to provide a sense of the cultural scene in which radical cheerleaders were operating in the early 2000s.

Maggie and I attended the FemSex event together. A young, very pierced woman in dominatrix-style black leather was at the cash register just inside the doors, and the spacious lobby was lined with a dozen tables laden with merchandise—baked goods, CDs, posters, T-shirts—along with informational brochures and pamphlets from local feminist organizations. The table nearest the door was stocked with dildos and sex toys; the baked goods all resembled female body parts. The entire back of the lobby was devoted to the radical cheerleaders. On their table were scrapbooks with photos and press clippings of radical cheerleading groups at various actions, cheerbooks and feminist zines, and T-shirts and tank tops bearing feminist slogans: "Boys can wear skirts too"; "Capitalism is the devil's wet dream"; "God is not welcome in my pants and neither, sir, are you." I recall hearing the radical cheerleaders practicing in an adjacent hallway ("T&A, all the way, occupation not okay! No border, no states, we just wanna masturbate!").

Inside the large auditorium, organizers were testing sound equipment and putting up homemade sex-positive posters as spectators filed in. The crowd was young, primarily female, and racially diverse. The typical uniform consisted of low-slung jeans, big belt, muscle shirt, lots of tattoos and piercings, and close-cropped hair or matted dreads. Some attendees, however, had a more femme, hippy style, while others were scantily dressed in leather and spike heels. It was a far cry from the women in the audience of a mainstream cheerleading competition. By the time the program started, the theater was packed and the audience ready for fun. The program delivered. There were two mistresses of ceremonies and thirteen acts—showcasing belly dancing, breakdancing, comedy, slam poetry, drag king performance, musical numbers, and of course radical cheerleading. The cheerleaders were the final act. The emcee introduced them as "badass activists with pom-poms and middle fingers extended" and enjoined the audience, "If you like what you see, join the squad or start your own—get mad and get loud!" There were seven participants (five white women, two women of color) in black or pink skirts, black camisoles exposing a lot of skin, leggings, and combat boots. Some had pink in their hair, just long enough for pigtails. Poms were made of cloth strips. Body types varied from tall to short and skinny to fat. The radical cheerleaders did a short, rousing cheer and then one of them, Sam, delivered a brief speech:

> We're cheerleaders, right? I mean, the short skirt, the pom-poms, the pigtails. But we're not your average cheerleaders, we're not on the sidelines cheering for some crazy aggro sport. No, we're out here voicing our opinions and talking about our politics. We're using our sexuality so that you'll pay attention to us, okay? Look, in high school a lot of cheerleading was fucked up, it was about anorexia and image. We're not about that. We're about loving ourselves, being loud, being proud, being sexy, and being out there.

The group performed a dozen or so additional cheers, lasting about twenty minutes. They were exuberant, playful, and lewd. They ended by spoofing the children's game ring-around-the-rosy: Yelling "We're here, we're queer, we're fabulous, don't fuck with us," they kissed each other and collapsed into a pile of sweaty, writhing bodies.

## Not Your Average Cheerleader, But . . .

Radical cheerleaders are drawn to political activism for various reasons, but the main rationale for choosing the cheerleader icon as a vehicle for this activism has to do with the complex nature of the icon itself. Simultaneously in the spotlight and relegated to the sidelines, revered and vilified, all-American sweetheart and oversexed bimbo, the cheerleader is a prime target for both appropriation and critique.

Given this, it's not surprising that radical cheerleaders themselves differ in attitude toward traditional cheerleading. Most would agree with Sam that they are not your average cheerleaders "on the sidelines cheering for some crazy aggro sport." Most would also agree with Sam's squad mate, who characterized the difference between radical cheerleading and conventional cheerleading this way: "Regular cheerleaders have to be happy and superanimated. Enthusiastic. Smiling. Appeasing. Made-up, with their hair all done. Uniformity. Conformity. Heterosexuality." Radical cheerleaders not only see conventional cheerleading as a popularity contest they would never want to win but also reject the beauty standards associated with it; some also find it outright laughable. When asked what she thought of the cheerleaders at her high school, one interviewee said, "I judged them, and I thought they were ridiculous." Interestingly, the key components of mainstream cheerleading that radical cheerleaders distance themselves from are the same components many straight male college cheerleaders reject in debates over whether the activity qualifies as a "real" sport: the historic sideline function of cheerleading, along with its continued feminine appearance and performance demands, which preclude its classification as a sport (see chapters 3 and 4)—the rise of competitive cheer notwithstanding.

At the same time, radical cheerleaders are not uniformly dismissive of mainstream cheer. After all, radical cheerleading was invented by former secondary school cheerleaders, and former cheerleaders reportedly participate on many radical cheerleading squads (as did three of my interviewees). My interviewees noted with approval that regular cheerleaders, especially sideline cheerleaders, must be assertive, bold, and confident and that mainstream squads bring girls and young women together in cooperation. Radical cheerleaders appreciate the athleticism of contemporary cheer, especially competitive cheer, even while acknowledging that it is a socially safe (i.e., girly and heterosexual-presenting) brand of athleticism. Virtually everyone I interviewed spoke fondly of *Bring It On*, released in 2000, some even naming it as their favorite film. As Tricky told me, "I've never known an instance of a radical cheerleading squad protesting actual cheerleaders."

Most important, interviewees recognized that cheerleading is ripe for appropriation precisely because of its juxtaposition of girly-girl sexiness (which they attempt to subvert) and brash, in-your-face assertiveness (which they attempt to reclaim). Ironically, while the former can prompt unwarranted harassment, the latter may serve as an antidote. Xena, a radical cheerleader from New York City, spoke of getting harassed by men on the street while walking home from protest events with her radical cheerleading squad and, in response, "busting out with anti-harassment cheers."

She added, "I found it useful in surprising contexts. When you're just on the subway and some sleazy dude is fucking with you, you can use cheerleading to scream at the top of your lungs at him." Xena also expressed gratitude that radical cheerleading's subversion of girly-girl sexiness didn't entail a rejection of femininity as she understood it. She explained her own participation this way:

> One major appeal [of radical cheerleading] is the femme nature of it . . . as a former fashion model, sex worker, and a radical feminist, I hadn't found a solid way of linking my experiences together. It was either one extreme or the other, but I had not heard of a way to be glamourous and ridiculously feminine without compromising my need to express feminism and anger. Radical cheerleading brings it all together in one pissed-off package!

If you substitute "athleticism" for "assertiveness," a similar juxtaposition draws young women to mainstream competitive cheerleading. Sexy attractiveness and athleticism conjoined enables women to claim the status of athlete without anyone questioning their "proper" feminine credentials.[9] But radical cheerleaders have a far more expansive view of what counts as sexy or attractive. They are not seeking approval from a dominant male gaze.[10] As Xena put it, "There's little room [in the mainstream] for larger bodies or for bodies that don't 'make sense.' But in radical cheerleading there is space to talk about bodies, to feel hot and complete, to be proud of what/whoever you are. So we have a lot of fat cheerleaders, a lot of gender-fuckers, a whole lotta body hair goin' on." Unsurprisingly, many radical cheers reference the emerging body-positivity movement: "I take up space and love my size, 'cause fat and fab are on the rise!"; "Raise those arms up in the air, let me see that armpit hair!"

And yet even radical cheerleaders, with their expansive view of sexual attractiveness, are subject to unwanted male attention—not only on the streets but also within activist spaces—because cheerleading is the medium of the message. My interviewees were well aware that the very act of cheerleading carried gendered connotations that were difficult to fully escape. To quote Rabbit, a participant from North Carolina, "Some men, like, who were even organizing the march, were being kinda creepy, in that, they were, like, 'Oooh, we definitely want you to come back next year.'" Rabbit noted that radical cheerleaders risk being trivialized as well as sexualized: "Some people will see it primarily as entertainment, like, 'Oh, isn't that cute, girls that are doing coordinated moves and have cute little outfits on.'" On occasion, when the radical cheerleaders had not been cleared to participate in a demonstration in advance, they would literally be cheering from the sidelines, amplifying their similarity to mainstream cheerleaders in the eyes of spectators.

## Performative Protest: A Double-Edged Sword

Radical cheerleading emphasizes the performative dynamics of social movement activism. In invoking comparison, contrast, and humor, the cheerleaders are playing off and against an old boys' network of "serious," "militant" activism.[11] Radical cheerleaders want to communicate via performance their opposition to various social injustices while also expressing dissatisfaction with the white, male-centric politics of the protest environment itself. But performance carries risks. In the case of radical cheerleading, participants walk a line between scriptedness and spontaneity, seeking to allow improvised, free-form expression within a loosely structured framework. One pitfall, oft repeated, is that such performances can become routine and predictable, thus reproducing the very, boring dynamic they set out to challenge. Another pitfall is that fun and energizing performances may seem ill-suited and even inappropriate to the gravity of the problems being protested. Social movement scholars have documented that while performative spectacular actions might be emotionally satisfying for participants and do important collective identity work, they can undermine the credibility of the activists involved and attract media attention over which they have little control.[12] Both the issue of the appropriateness of radical cheerleading in addressing certain injustices and the issue of media representation surfaced repeatedly in my interviews.

Regarding the challenge of using playful means to deliver a serious message, a Bay Area radical cheerleader said,

> I think [radical cheerleading] is cool and fun and important at protests because it lightens people's spirits when things are tense. But I also think that . . . by performing, putting things out there that are really important ideas and doing it in a sort of lighthearted way, at times it could be interpreted as not taking issues as seriously as they should be taken.

Xena, too, noticed that the main effect of radical cheerleaders on others in a protest context was levity and laugher. For her this was positive, even when the topic was depressing and sad. Yet not everyone agreed. The tension between medium and message became particularly acute in the wake of the September 11, 2001, terrorist attacks, as Americans grieved the loss of civilian life and anti-Muslim sentiment exploded. Dan, one of the few male radical cheerleading participants I interviewed, offered this: "There were vigils, peace marches, and that sort of thing, in which we just didn't really feel cheering was appropriate. Instead, we did things like presentations about the internment camps [of Japanese Americans during World War II], and about the profiling of Arab Americans."

Navigating media representation was equally challenging and, ironically, another issue that connects radical cheerleaders to traditional cheerleaders. Both groups feel misrepresented and misunderstood by mainstream media, and for similar reasons. The radical cheerleaders I interviewed were quick to notice that when they got mainstream media coverage, it focused on what they wore and how they looked as opposed to what they stood for; this coverage also sought the most conventionally attractive participants to represent the group, Xena included. Xena characterized the media representation of radical cheerleading as a "false archive"—a recorded history that's accessible to the public but doesn't represent its subject. Trixie, who is a Cuban American from Miami, could not have agreed more. Her tone incredulous, she told me that *The New York Times* ran a story ostensibly covering radical cheerleading activity at the Southern Girls Convention in Georgia, which she helped organize, and the one photo used by the newspaper showed a group of radical cheerleaders from the North, knitting: "Long hair, perfect girls, knitting, just knitting, and they weren't even Southern!" The British version of *Glamour* magazine reportedly ran a story whose photos airbrushed out the girls' armpit hair.[13] In the heyday of radical cheerleading activity, media outlets writing about the phenomenon also included *Bust*, *Spin*, and *Ms.* magazine, along with local news organizations.

Radical cheerleaders were consequently ambivalent about media coverage: They realized that mainstream media outlets are attracted to them for their subversion of cheerleading, yet at the same time, their status as cheerleaders becomes the ground on which to dismiss their seriousness and significance. Conventional cheerleading faces much the same dilemma; in its bid for legitimacy and respect, it has tended to foreground its competitive, sport-like "masculine" dimensions, and to downplay its aesthetic and performative "feminine" dimensions. Yet jettisoning the performative, feminine part of cheerleading, whether conventional or radical, is, arguably, to reproduce the stigma of femininity that has contributed to the historic marginalization of women (and other feminine-identified individuals) in the first place. This speaks to a broader tension in the radical cheerleading movement between using a culturally familiar form to reach broad audiences and maintaining radical political content. There is the additional challenge of using performance effectively without having it overshadow or trivialize the underlying message, a challenge amplified for feminist participants who use their bodies or sexuality as a core performative element.

## Movement Decline

Radical cheerleading has not completely disappeared, but contemporary manifestations appear confined to performance art spaces seeking to document its historic influence.[14] I can only speculate on the reasons for the movement's decline, but even in the early 2000s, interviewees grappled with questions about sustainability. In addition to the challenge of using humor and parody to deliver serious messages, radical cheerleaders spoke of organizational challenges, burnout, mainstream co-optation, lack of racial and class diversity, and a widening gulf between activists who use radical cheerleading as one arm of their wide span of activism, and those for whom radical cheerleading is the totality of their political involvement.[15]

Activist groups aiming for a nonhierarchical organizational structure with no clear leadership or decision-making body, like radical cheerleaders, often struggle to balance their commitment to cooperative governance with efficiency and efficacy.[16] Interviewees noted that collective decision-making can be as exhausting as cheering itself, raising questions about who gets to speak for the group, who controls its direction, and which causes are prioritized. The Bay Area radical cheerleaders had an opt-out clause, where cheerleaders could opt out of certain cheers during an event if they disagreed with the politics being promoted, but as one of the members said, "sometimes differences couldn't be dealt with so easily." Which events warranted their attention and energy in the first place was a thornier issue. The biggest controversy at the time of my interviews was whether to cheer at the Michigan Womyn's Music Festival (Michfest), which had recently adopted a trans-exclusion policy. On the one hand, the festival was an important cultural touchstone and had served as a radical voice against lesbian oppression since the mid-1970s. On the other hand, excluding trans women from the category of women was not cool. According to Tricky, it got to the point where one radical cheerleading squad was protesting outside the festival at the same time that another squad was inside performing. She told me that squads broke up over the decision of whether to boycott the festival or to overlook the policy.

The issues of co-optation, lack of race and class diversity, and increasing numbers of participants for whom radical cheerleading was divorced from a broader repertoire of political action were all interrelated. The relative whiteness and class privilege of radical cheerleading, combined with its sexy, badass sensibility, helped garner media attention, and media attention led to accusations of selling out, while also attracting new members uninterested in activism beyond radical cheerleading—unlike the original founders of the movement, who sought to bring the tools and trappings of cheerleading into preexisting political and wide-ranging commitments. As Tricky, Rabbit, and others told me, radical cheerleading was becoming the message rather than a vehicle for communicating radical politics, and this was another aspect of its co-optation. Rabbit saw co-optation as pretty much inevitable: "Subcultures always get co-opted. You know, Madonna on her last tour did like a WTO-fashion-esque thing, where she had, like, gas masks and baggy pants on. It always happens. Riot grrrl got co-opted, punk rock did, everything does, so . . . it had to happen [to radical cheerleading]."

Tricky, the only woman of color on her squad, also felt that the whiteness of the activity, along with that of the broader feminist punk scene, made radical cheerleading difficult to sustain:

> It's not intentional, but it's—they always asked the dumb question, "Why don't we have any ethnic people here?" And I'm sitting there and I'm just like, "Well, maybe if you didn't put up flyers in your COLLEGE DORM." They are not reaching out to the right communities. They are not reaching out to every community, they just reach out to pretty much, like, their own four walls. . . . Same thing with riot grrrl, it was extremely white, and a lot of people felt left out and marginalized by that.

Rabbit had an equally trenchant critique of the racial politics she witnessed:

> I think that when you are white, you totally have the privilege to be able to run around and scream and raise pom-poms, especially in the South, because if you're Black and do that, somebody is gonna assume you'll shoot them up or rob them or whatever, you know—it's a total white privilege to be able to be a [radical cheerleader] at all. I don't think people acknowledge that.

Rabbit, herself from the white working class, further objected to the tendency of radical cheerleaders and other (white) anarchist activists to, as she put it, "slum it":

> As a person who grew up working class, it kind of bugs me how people, like, slum—do you know what I mean? Like dreadlocks, living in houses full of dirty dishes, never taking a shower. . . . I know that makes me sound classist, but I am coming from a totally different background than they are. They grew up either rich or upper middle class, so I don't think they understand what it's like. Like, today I saw a sticker that said, "Being poor is an artform." I was like, no. Being poor sucks. It was just awful.

## Give Me an *F* (for Finale)

Although cheerleading itself appears to be a relatively stable fixture in the fabric of American culture, not so with radical cheerleading. And it has not been resurrected to any significant degree, perhaps partly because so much social movement activity is now happening online. As a campy, theatrical, sexy, punk-inspired mode of in-your-face performativity, radical cheerleading thrust a certain brand of feminist activism into the public sphere and onto a public stage—for a time. Its energy, physicality, and irreverence staged a DIY critique of both conventional social movement activity and conventional (mainstream) cheerleading—a critique shaped by irresolvable tensions between media representation and self-representation, the (performative) medium and the (political) message, and the retooled versus reinforced gender norms of cheerleading.

Radical cheerleading not only made people laugh and think about intersectional feminist issues but also revealed the tensions faced by feminist movements that use theatrical performances of familiar cultural icons to demand political change. Radical cheerleading further reveals the challenges faced by feminist movements that fail to draw participants from the diversity of communities they seek to support. All performance, political or otherwise, is a translation and distillation of processes unfolding elsewhere, even as it is also an event unto itself. Performance calls attention to, and complements, but cannot not replace, the everyday and often unspectacular, unglamorous efforts of those working to realize a more just society in less public, less visible spaces.

## Notes

1. Home page, Radical Cheerleaders, accessed November 1, 2025, https://radcheers.tripod.com.

2. Even in the literature on "new" social movements, in which scholars emphasize the role of emotion (James M. Jasper), community and identity formation (Alberto Melucci), and storytelling or narrative (Francesca Polletta) as crucial to movement success, such processes are still typically understood as cultural resources to be mobilized for "real" political action occurring elsewhere.

3. Christine Ro, "Hey Hey! Ho Ho! Where Did Radical Cheerleaders Go?," *Bitch Media*, August 10, 2016, https://www.bitchmedia.org/article/hey-hey-ho-ho-where-did-radical-cheerleaders-go.

4. Margaret Farrar and Jaime Warner, "Rah-Rah-Radical: The Radical Cheerleaders' Challenge to the Public Sphere," *Politics and Gender* 2, no. 3 (2006): 281–302; Abbie Jarman, "The Jennings Sisters: Aimee, 28, Cara, 25, and Coleen, 23," *Utne Reader*, September–October 2002, 55.

5. See Jessica Rosenberg and Gitano Garofalo, "Riot Grrrl: Revolutions from Within," *Signs* 23, no. 3 (1998): 809–841.

6. The names of all interviewees are pseudonyms, as is the name of my graduate student, "Maggie."

7. Home page, Radical Cheerleaders.

8. See Radical Cheerleading Archives, last updated 2002, https://doremifaso.ca/archives/radicalcheers/start.html.

9. For elaboration on this point, see Laura Grindstaff and Emily West, "Cheerleading and the Gendered Politics of Sport," *Social Problems* 45, no. 4 (2006): 500–518.

10. The male gaze is a scholarly concept emerging in the 1970s that theorized the gendered relation between image and spectator in Western media. In his classic monograph *Ways of Seeing* (1972), for example, John Berger argues that because a woman's worth in Western society is so heavily dependent on how she appears to others, especially how she appears to men, she is continually accompanied by

her own image of herself. Her very identity is split between surveyor and surveyed. Laura Mulvey's 1975 essay "Visual Pleasure and Narrative Cinema" was equally influential. Drawing upon psychoanalysis, Mulvey argued that female representation in mainstream cinema was ultimately little more than a projection of male sexual desire. The cinematic apparatus produced a male gaze—comprised of the gaze of male characters within the film, the gaze of the camera, and the gaze of the privileged male spectator—that fetishized women as objects and denied women a voice of their own outside of a discourse of male desire. See John Berger, *Ways of Seeing* (British Broadcasting Corporation, 1977); Laura Mulvey, "Visual Pleasure and Narrative Cinema," *Screen* 16, no. 3 (1975): 6–18.

11. Farrar and Warner, "Rah-Rah-Radical."

12. See Todd Gitlin, *The Whole World Is Watching: Mass Media in the Making and Unmaking of the New Left* (University of California Press, 1980).

13. Jeanne Vaccaro, "Give Me an F: Radical Cheerleading and Feminist Performance," *Women and Performance* 14, no. 2 (2005): 43–50.

14. One such event was hosted by the Antistatic International Festival for Contemporary Dance and Performance in Germany in 2024; see "Radical Cheerleading," Antistatic, performed May 14, 2024, https://antistaticfestival.org/en/project/radical-cheerleading/.

15. Ro, "Hey Hey! Ho Ho!"

16. Francesca Polletta, "Participatory Democracy in Social Movements," in *The Wiley-Blackwell Encyclopedia of Social and Political Movements*, ed. David A. Snow, Donatella della Porta, Bert Klandermans, and Douglas McAdam (Wiley-Blackwell, 2013).

PART III

# Not Just Any Girl

## MEDIATED REPRESENTATIONS OF CHEERLEADERS

CHAPTER 9

# Queering the All-American Girl

## CHEERLEADING, SAME-SEX DESIRE, AND THE (NOT SO) GOOD GIRL

*Barbara J. Brickman*

MEGAN: Cheers are supposed to be simple, make people feel good.
GRAHAM: Cheers make girls do stupid cartwheels. Orgasms make people feel good.

*But I'm a Cheerleader*

Described by its costar and cowriter Rachel Sennott as a movie about "two girls in a classic American football town who start a fight club under the guise of female empowerment, but it's actually so they can have sex with cheerleaders," the recent film festival darling *Bottoms* (Emma Seligman, 2023) irreverently—even violently—upends the classic teen sex comedy in which loss of virginity has always been not just a male prerogative but inexorably heterosexual.[1] As a result, we, an almost shell-shocked audience, are disarmed by the film's genre-bending, unashamed humor, as its two self-identified "ugly, untalented gays" (Rachel Sennott and Ayo Edebiri) resort to lies, amoral manipulation, bodily harm, and half-hearted gestures toward feminism just to get the girl(s), while the cherished all-American football team takes the brunt of the film's wicked, satirical ire. Not unlike one of its foremost influences, Michael Lehmann's dark teen classic *Heathers* (1989), *Bottoms* skewers the normative forces that seem to make life hell for misfit queer adolescents in the generic American high school—at the center of which is, of course, not just the adored football kings but also their sexy trophy queens: the apex cheerleaders.[2] Loser lesbian protagonists PJ and Josie do not create a fight club to get just any "coochie" in the school; they set their sights, predictably, on the dazzling head cheerleaders, Isabel and Brittany. Highlighted in the trailer with a clip of that generic staple, the seductive cheerleading routine, this iconic figure of American girlhood is queerly transformed by the film not just through the protagonists' desires but as a keystone of its bawdy, unrepentant, and ferocious derangement more generally, with Isabel even leading the pack of fight club members who line up to go "fuck up some football players" in the narrative's denouement. Blood dripping down their chins and romanced by lesbian bottoms, these cheerleaders clearly signal a new era.

For much of the twentieth century, as scholars and historians of cheerleading contend, the female cheerleader, particularly in the United States, has served as a nexus for two central conflicting and coconstitutive ideas of so-called womanhood or girlhood: that she is both the performing object of male sexual desire and simultaneously a paragon of ideal, wholesome femininity—a Madonna/whore with pom-poms, if you will. Needless to say, both mythic constructs codefine the cheerleader as compulsorily heterosexual. In other words, as the revisionary filmmakers of *Bottoms* well know, the (hetero) sexy cheerleader has become "a mainstay of American male fantasy," both in media and beyond, but this fantasy figure always remains in unique tension with her mirror image of "idealized heterosexualized femininity," in Pamela Bettis and Natalie Adams's terms, which circumscribes normative girlhood as necessarily chaste, moral, other-directed, and of course white.[3] She stands, at one and the same time, then, as both the gyrating prize of hetero-male aspiration in her short skirt, cropped top, and heavily styled appearance and the supportive, smiling, and pure all-American girl. What cultural historians and sociologists of sport have established quite clearly, therefore, is that she can never be queer and is very rarely figured as an agentic, self-possessed "athlete." Yet as *Bottoms* and its forerunners like the Fox television series *Glee* (2009–2015) and the indie film cult classic *But I'm a Cheerleader* (Jamie Babbit, 1999) demonstrate, popular media has been signaling a revision of this iconic cheerleader for over two decades. Through a close reading of these two earlier media texts—most centrally, Babbit's film—this chapter will interrogate how queer sexual desire and identity formation can trouble and redefine the supposed hetero-wholesome, anti-feminist, and sexually trivialized cheerleader in mainstream American culture.

Scholars of gender and sexuality in sport have established, since the 1980s, two axiomatic attributes of the female cheerleader that have been increasingly challenged by popular media texts: her inherent and unquestionable heterosexuality and her categorical exclusion from the classification of "athlete." In *Cheerleader! An American Icon*, Natalie Adams and Pamela Bettis recognize the commonplace belief that "female cheerleaders' sexual orientation is simply assumed to be heterosexual"; by contrast, other women and girls who participate in sports are censured for their apparent gender nonconformity (i.e., for being too "masculine") and questioned about their sexuality, since team sports have long been considered a lesbian "haven."[4] Often viewed as support and as mere spectators of the "true" athletes on the field, cheerleaders, then—presumed to be straight—symbolize one of the "last bastions of traditional femininity," even as Adams and Bettis document their increasing investment, since the turn of the new millennium, in establishing themselves as serious and tough competitive athletes.[5]

Indeed, the growing body of research on lesbians in sport overwhelmingly reinforces this dichotomy between ("masculine") lesbian athletes on the one hand and ("feminine") straight cheerleaders on the other. Beginning with one of the foundational works on sexuality in sport, *Out of Bounds: Women, Sport and Sexuality*, Helen Lenskyj initiates her consideration of sex and sport through this defining opposition, between women and girls who want to participate in sport and the sidelines they are so often relegated to as "spectators and cheerleaders," there to validate the (male) "display of masculinity and machismo on the playing field." Indeed, Lenskyj even repeats the conjecture that the "alleged 'high incidence' of lesbianism in sport" is due to the "tendency for many young heterosexual women to see themselves as cheerleaders, not participants."[6] Subsequent work in the field, including Lenskyj's own more recent work, has gone on to reinforce this principal divide, where studies examining queer women in sport seem to categorically disregard cheerleading.[7]

It is not the case, however, that studies of cheerleading fail to recognize nonnormative sexualities; they have just focused predominantly on queer men. Most notably, Eric Anderson's work establishing the homophobia, enforced heteromasculinity, and what he terms "homohysteria" surrounding male-identified athletes has explored the experiences of gay male cheerleaders particularly.[8] Nevertheless, even as Anderson and fellow researchers have more recently found that homophobia and homohysteria have been "dramatically" decreasing in men's sport (including in cheerleading), the same cannot be said of women's sport, where homohysteria "remains rife" yet has been underexamined.[9] One might even argue that a kind of "lesbohysteria" has plagued all female athletes until very recently, as the specter of what Pat Griffin calls the "image of the sick, masculine lesbian sexual predator"—lurking on sports teams, in locker rooms, and even in coach's offices—has exerted enormous influence on women's sport and its athletes.[10] Numerous studies have found that in response to being stigmatized for nonnormative gender expression (e.g., "masculine" strength, aggression, toughness) and to having their heterosexuality called into question, heterosexual athletes in women's competitive sports often react with homophobia and emphasized femininity or hyperfemininity that they use as a tool or an "apology" to distance themselves from deviance—but none of this work considers the inverse: How do queer female athletes respond to the experience of participating in an athletic world marked not by stigma but by "idealized heterosexual femininity," as Bettis and Adams characterize cheerleading?[11] In other words, what happens to our understanding of the cheerleader and the typical female athlete when the lesbian cheerleader enters into these debates? While sociologists and historians have yet to really address these questions, popular culture has become increasingly interested in them, exploring and even elevating female same-sex desire on the cheer squad.[12]

In the late 1990s and early 2000s—perhaps not coincidentally around the same time that competitive cheering started to expand rapidly in the United States—queer female cheerleaders began appearing in mainstream media texts.[13] Although lacking direct representation, Joss Whedon's influential, groundbreaking WB series *Buffy the Vampire Slayer* (1997–2003) might be proposed as an origin point, with its early episode "Witch" (season 1, episode 3) queering the villainous cheerleader through her use of dark magic and her clash with the young witch Willow—who will, of course, become one of the show's trailblazing lesbian characters.[14] Then, Jamie Babbit's 1999 independent film *But I'm a Cheerleader* marked a significant turning point, so that by the end of the first decade of the new millennium, queering the female cheerleader could become mainstream fare. For example, Karyn Kusama's campy horror film *Jennifer's Body* (2009) homoeroticizes its possessed succubus cheerleader (Megan Fox) through a climactic bedroom kiss with her "best friend" Needy (Amanda Seyfried), whose suspiciously close relationship to the head cheerleader and devourer of men has already been characterized as "totally lesbigay" by a fellow spectator at a pep rally. Then, perhaps more notably, the Fox hit *Glee*, which began in 2009, centralized the emotional journey of caustic Cheerio cocaptain and Glee Club stalwart Santana Lopez (Naya Rivera) as she struggled to come to terms with her sexuality, as well as her relationship with fellow cheerleader Brittany (Heather Morris), particularly after being outed as a lesbian in season 3. To be sure, the influence of Santana and Brittany's representation of queer female adolescence—and of cheerleaders—should not be underestimated, as its cherished precedent has clearly paved the way for another power lesbian couple, in the CW's popular, salacious update of the *Archie* comics. In *Riverdale* (2017–2023), the dramatic (and sexy) romance between self-designated "HBIC" and River Vixen cheerleader Cheryl Blossom (Madelaine Petsch) and one-time Southside Serpent Toni Topaz (Vanessa Morgan) has essentially stolen the show, and the ardor of the fan base.[15]

Indeed, one could argue that *Glee*'s Santana Lopez has made the greatest strides in queering the heteronormative cheerleader in American popular culture to date, but her image as a tough and sarcastic but ultimately eroticized cheer squad cocaptain does conform in some ways with the iconic fantasy figure of the "sexy" cheerleader presumably posed for a heterosexual male gaze. While the show does not exactly "demonize or trivialize" this particular mainstream media cheerleader, especially after its close focus on her identity struggles in seasons 2 and 3, it does capitalize on and emphasize her conventionally attractive, feminine sexual allure as its quintessential "bad girl."[16] Beginning with the "Duets" episode in 2010 (season 2, episode 4), which includes a significant scene of Santana, in her cheerleading uniform, and a (perhaps) bisexual Brittany engaging in "sweet lady kisses" and discussing their relationship on Brittany's bed, *Glee* foregrounds Santana's difficult coming-out narrative. The storyline follows the two girls as they question their possible "lesbian" identities with sex ed teacher Holly Holliday several episodes later ("Sexy," season 2, episode 15), and then culminates in two coming-out episodes for Santana in season 3: "Pot O' Gold" (episode 4), where she and Brittany are acknowledged as a couple, and "I Kissed a Girl" (episode 7), in which she is heartbreakingly disowned by her *abuela* after coming out to her. The two characters even marry in the show's final season ("A Wedding," season 6, episode 8). To be sure, *Glee* legitimates and centralizes Santana's queer adolescent journey—from "stereotypical jaded 'whore' to a young woman trying to navigate her sexual desire and agency"—but it also never fails to exploit her cisgender eroticized femininity, accentuating her traditional beauty with her long hair, makeup, and painted nails and featuring her slim but curvy body with tight girly outfits (and of course her cheer uniform).[17] Set up from the beginning as the show's "indiscriminate sexual deviant" whose promiscuity and unapologetic erotic drive fit too easily into a Latina stereotype, and yet who seems redeemed by her queer maturation, Santana still never stops being the "popular and desirable cheerleader."[18] She is just the "sexy" queer one.

To understand the larger consequences of queering the iconic American cheerleader, however, we need to return to the earlier independent film *But I'm a Cheerleader*, whose comically wholesome, lesbian "good girl" redefines this feminine icon more fundamentally than a stereotypically eroticized "bad girl" like Santana might. Certainly, the creators of *Glee* are politically invested in producing "positive, affirming images of [the] gay teen experience" for "queer viewers" validated by seeing these characters onscreen, but the series has also often been accused of employing stereotypes for its broad humor and messaging and so perhaps lacks the more shrewd critique of Babbit's film.[19] What makes *But I'm a Cheerleader* so radical, I would argue, is its ironic denaturalization of two conflicting types, as they are embodied in the same teenage girl: the pure, feminized heterosexual cheerleader and the deviant lesbian lover.[20] The film's protagonist, Megan Bloomfield (Natasha Lyonne)—who starts out so inculcated in the normative ideology of (hetero) cheerleading that she absurdly fails to recognize her own queer desires until she is confronted by an intervention and sent off to gay conversion camp—remains until the very end the clean-cut, feminine cheer lover we meet in the opening scene, even as she falls in love with the more experienced, and butch, Graham (Clea DuVall) and, ultimately, embraces her own lesbian identity. As Katrin Horn has claimed, this unusual rom-com's happy ending, where the two girls run off together and Megan's parents join PFLAG, allows Megan to "reconcile her attraction to Graham with her cheerleader identity," validating both of her identities and rejecting the notion that the cheerleader's "wholesome image and gayness are mutually exclusive."[21] Directly taking on that icon of American girlhood, then, the film presents Megan not as the dangerously masculinized athlete or the heterosexy object of the male gaze but as the idealized femme cheerleader and lesbian romantic lead with a female gaze all her own.

Roundly panned by critics on its initial release as "nothing to cheer about," due to its supposedly simplistic satire and crude attempts at a garish, campy Barbie aesthetic, Babbit's film has since grown into something of a "lesbian classic," mostly likely because it succeeds as a sweet, even disarming, romance.[22] Although its opening credit sequence alludes to the kind of male fantasies of cheerleading that the same year's *American Beauty* (Sam Mendes, 1999) would rely on to signal its protagonist Lester's midlife crisis, this montage of disarticulated bodily temptations—close-ups of midriffs, bouncing breasts in jog bras, thighs, and panties visible under lifted cheer skirts—attributes this fantasy to an altogether different, and seemingly innocent, subject: It ends by cutting to a buoyantly smiling Megan at the center of the routine, sincerely cheering, "Go Freemont!" Indeed, the central conceit, and joke, of the first act of the film ironically positions Megan so far outside of sexual knowledge and experience that these erotic visions of her fellow cheerleaders, which return again while she makes out with her football star boyfriend, do not register to her as queer. She may have a Melissa Etheridge poster on her wall, eat tofu, dislike kissing her boyfriend, and adorn the inside of her locker with swimsuit models, as we learn at her intervention, but she is shocked to discover that she might be a lesbian. As she protests at her first group therapy session at the gay rehab center True Directions, "I'm not perverted! I get good grades. I go to church. I'm a cheerleader!" Yet even as she makes this smiling, simple (to her) objection, her thoughts about other girls betray her, with the film cutting yet again to the eroticized, "isolated body parts" of her fellow cheerleaders so typical of that popularized male fantasy.[23]

Nevertheless, while poking fun at Megan's innocence and naïveté (and perhaps more importantly, at our own inability to even conceive of a queer female cheerleader), the film refuses to discipline and correct her femme identity or to ask her to abandon her cheer enthusiasm as she does the apparently unconscionable—falling in love with another girl. In other words, Megan does not stop being the girl who gets good grades or wears modest, feminine clothing (like matching sweater sets), or goes to church, just because she has same-sex desires. In fact, the viewer can easily discern the gold cross she wears around her neck at two key moments in her journey of sexual and emotional discovery: her first time with Graham and her declaration of love that spurs their final escape. If, as Adams and Bettis assert, the cheerleader still represents for so many the "ideal American girl" next door whose cheerful smile, optimism, wholesomeness, and "loyalty and devotion" make her a kind of "model" citizen and student, Babbit resolutely refuses to let Megan lose those qualities as she comes to act on and accept her lesbian identity.[24] Instead, the film uses those aspects of the cheerleader that make her one of the "last bastions of traditional femininity" to endear Megan to Graham (and to the audience).[25] Despite Graham's initial snide assessments of Megan as a "princess" or a "prom queen," in their tender postcoital moments Graham appears won over by Megan's guileless enthusiasm and sincere "love" for cheerleading, expressing what appears to be an authentic wish to see her cheer.[26] The film's initial joke then—that cheerleading and lesbian identity are so incommensurate that Megan must be convinced she has these "tendencies"—is ultimately harnessed to carry its central emotional aim: to bring the two lovers together. Graham does, happily, get to see Megan cheer at the film's conclusion, when her cheerleader in shining armor disrupts True Directions' "happy heterosexuals" graduation ceremony with a sweet "One, two, three, four, you're the one that I adore!" and then drops her pom-poms to embrace as the two girls run off together.

In interviews at the time of the film's release and since, director Jamie Babbit has been outspoken about her intention to create a sympathetic protagonist who remains true to herself as a cheerleader and as a burgeoning lesbian. As she shared with Cynthia Fuchs in 2000, she wanted Megan to begin the film as a cheerleader, "that icon of American femininity," and to end the film as one, keeping her "identity as a cheerleader," staying "who she was," but just adding "and I'm gay" to her sense of self.[27] Rejecting the notion that Megan must transform into a butch icon—for example, riding off on a motorcycle to fit the mold of established lesbian representation—Babbit created instead, as she put it more recently, a character who "embraces her lesbianism" as a "girly girl" through to the very end.[28] What others now call Megan's "irreverent lesbian femininity" clearly came from the director herself, who had seen too little lesbian comedy and far too few lesbian femmes for her liking, either in mainstream fare or independent queer film.[29] With her good girl cheerleader Megan, therefore, Babbit sought to challenge "gender expectations," even in the queer community, but significantly, she connects this contestation with her own failure at sports: "When I was coming out as a lesbian, a lot of people made fun of me because I was bad at sports. . . . One of the many bizarre gender expectations is that lesbians are supposed to be really good at sports. But I'm not; I'm femme, and that's it."[30] So, she made her lesbian lead a cheerleader, the ultimate femme.

Yet, with this decision, Babbit subverted not just the typical expectations and representational iconography for lesbians; she upended the expectations for cheerleaders as well. In their discussion of the explosion in competitive cheer squads since the 1990s, Adams and Bettis provide the history, which I alluded to above, wherein female-dominated cheerleading has in "no shape, form or fashion" been viewed as a "sport," and instead is designated as the "feminine sphere" (opposed to the "masculine" one) in the dichotomy between supporters and "athletes"—all of which has been seriously challenged by recent competitive cheerleaders whose difficult routines, grueling schedules, and frequent injuries signify their athletic credentials.[31] But of course, as I have emphasized, this cheerleader has been historically defined as heterosexual and feminine, and Adams and Bettis assert that until she gets rid of her "highly sexualized"—meaning heterosexualized—image, she will not garner "respect" as a serious athlete.[32] I would argue, however, that recent cheerleading's engagement with masculinized concepts of sport and the figure of the athlete was inevitably going to raise the specter of the lesbian cheerleader, whether sociologists want to address it or not. As Babbit's interview comments suggest, sports feel as compulsory for lesbians as feminine display does for female cheerleaders. In *But I'm a Cheerleader*, then, we have a representation of the cheerleader that disrupts and disturbs these simple dichotomies, binaries, and normative expectations. It refuses the easy divide between Madonna and whore—wholesome booster and sexy object—by warmly embracing the sexual awakening of its sweet, feminine, lesbian cheerleader, and it complexifies the debate about what qualities a female athlete should have or who gets to count as an athlete by questioning the association of (masculinized) lesbians with sport. The impact of this revisionary story, as the recent outrageousness of the film *Bottoms* suggests, has been significant in popular culture. Perhaps now, though, it is time for the scholarship to catch up.

## Notes

1. Megan Conway, "Rachel Sennott Just Wants You to Have the Time of Your Life," *New York Times*, September 12, 2022, https://www.nytimes.com/2022/09/12/t-magazine/rachel-sennott-bodies-bodies-bodies.html. Signaling its revisionary potential for the genre, *Rolling Stone* dubbed the film the "horniest, bloodiest high school movie" of the century. David Fear, "'Bottoms' Is the Horniest, Bloodiest High School Movie of the 21st Century," *Rolling Stone*, March 12, 2023, https://www.rollingstone.com/tv-movies/tv-movie-reviews/bottoms-review-ayo-edebiri-rachel-sennott-sxsw-lesbian-fight-club-1234692636/. Similarly, the reviewer in *Sight and Sound* praised the film for its refreshing take on the "raucous, filthy, take-no-prisoners high-school comedy" of the past. Isabel Stevens, "Smells Like Teen Spirit," *Sight and Sound*, December 2023, 34.

2. Noting the influence of precursors like Jamie Babbit's *But I'm a Cheerleader* (1999) and Lehmann's *Heathers* for the film's "comedy of vicious gamesmanship, at once confessional and surreal," *Variety*'s reviewer finds *Bottoms*' "caustic relentlessness" in an almost "dementedly over-the-top" league of its own—a "gonzo gay 'Fight Club' meets 'Heathers.'" Owen Gleiberman, "Emma Seligman's Wild Ride of a High School Comedy Is a Gonzo Gay 'Fight Club' Meets 'Heathers,'" *Variety*, March 12, 2023, https://variety.com/2023/film/reviews/bottoms-review-rachel-sennott-1235550522/.

3. Pamela J. Bettis and Natalie G. Adams, "Interrogating the Body in Contemporary Cheerleading," in *The Routledge Handbook of Sport, Gender and Sexuality*, ed. Jennifer Hargreaves and Eric Anderson (Routledge, 2014), 212–213.

4. Natalie G. Adams and Pamela J. Bettis, *Cheerleader! An American Icon* (Palgrave Macmillan, 2003), 66–67.

5. Adams and Bettis, *Cheerleader!*, 66–67.

6. Helen Lenskyj, *Out of Bounds: Women, Sport and Sexuality* (Women's Press, 1986), 101, 103.

7. See Helen Lenskyj's *Out on the Field: Gender, Sport and Sexualities* (Women's Press, 2003) for her updated examination of gender and sexuality's impact on female-identified athletes in sport. The book devotes considerable space to lesbian athletes and discusses a wide range of sports (including soccer, softball, tennis, golf, hockey, basketball, volleyball, track and field, martial arts, and even "aesthetic" sports like gymnastics and figure skating) but does not examine cheerleading. Other early works—for example, Pat Griffin, "Changing the Game: Homophobia, Sexism, and Lesbians in Sport," *Quest* 44, no. 2 (1992): 251–265; Maria J. Veri, "Homophobic Discourse Surrounding the Female Athlete," *Quest* 51, no. 4 (1999), 355–368—similarly equate "sport" with predominantly competitive team sports like soccer and basketball and never mention cheerleading, although Veri does differentiate between more "feminine" sports like figure skating and "masculinely defined" team sports (364). This distinction and exclusion of cheerleading continues to the present. For updated discussions of lesbian athletes in various sports, but not cheerleading, see Helen Lenskyj, "Sexuality and Femininity in Sport Contexts: Issues and Alternatives," *Journal of Sport and Social Issues* 18, no. 4 (1994): 356–376; Gill Clarke, "Queering the Pitch and Coming Out to Play: Lesbians in Physical Education and Sport," *Sport, Education and Society* 3, no. 2 (1998): 145–160; Jayne Caudwell, "Femme-Fatale: Re-Thinking the Femme-inine," in *Sport, Sexualities and Queer/Theory*, ed. Jayne Caudwell (Routledge, 2006), 145–158; Kerrie Kauer and Vikki Krane, "'Scary Dykes' and 'Feminine Queens': Stereotypes and Female Collegiate Athletes," *Women in Sport and Physical Activity Journal* 15, no. 1 (2006): 42–55; Scarlett Drury, "'It Seems Really Inclusive in Some Ways, but . . . Inclusive Just for People Who Identify as Lesbian': Discourses of Gender and Sexuality in a Lesbian-Identified Football Club," *Soccer and Society* 12, no. 3 (2011): 421–442; Suzanne Stoelting, "Disclosure as an Interaction: Why Lesbian Athletes Disclose Their Sexual Identities in Intercollegiate Sport," *Journal of Homosexuality* 58, no. 9 (2011): 1187–1210; Laurel Davis-Delano, "Sport as Context for the Development of Women's Same-

Sex Relationships," *Journal of Sport and Social Issues* 38, no. 3 (2014): 263–285; Jennifer Waldron, "It's Complicated: Negotiations and Complexities of Being a Lesbian in Sport," *Sex Roles* 74 (2016): 335–346; Jamie Cleland, Kevin Dixon, Ellis Cashmore, and Connor MacDonald, "Fan Reflections on Sexuality in Women's Football in the United Kingdom," *Journal of Sport and Social Issues* 46, no. 5 (2022): 458–476; Austin R. Anderson, Sarah Stokowski, Chase M. L. Smith, and Megan R. Turk, "'You Have to Validate It': Experiences of Female Sexual Minority Student-Athletes," *Journal of Homosexuality* 70, no. 3 (2023): 497–518.

8. Eric Anderson, *In the Game: Gay Athletes and the Cult of Masculinity* (State University of New York Press, 2005), 119–134. See also Anderson, "Orthodox and Inclusive Masculinity: Competing Masculinities Among Heterosexual Men in a Feminized Terrain," *Sociological Perspectives* 48, no. 3 (2005): 337–355; Anderson, "'I Used to Think Women Were Weak': Orthodox Masculinity, Gender Segregation, and Sport," *Sociological Forum* 23, no. 2 (2008): 257–280; Anderson, "'Being Masculine Is Not About Who You Sleep With . . .': Heterosexual Athletes Contesting Masculinity and the One-Time Rule of Homosexuality," *Sex Roles* 58 (2008): 104–115; Anderson, *Inclusive Masculinity: The Changing Nature of Masculinities* (Routledge, 2009). Similarly, Michelle Bemiller has investigated how this sort of homohysterical atmosphere can encourage self-identified straight male cheerleaders to assert heteromasculinity and dominance by objectifying fellow female cheerleaders. Michelle Bemiller, "Men Who Cheer," *Sociological Focus* 38, no. 3 (2005): 205–222.

9. Rachael Bullingham, Rory Magrath, and Eric Anderson, "Changing the Game: Sport and a Cultural Shift Away from Homohysteria," in Hargreaves and Anderson, *Routledge Handbook of Sport*, 278. Bullingham, Magrath, and Anderson lament that "there has been no empirical investigation of the experiences of lesbian athletes on ostensibly heterosexual teams" (279), which they seem to rectify with later work in 2015, although none of the female athletes are cheerleaders. See Eric Anderson and Rachael Bullingham, "Openly Lesbian Team Sport Athletes in an Era of Decreasing Homohysteria," *International Review for the Sociology of Sport* 50, no. 6 (2015): 647–660.

10. Griffin, "Changing the Game," 252.

11. Anderson and Bellingham, "Openly Lesbian Team Sport Athletes," 648; Bettis and Adams, "Interrogating the Body," 213.

12. In their chapter examining cheerleaders who break the mold or challenge traditional notions about cheerleading, Natalie Adams and Pamela Bettis *do* recognize the "unstraightening" of cheerleading achieved by predominantly gay and lesbian squads like CHEER San Francisco (discussed in chapter 7 of this volume), but while these groups do perform at cheerleading camps where "most squads are heterosexual," they, for the most part, are not; therefore, the question of how a lesbian cheerleader might fare on a heterosexual squad remains unexamined. Adams and Bettis, *Cheerleader!*, 31–33.

13. Not surprisingly, the lesbian cheerleader appears much earlier in feminist independent film—with, for example, Jan Oxenberg's *Home Movie* (1972), which features a significant segment where the lesbian filmmaker counterposes home

movies of her as a high school cheerleader with a voice-over that knowingly observes, "The thing I liked best about being a cheerleader was being with the other cheerleaders." The critic Andrea Weiss contends that Oxenberg uses this ironic commentary about her own girlhood to confirm her "distance from a culturally-mandated feminine model," and the film ultimately concludes by rejecting this model altogether, which Weiss supports with, notably, a final scene where women together enjoy a "sensuous, non-competitive disorderly game of football," rather than "cheering from the sidelines." Andrea Weiss, "Transgressive Cinema: Lesbian Independent Film," in *Queer Cinema: The Film Reader*, ed. Harry Benshoff and Sean Griffin (Routledge, 2004), 45.

14. Whedon's screenplay for the film *Buffy the Vampire Slayer* (Fran Rubel Kuzui, 1992) makes the connection between the disturbance and subversion of the wholesome suburban teenage world and cheerleading when Buffy must interrupt one of her routines at a basketball game to battle with an avenging male vampire/player.

15. The fan fervor over and devotion to the Brittany-Santana plotline and relationship, which the showrunners reward in the end with a marriage episode, is unquestionable. Researchers in 2014 were in fact stunned to find in their audience reception study that fans overwhelmingly favored Santana and Brittany's romance over the more central one between the male characters Kurt and Blaine, with twice as many tweets devoted to the hashtag #Brittana than to the hashtag #Klaine. Alice Marwick, Mary L. Gray, and Mike Ananny, "'Dolphins Are Just Gay Sharks': *Glee* and the Queer Case of Transmedia as Text and Object," *Television and New Media* 15, no. 7 (2014): 639.

16. La'Tonya Rease Miles, "American Beauty: The Cheerleader in American Literature and Popular Culture," *Women's Studies Quarterly* 33, no. 1/2 (2005): 227.

17. Melissa Esh, "'I'm a Slave 4 U' but Only When I Want to Be: Female Sexual Agency," in *Queer in the Choir Room: Essays on Sexuality in "Glee,"* ed. Michelle Parke (McFarland, 2014), 211. Kathryn Hobson similarly assesses Santana's gender expression as "hypersexualized" and "feminized" so that she appears as a clichéd Latina version of "normative, stereotypical femininity." Kathryn Hobson, "Sue Sylvester, Coach Beiste, Santana Lopez, and Unique Adams: Exploring Queer Representations of Femininity on *Glee*," in *"Glee" and New Directions for Social Change*, ed. Brian C. Johnson and Daniel K. Faill (Sense, 2015), 102.

18. Christina Belcher, "'I Can't Go to an Indigo Girls Concert, I Just Can't': *Glee*'s Shameful Lesbian Musicality," *Journal of Popular Music Studies* 23, no. 4 (2011): 412; Kate Norbury, "Embodied Performances by Lesbian Cheerleaders and Dancers in *Glee* and *Leading Ladies*," in *The Embodied Child: Readings in Children's Literature and Culture*, ed. Roxanne Harde and Lydia Kokkola (Routledge, 2018), 245. Norbury recognizes the show's play with the "hot Latina stereotype" so often used in mainstream media.

19. Jason Jacobs, "Raising Gays: On *Glee*, Queer Kids, and the Limits of Family," *GLQ* 20, no. 3 (2014): 320.

20. Miles, "American Beauty," 226. If we are to accept cheerleaders as athletes—

and it is not clear that Babbit's film does—then *But I'm a Cheerleader* is also radical in its depiction of a lesbian teenage athlete, since the few films that have centered on girls in sport typically "privilege heterosexuality," despite raising the specter of lesbianism. Jayne Caudwell, "*Girlfight* and *Bend It Like Beckham*: Screening Women, Sport, and Sexuality," *Journal of Lesbian Studies* 13, no. 3 (2009): 256.

21. Katrin Horn, *Women, Camp, and Popular Culture: Serious Excess* (Palgrave Macmillan, 2017), 85.

22. Kate Stables, "But I'm a Cheerleader," *Sight and Sound*, September 2021, 97. The title of the review in *The Advocate*—which likened the film to "a five-minute Kids in the Hall–type sketch that has been inflated into a numbingly crude full-length satire"—was blunt, but others were equally dismissive of this "one-joke" film. Jan Stuart, "Nothing to Cheer About," *The Advocate*, July 18, 2000, 59. See also Owen Gleiberman, "Dipstick Lesbian," *Entertainment Weekly*, July 14, 2000, 54; Amy Taubin, "Anti-Essential Viewing," *Village Voice*, July 11, 2000, 124; Elvis Mitchell, "Don't Worry: Pink Outfits Will Straighten Her Out," *New York Times*, July 7, 2000.

23. Mary Ellen Hanson, *Go! Fight! Win! Cheerleading in American Culture* (Bowling Green State University Popular Press, 1995), 3. Hanson refers to the way in which the isolating of female body parts in images of cheerleaders contributes to the devaluing and trivializing of the female cheerleader, while denying her respectable status as an athlete.

24. Adams and Bettis, *Cheerleader!*, 10, 17.

25. Adams and Bettis, *Cheerleader!*, 67.

26. Indeed, the film uses the sweet postcoital scene to upend one of its funniest earlier jokes. The first time that Graham interrogates Megan about her investment in cheerleading, she defends it by saying, "Cheers are supposed to be simple, make people feel good." To which a smoking, world-weary Graham responds, "Cheers make girls do stupid cartwheels. Orgasms make people feel good." Yet after they have sex for the first time, Graham (clearly falling in love) is moved to take Megan's enthusiasm and passion for cheering seriously, not mocking but appreciating Megan's comparison of their lovemaking to the happiness and exhilaration she feels while cheering.

27. Cynthia Fuchs, "So Many Battles to Fight: Interview with Jamie Babbit," *Nitrate*, July 21, 2000, https://nitrateonline.com/2000/fcheerleader.html.

28. Rebecca Rubin, "*But I'm a Cheerleader* Director Jamie Babbit on the Queer Classic 20 Years Later: 'I Wanted to Make a Gay *Clueless*,'" *Variety*, December 4, 2020, https://variety.com/2020/film/features/but-im-a-cheerleader-director-jamie-babbit-20th-anniversary-1234842163/.

29. Clara Bradbury-Rance, "Ambivalent Masculinities in Contemporary Film and TV: On Lesbian and Trans Representability," *Film Quarterly* 77, no. 3 (2024): 35.

30. Wheeler Winston Dixon, "An Interview with Jamie Babbit," *Post Script* 21, no. 1 (2001): 19–20.

31. Adams and Bettis, *Cheerleader!*, 60, 67.

32. Adams and Bettis, *Cheerleader!*, 68.

CHEER NOTE #6

# Cheerleaders in Popular Culture

Cheerleaders are a mainstay in popular culture, although who and what they represent (e.g., mean girl, popular girl, promiscuous girl) varies. How well do you know cheerleading in popular culture?

1. Which of the following movies features a high school cheerleader sent to a conversion camp to "cure" her lesbianism?
   A. *Attack of the 50 Foot Cheerleader*
   B. *But I'm a Cheerleader*
   C. *Heathers*
   D. *Debbie Does Dallas*

2. How old was Olivia Newton-John when she played a high school cheerleader in the blockbuster movie *Grease*?
   A. 18
   B. 25
   C. 28
   D. 30

3. In the film *Bring It On*, Torrance does something that in cheerleading folklore foretells bad luck. (And later the Toros come in second at Nationals.) What does she do?
   A. drop the spirit stick
   B. have sex with her boyfriend the night before Nationals
   C. remove her tiny megaphone necklace
   D. forget to lead her team in prayer before they hit the mat at Nationals

4. Which of the following actors, after being nominated for an Oscar, revealed that she had once been dismissed by a fellow actor for being in a "dumb cheerleader movie"?
   A. Natasha Lyonne
   B. Olivia Newton-John
   C. Kirsten Dunst
   D. Alicia Silverstone

5. Which of the following popular TV series featured two female characters, both high school cheerleaders, getting married?
   A. *Gossip Girl*
   B. *Riverdale*
   C. *Euphoria*
   D. *Glee*

6. Which of the following actors from *Bring It On* had not been a cheerleader in real life?
   A. Carla Mackauf
   B. Gabrielle Union
   C. Kirsten Dunst
   D. Eliza Dushku

7. Which powerhouse high school cheerleader team is featured in the reality TV show *Cheerleader Nation*?
   A. Christian Brothers High School
   B. Paul Laurence Dunbar High School
   C. Houston High School
   D. St. Joseph's Academy

8. Who played Navarro College assistant coach Andy Cosferent in *Saturday Night Live*'s parody of the Netflix docuseries *Cheer*?
   A. John Krasinski
   B. Chris Pratt
   C. Adam Driver
   D. Ed Sheeran

9. Which Taylor Swift music video featured Taylor as a cheerleader?
   A. "Shake It Off"
   B. "Fearless"
   C. "Picture to Burn"
   D. "All Too Well"

10. Which of the following music videos featured black-clad anarchist cheerleaders?
    A. "Jeremy" by Pearl Jam
    B. "Smells Like Teen Spirit" by Nirvana
    C. "Black Hole Sun" by Soundgarden
    D. "Doll Parts" by Hole

(Answers found on page 283.)

CHAPTER 10

# Cheerleading and the Body

## DISORDERED EATING, PUBLIC SURVEILLANCE, AND SELF-REGULATION

*Caitlyn M. Jarvis and Ashleigh N. Shields*

Abs, thighs, buns of steel
Puking after every meal
Tummy tucks, liposuction
Gotta get a breast reduction
Legs too short, butt too big
Get fake nails, buy a wig
Weight Watchers, Lean Cuisine
I gotta be what's on the screen.
Perfection! Perfection! Perfection!

X-Cheerleaders chant, circa 1990s

"It's harder for girls not to even just . . . not wanna starve themselves," veteran Dallas Cowboys Cheerleader and professional dancer Victoria Kalina says during a confessional on the Netflix docuseries *America's Sweethearts: Dallas Cowboys Cheerleaders*.[1] In the scene, Victoria sits in her childhood bedroom, which is bedecked in Cowboys paraphernalia, vulnerably admitting to disordered eating as she discusses the pressure to stay thin and appear in line with what is expected of Dallas Cowboys Cheerleaders. Another veteran member of the team, Kat Puryear, explains the pressure all the women face to maintain their figure when they are issued one uniform at the start of their rookie year and expected to fit into it throughout their remaining tenure on the team. For many women, this means maintaining the weight and shape of their nineteen-year-old selves even as they enter their mid-twenties. For Kat, Victoria, and the other young women on the squad, failure to maintain their rookie weight is met with judgmental comments, strong insinuations that something is wrong with them, and the risk of not making the team the following year, since the cheerleaders must audition every year for a coveted spot on the team.

In the world of sports, athletes often feel pressure from their coaches to ascribe to specific body types. This is particularly true for female athletes in aesthetic sports like gymnastics or cheerleading.[2] For instance, in their study of the athlete-coach relationship, Robyn Jones, Niki Glintmeyer, and Alex McKenzie relate the story of a collegiate swimmer whose eating disorder was precipitated in part by her coaches' criticism. They write that the athlete's body "became a source of humiliation and degradation. . . . Chained to her coaches' discourse and feeling that her core identity was under threat, she began to regulate her caloric intake and weight, which soon led to drastic dieting and vomiting."[3] The *America's Sweethearts* docuseries illustrates the influence of coaches on body expectations when Charlotte Jones, chief brand officer and co-owner of the Dallas Cowboys, advises coach Kelli Finglass which rookies should be dropped because their torso proportions or body shapes don't conform to expectations (not too skinny or too big, not too tall or too petite, not too much cleavage, and not too big of a butt). The influence of cheer coaches coupled with cheerleaders' own self-surveillance is not relegated to professional cheerleading squads. All cheerleaders, of every age, are subjected to rigid (and often unrealistic) expectations about their bodies. This often creates a culture of fear and anxiety, sometimes leading to harmful practices and behaviors.

Despite the ample research into gender performance and the rampant sexualization of cheerleaders, scant research has sought to understand how cheerleaders navigate the pressures to maintain a slim body. This chapter examines the communication tactics and everyday language of cheerleaders and coaches when discussing the cheerleading body. Through an ethnographic analysis of popular online cheerleading communities, including r/Cheerleading and FierceBoard, and popular media programs such as the Netflix series *America's Sweethearts* and *Cheer*, this chapter seeks to understand how unrealistic and often harmful expectations are produced, perpetuated, and resisted within the cheerleading community, and popular media's role in these processes.

A quick word about methodology: In its most basic form, online ethnography is a technique used to study virtual or digital environments to understand culture and human behavior.[4] Ethnography requires immersed and sustained observation of communities to observe how people communicate, engage, and participate. For this study, we observed the subreddit r/Cheerleading and the online community FierceBoard, two social media platforms for cheerleaders, over two months, reading and recording comments that discussed weight, body perception, and identity. While r/Cheerleading explicitly bans discussions of cheerleaders being too heavy or too light, we nonetheless found evidence of how the commenters participating in the forum, mainly girls and women, discussed their bodies and self-presentation. We also followed other strains of inquiry, such as observing the social media presence of various cheerleaders who became popular for appearing on *Cheer* and the Dallas Cowboys Cheerleaders TV shows. This observation gave us a more holistic, deeper understanding of the many forms of influence that shape perceptions of cheerleaders online and in the larger culture. In what follows, we discuss two dominant forms of surveillance: one rooted with the individual cheerleader and the other traced to the influence of coaches.

## Roots of Surveillance

As discussed throughout this volume, cheerleaders have long been a cultural artifact of sexualized perfection; their bodies are a site of both objectification and condemnation. Emma Jane (Tom) has written extensively about the paradoxical fetishization the news media employs to overtly sexualize cheerleaders while also claiming that they serve no value in society.[5] Writing about their representation in both pornography and mainstream media, Jane argues that the "sexualizing and trivializing representations of cheerleaders in porn—combined with similar and complementary framings in other domains [i.e., mainstream media and sports coverage]—both constitute and are constituted by a prejudice against cheerleaders so ubiquitous that it seldom prompts comment."[6] Even with the progress made during the #MeToo era in recognizing and critiquing oppressive systems of gender inequity, the media continue to frame cheerleaders as accomplices in their own victimization, as if their choice to participate in cheerleading should render them compliant in sexual harassment.[7] This may result in sexual assault and harassment going underreported or underinvestigated.[8] For instance, in season 1, episode 7, of *America's Sweethearts*, we learn that veteran cheerleader Sophy Laufer was assaulted by a cameraman. Even after Laufer tearfully reported the incident to her coaches and the police, the assault was not investigated. The reason: lack of evidence. The contradictory representation of cheerleaders renders their bodies as sites for public consumption and critique while negating their individuality and emotional well-being.

Public consumption is a constituent of surveillance, the ubiquitous yet often unacknowledged process of monitoring social practices and behavior. The study of surveillance is traced to the French philosopher Michel Foucault through his theory of panopticism.[9] The panopticon, in short, is a theorized prison in which a guard can monitor all inmates from a central position. Foucault's theory highlights the ever-present possibility that given the mere potential of being watched by the guard, the inmates will feel pressured to behave in accordance with prison regulations. The same idea applies to drivers who stop at red lights even when no one else is on the road; the potential of being surveilled is enough to motivate individuals to engage in certain behaviors.

In the age of social media, the concept of surveillance has narrowed, shifting the ability of "the many to see and contemplate the few."[10] Thus surveillance has evolved from a hierarchical power structure (i.e., one that exists because of the mere potential of the prison guard's authority) to one that is "lateral" or "peer-to-peer" (i.e., the perceived threat of the other prisoners watching and judging).[11] This form of distributed surveillance "relies on the internalized discipline not just of the watched, but also of the watchers."[12] Today's social media users may adopt self-censorship and self-regulating behaviors, recognizing that what they do or post will be seen by multiple audiences.[13] For cheerleaders, this shift may result in a stronger internalized demand to configure and comport themselves as the figureheads of American womanhood and the paragons of femininity.[14]

This need to self-monitor one's online presentation is particularly prevalent among girls and women, who often rely on the "girlfriend gaze" to normalize self-surveillance practices through the guise of being a role model for younger girls.[15] Surveillance of the self emerges through a variety of choices, including how one presents one's identity and body through profile pictures and posts. The girlfriend gaze also exists as a source of "evidence" for those consuming this content and thus strengthens peer-to-peer surveillance. For example, Victoria Jaynes has examined the role of screenshots in creating "digital evidence" that can be strategically shared to engender sympathy for a person or, conversely, to slander them. When considering the sharing and screenshotting capabilities of social media as a panopticon practice, this allows users, particularly girls, to constantly monitor their self-presentation.[16] Jaynes's study further argues that among girls, "the fear of having one's content screenshotted and the awareness of imagined or realized surveillance by friends informed . . . everyday mediated practices."[17] In short, the panopticon on social media challenges girls not only to monitor others but also to closely monitor themselves, ensuring that they are not stepping outside the bounds of what is considered acceptable.

The panopticon is an especially visible force in disciplining the body, particularly on social media, where thinness and feminine muscularity remain the markers of the ideal body. Through mass media and social media, girls internalize the images of the ideal body as one that must be thin and taut to be feminine.[18] In cheerleading, these pressures to maintain thinness may be further compounded by the threat of surveillance, leading to heightened self-regulation and self-surveillance.[19] We use the term "self-regulation" in this context to mean the thoughts, actions, and behaviors one takes to change, alter, or modify one's body and present oneself in (what are considered) physically healthy ways. Martin Hagger has identified three features of self-regulation in relation to health.[20] First, self-regulation involves actions, thoughts, and behaviors adopted to change or alter health. Second, individuals adopt these self-regulating behaviors consciously and intentionally. Finally, self-regulation is goal oriented, although it may be challenging to separate the goal from the behavior itself.[21]

Self-regulating behaviors, particularly those centered on diet and weight, are especially prevalent among female cheerleaders.[22] Researchers report that one in three cheerleaders are likely to experience a risk of disordered eating, with the highest risk among flyers, the petite women who grace the top of the pyramid.[23] Further, college students, especially those on coed teams, are at greater risk for body dissatisfaction and unhealthy dieting.[24] Self-regulating behaviors, including those related to weight and dieting, are an embedded component of self-surveillance and particularly prevalent on social media. As Rosalind Gill argues, self-surveillance has proliferated alongside social media and beauty filter apps, allowing women to engage in regulatory behaviors that place value solely on the body.[25] The types of self-surveillance made possible by technology have engendered a "hitherto unprecedented degree of scrutiny" for women beyond mere self-care and beauty regimes.[26]

Research is rife with examples of how social media negatively affects body image. Long-term social media use is consistently associated with negative body image, which likewise increases the risk of unhealthy dieting and disordered eating.[27] Social media can lead women to perceive themselves and their bodies more negatively, resulting in stronger desires to change their hair, face, and skin.[28] Online fitness communities can be a breeding ground for "fitspiration" posts that showcase unrealistic or unattainable bodies.[29] While fitspiration posts appear ostensibly positive, with uplifting messages about mental and physical health, research has found that they typically only contain one type of body—one that is excessively thin and toned.[30] As a result, the sharing of fitspiration content promotes higher levels of body dissatisfaction, anxiety and depression, and excessively controlled eating habits among young adults.[31]

## "Am I Too Fat to Be a Flyer?": Surveilling the Self in Online Cheer Communities

Despite the subreddit's regulation of comments pertaining to weight, much of the conversation on r/Cheerleading attends to weight loss and weight management topics. Typically, these comments are situated within a larger narrative of fitting into a role on the team. For example, a typical comment does not explicitly critique a person's weight or body type but questions whether the individual is suited for the team, especially as a hopeful flyer. Most comments on this topic appear to come from petite women and girls who weigh just over or under one hundred pounds, yet they worry they are too tall or too heavy to be at the top of the stunt. Such comments are present throughout r/Cheerleading, with a number of posts fitting this pattern, including the following examples:

> I'm about 5'2 and 108ish, is that too tall for a flyer?
>
> I have been told I am too heavy to be a flyer. I am starting a new all star gym tomorrow and I really want to fly. I am 5' and 87 pounds. Is that too big to fly?
>
> I'm concerned I'm too fat to fly in high school. Or maybe I just compare myself too much. I'm 13, female, 4'11/5'0, and 97/98 pounds. Can someone be bluntly honest?

The pressure for flyers to maintain thinness is so totalizing, in part because flyers often exist at the peak of the cheerleader social hierarchy, leading many girls, especially those in high school, to see making the team, particularly as a flyer, as a pathway to popularity.[32]

While flyers are often the cheerleaders most frequently spotlighted, other members of the team also struggle with body issues, including the other primary members of a stunt team: the base (one or two members of the team who hold the flyer in the air) and the back spot (the person who stands behind the stunt and monitors the safety and stability of the flyer). Typically, the bases are stronger and more muscular, while back spots tend to be taller so as to more safely hold on to a flyer. While the body standards for these positions are not as strict as those of a flyer, many girls continue to feel the pressure to fit in with normative expectations about the ideal cheer body. For example, one commenter on r/Cheerleading describes feeling insecure as a small base: "I feel ridiculous because I am so small and even when we do extended it doesn't look as great as with others because I am so fucking tiny. I hate it." And although commenters across the community are quick to respond that anyone can serve in any position if they are skilled and capable (e.g., "The best cheerleaders are skilled in all stunt positions"), many also affirm that certain body types are expected for certain positions. In other words, even while commenters proclaim all positions are accessible to anyone, they nonetheless reproduce stereotypical rules for size that most coaches expect and enforce, as one coach commenter explains: "A lot of the time flyers are given a chance to fly based on size. It's easier to put the smaller people in the air and have your bases be stronger and/or heavier. Back spots are generally the taller people on the team." This contradictory stance, which claims the acceptability of different body shapes for different positions but nonetheless enforces strict standards for all participants, perpetuates a sporting culture in which girls' and women's bodies are defined and regulated by very narrow notions of the acceptable cheerleading body.

Another way that cheerleaders attempt to control and regulate their bodies, without explicitly discussing weight-loss strategies, is through discussions of snacks and healthy eating. For example, many healthy-eating recommendations center on high-protein or low-calorie foods, like protein shakes and rice cakes. What becomes more concerning are the communication tactics these types of recommendations reflect. For example, commenters talk about healthy eating by using phrases like "Eat on an if-needed basis." They recommend foods that are "not too heavy" or allude to a "less is more" mentality in eating. In this way, many of the comments hint at eating "just enough," as illustrated in this statement: "I have this one rule I stick to which is that [competition] morning breakfast is always porridge (homemade) and only a sip of water. It helps me feel less anxious because I'm not full but I'm not hungry either." Similarly, another commenter gives advice to eat "just a little bit" before games. This discourse hints at a highly regulated, restrictive pattern of rules surrounding what to eat and how to limit hunger pains without feeling full.

The popular Netflix docuseries *Cheer* reinforces many of these beliefs surrounding ideal size and hypercontrolled eating habits. Over the course of the series, many of the young, college-aged women display unhealthy relationships with food and abide by strict regulatory practices. Gabi Butler, the series's breakout star and social media "cheerlebrity," is the epitome of a "perfect" flyer with her toned muscles and endless tan. As the series unfolds, she sets the standard for perfection that the other Navarro College cheer girls judge their bodies by and strive to attain. For many viewers, this presentation has a negative impact on their own relationship to eating and body image, resulting in the strengthening of their self-regulating behaviors. Evidence of this was discussed online in a Reddit forum for eating disorder support, r/EDAnonymous. Here girls and women described the negative impact of seeing the strict regulation of eating and fitness habits of the girls on *Cheer*. As one commenter describes, "In one scene, they did weigh-ins and one of the girls was 98 pounds and was like 'Ugh, guess I'm not eating tonight.' I was SHOOK. Guess who also didn't have dinner that night and is now looking at cheerleading workout routines." Similarly, another commenter describes the scenes featuring strict dieting and how it aligns with her own experiences, writing, "One girl is talking about hopefully being skinny enough in their uniforms so her ribs would show. And the other girl is like 'we're gonna get weighed at practice anyways . . . so I need to know how much food to not eat.' I felt that." Clearly, the thoughts, feelings, and commentary of the Navarro cheerleaders resonated with the real-world experiences of many cheerleaders. This expectation to be perfect is real and leaves many cheerleaders dejected because they cannot measure up to this ideal. As discussed in the next chapter, these thoughts of inferiority lead many girls to quit cheerleading.

It is important to note that while many comments and concerns focused on body image, many of the posts also reflected resistance to rigid compliance with thinness and a move toward acceptance of one's body. For example, one commenter celebrates her size by describing herself as "a fellow chunky cheerio." Another commenter advises fellow cheerleaders to take a more body-positive approach by moving away from weight-focused behavior. She writes, "gaining weight is nothing to be ashamed of." These types of comments focus on integrating positive lifestyle changes and taking on perception shifts, such as focusing on eating enough calories and being proud of one's physical appearance.

## "I Can't Teach Tiny": The Role of Coaches in Surveillance

Cheerleading communities are tight ecosystems, and cheer coaches wield significant power within them. Athletic coaches can have an indelible impact on participants' self-esteem and life satisfaction, especially for female athletes.[33] They play a pivotal role in determining and executing expectations about weight, fitness, and overall physical presentation. Unfortunately, many cheer coaches, whether intentionally or not, become the enforcers of rigid rules about the appropriate cheerleader body, as well as vocal critics of a cheerleader's lack of progress in reaching perfection. For example, on *Cheer*, head coach Monica Aldama, whom *The Atlantic* described as a "take-no-prisoners" leader, frequently forced her athletes to work through injuries and pain.[34] Hannah Einbinder, a comedian and costar of the HBO comedy series *Hacks*, told the host of *Fresh Air* that her coaches were closely akin to army generals: "I really do attribute my desperate pursuit of perfection and my high personal standard to cheerleading, for better or for worse, because my coaches were really, really intense and they did not accept anything other than perfection. And we won every competition we entered. I compare cheerleading to being a part of the United States military."[35]

Across r/Cheerleading, cheerleaders frequently discuss their coaches' obsession with standards of perfection, often citing these expectations as contributing to their own negative body image. For example, one commenter explains how her coaches' passive comments about the weight of others amplifies her own negative self-image: "One of my coaches was judging other coaches and said 'a fat coach is a lazy coach.' Me being a bit chubby was kinda offended. She wasn't talking about me, however, I know I am chubby." Coaches are paramount in creating and shaping team culture. While the coach's commentary did not explicitly condemn the cheerleader herself, it did create a ripple effect of body shaming, leading this cheerleader to feel badly about her body. She felt the coach was implying that her body was the "bad" cheerleader body, because "good" cheerleaders aren't "chubby."

Just as cheerleaders worry about their own fit appearance and size, so too are coaches acutely aware of the size standards, especially for flyers, that must be met for a strong cheerleading team. For example, on FierceBoard, one coach describes the importance of technique and form, yet admits, "I can teach most talented athletes technique and form. I can't teach tiny." Cheerleading coaches may be acutely aware of the negative impact of size standards in cheerleading, and likewise the resulting risks those standards pose to their athletes' mental and physical health. Nevertheless, many coaches exchange strategies online for discussing weight with their cheerleaders. For example, one commenter makes clear that while she will never critique an athlete's body size, she will discuss eating habits: "You can't say 'I want to cheer in college' or 'I want to get in shape for cheer season' when you: Drink Starbucks before every practice. Hit Chick-FilA after every practice. Eat every single unhealthy thing in the venue on [competition] days." Coaches, many of whom are former cheerleaders, understand well the level of surveillance cheerleaders will experience on game day and at competitions. This coach sought to convey to her cheerleaders the need to adhere to self-regulatory practices such as dieting and healthy eating to protect them from harmful criticism or exclusion from cheerleading itself. The comment could be read as simultaneously signifying surveillance and compassionate care.

In considering the impact of coaches on team culture, many of the examples drawn from r/Cheerleading reveal toxic surveillance patterns as coaches try to exert control in many, if not all, aspects of a cheerleader's life. For example, one commenter received criticism from her coach for her natural hair, explaining, "Last practice my coach told me that I'll need to straighten my 3c curly hair for high school competitions, because she says my hair is against Varsity's rules." The implication that naturally textured hair would go against competition rules evokes decades of racist ideology that has stereotyped Black women's hair as unprofessional and othered women of color in cheerleading.[36] As Yago Ramis, Miquel Torregrosa, Carme Viladrich, and Jaume Cruz discuss, coaches with controlling coaching styles cause heightened anxiety in athletes, which in turn can amplify risks of burnout for the athlete.[37] Commenters in online cheer communities describe similar outcomes: "I went from loving a sport and being obsessed with it to hating it and now getting anxious just from watching random routines." Often these commenters describe feeling too anxious or depressed to continue cheerleading because of the impact of negative coaches. Many girls turn to r/Cheerleading for advice on navigating cheerleading coaches and quitting cheerleading.

From telling young women how to dress and how to style their hair, to what to post on social media, negative coaches can make cheerleaders feel like they have less control and ownership over their own identities. The negative culture created by toxic coaches can also leave cheerleaders feeling a heightened sensitivity to the perception of being watched. As one commenter writes, "One time I looked at the clock during practice and my coach thought I rolled my eyes so she silently came toward me and pulled me off of the mat and made me sit out the rest of practice." Coaches have an impressive level of power and authority over their cheerleaders' presentation and perception. Much like the gaze of a prison guard in the panopticon, their commentary creates a feeling of being watched, creating a ricochet of emotions for many young women both on and off the mat.

It is important to acknowledge, however, that discussions on Fierce-Board also highlighted the ways in which coaches exert positive influence on the lives of their cheerleaders. For example, one coach discusses her commitment to encouraging healthy eating habits: "I really want my athletes to be healthy and make good choices for themselves. So this is where I ask myself what can I do as a coach . . . or what is my duty as a coach in a sport like this, which is very difficult for young girls with possible body image problems." Several cheerleaders commented on the important role their coaches held in helping them seek treatment when they were struggling. One commenter writes, "My college coaches pulled me aside a few years into my cheer career to inquire about my rapid weight loss, dizziness, and lack of energy. They recommended I see the psychologist available to athletes at my school." These examples illustrate that surveillance is not always configured as an omnipresent threat. Rather, the watchful eye of the coach can be a guiding light to protect and mentor athletes through not only the difficulties of cheerleading in a challenging and pressure-ridden sport but also the struggles in their personal lives outside the sport.

## Disrupting Perfection: Creating New Patterns of Being

Many young women and girls who cheer engage in various forms of self-regulation and self-surveillance to ensure that they meet the expectations embedded in the culture of cheerleading and as part of a group viewed as paragons of American femininity. As previous chapters discuss, the culture of cheerleading has dramatically shifted throughout its history, often challenging gender norms and boundaries.[38] Despite changes in the last thirty years from a sideline activity to an activity showcasing athletic prowess, cheerleading's complicated entanglement with sexualized femininity remains.[39] Further, the culture of cheerleading has continued to insist on rigid standards of perfectionism. With lauded cheerlebrities like Gabi Butler of *Cheer* and the hypersexy Dallas Cowboys Cheerleaders as modern-day heroes of cheerleading, the standards they epitomize create an almost unachievable benchmark for aspiring cheerleaders. The pressure to achieve and maintain the ideal cheerleading body and high-level performance can lead to hypervigilant self-surveillance and self-regulation. This emphasis on perfectionism, especially during adolescence, can affect self-esteem and self-worth and lead to mental health issues such as disordered eating. As significant and influential adults in cheerleaders' lives, coaches play a key role in reproducing these unrealistic expectations. In closing, we urge coaches to develop a positive team culture that disrupts the unrealistic, and often harmful, environment prevalent in many high school, college, and All Star teams.

## Notes

1. *America's Sweethearts: Dallas Cowboys Cheerleaders*, season 1, episode 2, 2024, Netflix.
2. Tanya R. Berry and Bruce L. Howe, "Risk Factors for Disordered Eating in Female University Athletes," *Journal of Sport Behavior* 23, no. 3 (2000): 207.
3. Robyn L. Jones, Niki Glintmeyer, and Alex McKenzie, "Slim Bodies, Eating Disorders and the Coach-Athlete Relationship: A Tale of Identity Creation and Disruption," *International Review for the Sociology of Sport* 40, no. 3 (2005): 385.
4. Tabitha Hart, "Online Ethnography," in *The International Encyclopedia of Communication Research Methods*, ed. Christine S. Davis and Robert F. Potter (Wiley, 2017), https://doi.org/10.1002/9781118901731.iecrm0172.
5. Emma Tom, "Flip Skirt Fatales: How Media Fetish Sidelines Cheerleaders," *Platform: Journal of Media and Communication* 1 (2010): 52–70.
6. Emma Jane, "Is *Debbie Does Dallas* Dangerous? Representations of Cheerleading in Pornography and Some Possible Effects," *Feminist Media Studies* 17, no. 2 (2017): 275.
7. Caitlyn M. Jarvis and Jessica R. Welch, "'The Year of the Cheerleader Lawsuits': Paradoxical Sensemaking and Postfeminism in Reporting on Gender-Based Harassment," *Communication, Culture and Critique* 14, no. 4 (2021): 622–638, https://doi.org/10.1093/ccc/tcab046.
8. Carolina Lundqvist, "Prevalence of Harassment, Abuse, and Mental Health Among Current and Retired Senior Swedish Cheerleaders," *Journal of Sports Sciences* 42, no. 18 (2024): 1673–1684.

9. Michel Foucault, "Panopticism (1977)," in *Crime and Media: A Reader*, ed. Chris Greer (Routledge, 2019), 493–505.

10. Thomas Mathiesen, "The Viewer Society: Michael Foucault's 'Panopticon' Revisited," *Theoretical Criminology* 1, no. 2 (1997): 215–234.

11. Mark Andrejevic, "The Work of Watching One Another: Lateral Surveillance, Risk, and Governance," *Surveillance and Society* 2, no. 4 (2004): 479–497.

12. Mark Andrejevic, "The Discipline of Watching: Detection, Risk, and Lateral Surveillance," *Critical Studies in Media Communication* 23, no. 5 (2006): 391–407, https://doi.org/10.1080/07393180601046147.

13. Ivan Manokha, "Surveillance, Panopticism, and Self-Discipline in the Digital Age," *Surveillance and Society* 16, no. 2 (2018), https://ojs.library.queensu.ca/index.php/surveillance-and-society/article/view/8346.

14. Natalie G. Adams and Pamela J. Bettis, "Commanding the Room in Short Skirts: Cheering as the Embodiment of Ideal Girlhood," *Gender and Society* 17, no. 1 (2003): 73–91, https://doi.org/10.1177/0891243202238979.

15. Akane Kanai, "Thinking Beyond the Internet as a Tool: Girls' Online Spaces as Postfeminist Structures of Surveillance," in *eGirls, eCitizens* (University of Ottawa Press, 2015), 83–106; Alison Winch, *Girlfriends and Postfeminist Sisterhood* (Palgrave Macmillan, 2013).

16. Victoria Jaynes, "The Social Life of Screenshots: The Power of Visibility in Teen Friendship Groups," *New Media and Society* 22, no. 8 (2020): 1378–1392, https://doi.org/10.1177/1461444819878806.

17. Jaynes, "Social Life of Screenshots," 1390.

18. Laura Azzarito, "The Panopticon of Physical Education: Pretty, Active and Ideally White," *Physical Education and Sport Pedagogy* 14, no. 1 (2009): 19–39, https://doi.org/10.1080/17408980701712106.

19. Ginger Bihn, "On The Sidelines: Collegiate Cheerleading and Organizational Discourses" (PhD diss., Bowling Green State University, 2003).

20. Martin S. Hagger, "Self-Regulation: An Important Construct in Health Psychology Research and Practice," *Health Psychology Review* 4, no. 2 (2010): 57–65, https://doi.org/10.1080/17437199.2010.503594.

21. Hagger, "Self-Regulation."

22. Melissa G. Witt and Wendy Wood, "Self-Regulation of Gendered Behavior in Everyday Life," *Sex Roles* 62 (2010): 635–646, https://doi.org/10.1007/s11199-010-9761-y.

23. Toni M. Torres-McGehee, Eva V. Monsma, Thomas P. Dompier, and Stefanie A. Washburn, "Eating Disorder Risk and the Role of Clothing in Collegiate Cheerleaders' Body Images," *Journal of Athletic Training* 47, no. 5 (2012): 541, https://doi.org/10.4085/1062-6050-47.5.03.

24. Allison B. Smith, Jennifer L. Gay, Eva V. Monsma, et al., "Investigation of Eating Disorder Risk and Body Image Dissatisfaction Among Female Competitive Cheerleaders," *International Journal of Environmental Research and Public Health* 19, no. 4 (2022): 2196, https://doi.org/10.3390/ijerph19042196.

25. Rosalind Gill, "Surveillance Is a Feminist Issue," in *The Routledge Hand-*

*book of Contemporary Feminism*, ed. Tasha Oren and Andrea L. Press (Routledge, 2019), 148–161.

26. Ana Sofia Elias and Rosalind Gill, "Beauty Surveillance: The Digital Self-Monitoring Cultures of Neoliberalism," *European Journal of Cultural Studies* 21, no. 1 (2018): 59–77, https://doi.org/10.1177/1367549417705604.74.

27. Jasmine Fardouly and Lenny R. Vartanian, "Social Media and Body Image Concerns: Current Research and Future Directions," *Current Opinion in Psychology* 9 (2016): 1–5, https://doi.org/10.1016/j.copsyc.2015.09.005; Kim Rounsefell, Simone Gibson, Siân McLean, et al., "Social Media, Body Image and Food Choices in Healthy Young Adults: A Mixed Methods Systematic Review," *Nutrition and Dietetics* 77, no. 1 (2020): 19–40, https://doi.org/10.1111/1747-0080.12581.

28. Jasmine Fardouly, Phillippa C. Diedrichs, Lenny R. Vartanian, and Emma Halliwell, "Social Comparisons on Social Media: The Impact of Facebook on Young Women's Body Image Concerns and Mood," *Body Image* 13 (2015): 38–45, https://doi.org/10.1016/j.bodyim.2014.12.002.

29. Stephanie Easton, Katherine Morton, Zara Tappy, Daniella Francis, and Laura Dennison, "Young People's Experiences of Viewing the Fitspiration Social Media Trend: Qualitative Study," *Journal of Medical Internet Research* 20, no. 6 (2018): e219.

30. Marika Tiggemann and Mia Zaccardo, "'Strong Is the New Skinny': A Content Analysis of #Fitspiration Images on Instagram," *Journal of Health Psychology* 23, no. 8 (2016): 1003–1011, https://doi.org/10.1177/1359105316639436.

31. Ilaria Cataldo, Ilaria De Luca, Valentina Giorgetti, et al., "Fitspiration on Social Media: Body-Image and Other Psychopathological Risks Among Young Adults. A Narrative Review," *Emerging Trends in Drugs, Addictions, and Health* 1 (2021): 100010.

32. Pamela J. Bettis and Natalie G. Adams, "Short Skirts and Breast Juts: Cheerleading, Eroticism and Schools," *Sex Education* 6, no. 2 (2006): 121–133.

33. Eylem Gencer, "The Relationship Between Self-Esteem, Satisfaction with Life and Coach-Athlete Relationship," *Journal of Educational Issues* 6, no. 2 (2020): 493–505.

34. Amanda Mull, "Cheer Is Built on a Pyramid of Broken Bodies," *The Atlantic*, January 23, 2020, https://www.theatlantic.com/health/archive/2020/01/athletes-cheer-deserve-better/605326/.

35. Terry Gross, host, "Comic Hannah Einbinder on 'Hacks,' Cheerleading and Laughs as a Love Language," *Fresh Air*, NPR, June 17, 2024, https://www.npr.org/transcripts/nx-s1-5006044.

36. Tina R. Opie and Katherine W. Phillips, "Hair Penalties: The Negative Influence of Afrocentric Hair on Ratings of Black Women's Dominance and Professionalism," *Frontiers in Psychology* 6 (2015): https://doi.org/10.3389/fpsyg.2015.01311.

37. Yago Ramis, Miquel Torregrosa, Carme Viladrich, and Jaume Cruz, "The Effect of Coaches' Controlling Style on the Competitive Anxiety of Young Ath-

letes," *Frontiers in Psychology* 8 (2017): 572; Hunhyuk Choi, Yunduk Jeong, and Suk-Kyu Kim, "The Relationship Between Coaching Behavior and Athlete Burnout: Mediating Effects of Communication and the Coach–Athlete Relationship," *International Journal of Environmental Research and Public Health* 17, no. 22 (2020): 8618.

38. Laura Grindstaff and Emily West, "Cheerleading and the Gendered Politics of Sport," *Social Problems* 53, no. 4 (2006): 500–518.

39. Amy Moritz, "Cheerleading: Not Just for the Sidelines Anymore," *Sport in Society* 14, no. 5 (2011): 660–669.

CHEER NOTE #7

# The Booty Bill

In 2005, Al Edwards, a lay preacher and legislator in the Texas House of Representatives, proposed a bill banning cheerleaders, band members, and dance teams from performing "in a manner that is overtly sexually suggestive" at school events. Formally classified as HB 1476, the proposed legislation came to be known as "the booty bill."[1] According to *Texas Monthly*, legislators debated the merits of the bill for two hours on the house floor, even blasting the song "Shake Your Booty" and shaking pom-poms. John Kelso, a columnist for the *Austin American-Statesman*, quipped that perhaps the legislature should form a watchdog group to ensure compliance with the law. He suggested it be called the Bipartisan Observational Organization on Booty—or BOOB, for short.[2]

While the rest of the world laughed at the absurdity of the bill, some Texas legislators dug in their heels. They linked provocative cheerleading moves with increased rates of sexually transmitted diseases, AIDS, unplanned pregnancies, and the general moral decay of today's youth. "If I take my twelve-year-old son to a high school football game, I don't want to have to cover his eyes when the cheerleaders are on the field," Carl Isett told his fellow representatives. Even conservative talk show host Bill O'Reilly poked fun at the proposed bill, asking its sponsor, Edwards, "You wouldn't have the Texas Rangers out there busting the cheerleaders and putting them in cuffs, would you?"[3] The bill passed the house with a 65–56 vote and was sent to the Senate Education Committee, where the Booty Bill died in committee.

### Notes

1. Pamela Colloff, "Flipping Out," *Texas Monthly*, October 2005, https://www.texasmonthly.com/news-politics/flipping-out-3/.
2. Quoted in Colloff, "Flipping Out."
3. Quoted in Colloff, "Flipping Out."

CHAPTER 11

# For the Love of Cheer

## AN INSIDER'S VIEW

*Isabelle Bennington*

C-H-E-ER-LEA-DERS,
Oh yes, and we are the best!

Popular chant at National Cheerleaders Association cheer camp, 1970s

Cheerleaders occupy a nebulous space in the public imagination as well as in media and popular culture. They are seen as talentless, shallow, and promiscuous by some, while pressured to be enthusiastic, smiling, good-willed role models by others.[1] For decades, cheerleaders have been reliable fodder for public derision and ridicule. The vapid, not-so-bright Spartan Cheerleaders have appeared fifteen times on *Saturday Night Live*, yelling such cheers as "K-I-N-G, you can't take my king from me!" (at a chess tournament, because of course that is where you typically find cheerleaders). In movies and television series about high school life, cheerleaders are a staple. They are often depicted as cutthroat, duplicitous girls who relish their spot at the top of the high school food chain and will do whatever it takes to make sure they stay there. Their critics are many. Since the passage of Title IX, feminists have routinely characterized cheerleading as nothing more than a medium for female oppression, objectification, and sexualization. Cheerleaders' sole purpose, not only on the sidelines but in life, is to appeal to men. They have been equally denigrated by many male sports writers and commentators, such as Rick Reilly, who wrote in *Sports Illustrated*, "Cheerleaders have no more impact on the game than the night janitorial staff. They don't even face the game. They face the crowd, lost in their bizarre Muffy World."[2] Marty Beckerman, the teenage author of *Death to All Cheerleaders*, summarized his perception of cheerleading with this pithy comment: "They are a urine stain on the toilet seat of America."[3]

The negative depictions of cheerleaders by those outside the cheerleading world have implications for the millions of cheerleaders who participate in the sport. The many hardships they endure are diminished, and the real-world challenges and joys of cheer are obscured.[4] This chapter takes readers inside the world of collegiate, high school, and All Star cheer to highlight not only the joys of cheerleading but also the contemporary challenges cheerleaders face, including the following: (1) the constant fight against sexualization of the sport, (2) online hate speech, (3) toxic coaches and coaching, and (4) the invisibility of queer women in cheer. Drawing from over ten years of my experience as an All Star and high school cheerleader and several years as a coach, as well as from interviews with current and former cheerleaders, I present a cheerleader-positive insider view of the sport—a testimony to the strength, integrity, athleticism, and persistence of cheerleaders despite the many challenges they face.

## Short Skirts and Booty Pops: Sexualization in Cheerleading

Historically, women's bodies have been treated as a commodity, bought and sold for sexual pleasure. Nowhere is this more evident than in the oversexualization and selling of cheerleaders. Scholars attribute cheerleading's sexualization to several factors. For example, the short skirts and "infantile bows and ruby red lips" are said to invoke child pornography, while the "dance moves emulate strippers."[5] Some of the most well-known and widely recognized cheerleaders are the often scantily clad, gyrating dancers who cheer for professional National Football League (NFL) teams. While many argue that these squads aren't cheerleaders at all, their ubiquitousness in American culture contributes greatly to cheerleading's overly sexualized image. Media and popular culture reinforce the sexualization of cheerleaders through movies, television, and the adult film industry. Media of all types use vitriolic discourse that frames cheerleaders as purely sexual beings rather than the strong, powerful athletes they are.[6] Some scholars argue that cheerleading's sexualized aspects draw many middle and high school girls to the activity because cheerleading is one of the few places for young girls to "try on" sexuality without being labeled as sluts, whores, or skanks.[7] While this may draw some to the sport, most cheerleaders do not see themselves as sex objects, and many—especially those who compete—work diligently to distance themselves from the overly sexualized cheerleader represented in pop culture.

While cheerleaders usually do not see their involvement in cheerleading as sexual, they are aware that sexualization leads to cheer being trivialized in the larger culture. Cheer athletes believe that outsiders place too much emphasis on cheerleading's sexualized aspects when assessing the worth of the sport. Cheerleading insiders, including many in the cheer industry, have taken steps to distance cheerleading from its sexualized image. For example, many cheer competitions have instituted rules about "provocative uniforms and moves," and judges deduct points at competitions and tryouts for "inappropriate" (i.e., sexually provocative) dance moves, cheers, or motions.[8] Some critics claim that these penalties are a form of censorship that restricts creativity and expression. Others contend that these restrictions are a positive step in keeping routines and performances age appropriate while allowing athletes to continue to enjoy the performative aspects of cheer. This eschewal of the erotic in cheerleading within the cheer world runs counter to the depictions of cheerleaders in popular culture. Nevertheless, most cheerleaders accept the artifice, adornment, and performative aspects of cheerleading that lead to its sexualization. And many cheerleaders would say they enjoy the glitter, bows, and makeup. They do not see them as inherently sexual; they simply consider them a "fun bonus" and a part of what makes the sport what it is.[9]

This contradictory stance within cheerleading of renouncing the erotic while incorporating some feminized and sexualized aspects presents a challenge to cheerleaders and their coaches. One approach to reconciling this contradiction is to remove the blame for sexualization from the athletes and the spirit industry and to place it on those who are doing the sexualization. As one Reddit user, PracticallyPerfectMP, explains, "Cheerleading in and of itself is not creepy or sexualized. The viewer sexualizes things, such as cheerleading." This approach, unfortunately, does not mean that cheerleaders are unaffected by their intense sexualization. In fact, many believe it to be one of the major problems cheer athletes face and a primary impediment to official recognition as a National Collegiate Athletic Association (NCAA) sport. Gymnastics coach and current collegiate cheerleader Penelope H. notes, "Sexualization is so evident everywhere in this sport."[10] Kendall S., a cheerleader with twelve years of experience, concurs: "Cheer is often sexualized in ways that aren't true to the sport." Interviewee Kristin S., who cheered for nine years, cites the intense sexualization as the reason she is hesitant to allow her children to cheer. Cheerleaders who have participated in the sport for years can attest that the sexualization of cheer begins early, and the accompanying discomfort and shame associated with the sport follow many cheerleaders into adulthood. Cheerleaders know that this sexualization does not reflect who they are or what their sport is, but they often feel powerless to change it. Kendall S. explains, "People who make these unjustifiable comments just don't understand the sport and don't respect it for what it is."

The continued sexualization of cheerleaders in the public imagination, as well as in media and popular culture, means that cheerleaders, even minors, are often subject to highly sexualized and degrading speech, stares, and unwanted gestures. Worse still, cheerleaders are blamed for their own sexualization and sexualized treatment in ways closely akin to a woman being blamed for her own sexual harassment or assault. The framing of cheerleaders as complicit in their own sexualization is rampant on social media, where both internet trolls and feminists seem to take great delight in vilifying women and girls who cheer.

## Shake It Off! Online Criticism of Cheerleaders

Like traffic jams, annoying commercial jingles, or a rival sports team, for decades cheerleading has been one of those things that people just love to hate. The scholar Emma Jane (Tom) has written extensively about how cheerleaders are often the subject of contemptuous representation both by mainstream media outlets and in public forums, blogs, and readers' comment sections.[11] She argues that cheerleaders are often "used as multi-purpose scapegoats, becoming socially sanctioned outlets for misogyny," as they are subject to virulent speech that would be socially and professionally unacceptable in most contexts, especially in journalism and academia.[12] As discussed in chapter 3 of this volume, many observers and participants believe that the resistance to recognizing cheerleading as a sport, which would lead to greater regulation and enhanced safety, is fostered by this continued maligning of cheerleaders and their sport in mainstream media.

Jane compares the hatred of cheerleaders and the vitriol directed toward them to fetishism. She writes, "The nature of the discourse suggests that many of these critics gain pleasure from publicly expressing their objections to cheerleading to the point where their interest in this activity can be interpreted as fetishistic."[13] Many public forums about cheerleading have turned into competitions over who can create the most unsettling and socially impermissible comments about cheerleaders, many of whom are real-life women and girls, not fictionalized characters. Jane references a video uploaded in 2008 of a high school cheerleader falling from a stunt that is accompanied by the caption "Cheerleader falls on her face in front of the school. Watch the two girls in the audience give each other [a high] five when the slut falls on her face."[14] The video and caption were followed by comments such as "Haha stupid cunt" and "Odd that she was splitting her minge lips for the audience one second then splitting her other lips on the floor the next."[15] One comment even ponders if the injured girl might be better able to perform oral sex because she lost her front teeth. Over a decade ago, Jane argued that such comments reflected domains of speech that would be considered sexist or misogynist in other contexts.[16] An examination of more recent online discussions, specifically on Reddit, reveals that this is still true.

On the subreddit r/NoStupidQuestions, user diliberto123 asked in 2021, "What is the point of cheerleaders?" As evidenced by the question and its various responses, many outside the world of cheerleading still have no idea what contemporary cheerleading is or what cheerleaders do. User EmotionalMycologist replied, "I was always told the crowd is for the players, and cheerleaders are for the crowd." On the subreddit r/unpopularopinion, user Codymichael511 stated that "cheerleading is a weird, creepy tradition." As the following sampling of comments posted to r/unpopularopinion and r/NoStupidQuestions in 2019 and 2021 illustrates, the most frequent type of commentary reflects the sexualization of cheerleaders:

> Yeah, I never understood the concept of Cheerleading. It's like teaching girls to be attention whore[s] to get all the Jocks. Our world is truly fucked.
>
> To look hot for the dads and to bang their boys on the team.
>
> It's eye candy. What more do we need to explain?
>
> A future stripper has to start somewhere.

> So the pretty girls don't have to compete in a real sport.
>
> Cheerleading is stripping. I have always thought it was funny that they let kids do it, but hey, I'm not complaining.

These comments highlight that sexism, sexualization, and caustic public speech against cheerleaders are still prevalent and accepted.

It is not just internet trolls who participate in the denigration of cheerleaders in public discourse. As discussed throughout this book, feminists, including scholars and journalists, are often highly critical of cheerleaders and their sport.[17] On the r/Feminism subreddit in 2022, user Flat-Ad1599 asked why cheerleading at games is still "a thing." In response, user cockyUma stated that they couldn't believe it, calling cheerleading "beyond stupid and everything trashy." Others who responded expressed a feeling of ambiguity toward cheerleading. On the one hand, many expressed their respect for cheerleaders' athleticism, calling them daredevils and incredible athletes. On the other hand, most still felt that cheerleading's connection to sexualization—which was most often attributed to the uniforms—made the activity exploitative and demeaning. One now-deleted account commented, "I'm a huge NFL fan, and yeah totally agree, it's gross. Not the act of cheerleading itself but how they are used—as objects." "It's so goddamn stupid that the women are virtually nude," echoed user RowynWalkingwolf. It is important to note, however, that both comments refer to adult cheerleaders performing for NFL teams. When speaking about competitive cheer, Reddit user Friday-cat and others acknowledged its difference from professional cheerleading and agreed that cheerleading is a sport in its own right. Perhaps if a greater number of those outside the world of cheerleading understood the differences between the extremely sexualized dancing of NFL professional squads and the competitive athletics of high school, collegiate, and All Star cheer teams, cheerleaders would finally begin to shed their close association with a hypersexualized image.

Undoubtedly, the sexualization and idealization of emphasized femininity within cheer without a formal sport designation may explain why it seems to invite more haters than other similar sports, such as gymnastics. It's beyond the scope of this chapter to speculate on the motivations for their hatred. Perhaps they hate girls and women in general, or sexual objectification of any kind, or cheer's association with popularity and conventional femininity, from which critics themselves may have been excluded.

Regardless of the reason or motivation behind the criticism and rancor, harmful characterizations of cheerleaders often emanate from outsiders who lack adequate knowledge and understanding of contemporary cheer, or who gain pleasure in the vilification or fetishization of cheerleaders. That said, cheerleaders also face problems from within.

## There's No Hiding in the Back: Coaches, Surveillance, and Unobtainable Expectations

Cheerleaders are constantly aware that they are being watched—by teammates, coaches, peers, and spectators. As discussed in the preceding chapter, cheerleaders' bodies are assumed to be sites for public consumption and critique. Participants are constantly criticized for their weight, their hair, their breast size, their body type, and their overall physical attractiveness.[18] While this criticism often emanates from strangers online, many cheerleaders attribute their continued struggles with self-surveillance to the harsh critiques of their coaches.

Cheerleading takes place in an incredibly competitive environment. As do all athletes, cheerleaders compare themselves to others, especially those with more advanced skills or who compete on higher-level teams. This leads some, such as high school freshman Avery B., to question their abilities and even their placement on the team: "Sometimes you just have to try and let it go, even if the feeling never goes away." Coaches can either quash or foster such highly competitive environments. Former All Star and collegiate cheerleader Kayla A. felt that she received no support from her coaches when she was struggling with mental blocks during tumbling. A mental block occurs when an athlete is suddenly unable to force their body to perform a skill in which they were formerly confident. These blocks happen for a variety of reasons. Some cheerleaders attribute them to bad falls; others say they appear out of nowhere or arise from factors external to cheerleading. A mental block can cause an athlete immense anxiety and fear, especially when a coach doesn't believe the struggle is real. This was the case with Kayla, who received little support from her coaches when she struggled with executing difficult tumbling moves. She believes that the contentious relationship with her coaches contributed heavily to her struggles with mental health and eventually killed her love for cheerleading. Former All Star cheerleader Savannah S. reports that her coaches "instilled an idea within me that I would never be as good as the girl next to me, and that my friends were with my competitors. . . . It destroyed me." Some coaches may believe that fostering a competitive environment pushes cheerleaders to be the best athletes possible, but in doing so, they run the risk of creating a negative environment that may cause serious damage to the emotional and mental health of the athletes in their care.

Even worse, some coaches draw comparisons that go beyond discussions of skill. Collegiate cheerleader Ainsley R. tells the story of a former coach who lined up athletes in front of the mirror to inspect their appearance: "After she looked at each athlete individually, she proceeded to go down the line and tell each athlete in front of the whole team what was wrong with their bodies. She made sure she found something wrong with every single athlete's body, most of which were teammates' biggest critiques about themselves, which in turn made them even more self-conscious." Another former All Star cheerleader, Chloe T., shares that she still struggles with disordered eating because of the comments and actions of an adult figure within her cheerleading community. When the individual decided to change the size on Chloe's order for practice wear without her knowledge, it led to spiraling thoughts that she was getting too big for the sport. "Ever since then, I have struggled with eating consistently, not feeling guilty for eating, or feeling sick after," states Chloe. As noted in the previous chapter, coaches' failure to support their athletes, the unrealistic expectations they place upon them, and the constant and intense scrutiny of athletes' bodies can lead to long-term, harmful beliefs and behaviors that leave lasting impacts. Further, these negative experiences with coaches are often the primary reason why cheerleaders leave the sport they love. Former college cheerleader Kaitlyn B. states that she pursued cheer in college because she loved the sport, but was "disappointed with the team environment and coaching staff," leading to her retirement from competitive cheerleading. Kaitlyn continues to stay involved with cheerleading as a Universal Cheerleaders Association (UCA) staff member. But her experience is not unique among the many thousands of athletes who have chosen to leave cheerleading behind because of the impacts of toxic coaching.

Fortunately, many cheer coaches are supportive of their athletes and have managed to find an appropriate balance between high expectations and compassionate care. Fans of the Netflix hit *Cheer* often point to Navarro College coach Monica Aldama as one such coach. She has been compared to football coaching icons like Nick Saban and Andy Reid for her ability to motivate her athletes to execute, perform, and win. She also earned some unexpected praise for her unequivocal support of her openly gay (primarily Black) male cheerleaders, particularly La'Darius Marshall, who pops, dances, smiles, and performs in a gender-nonconforming way.[19] While this support is notable, it has also led many to question whether Aldama would have been as supportive of an openly gay female cheerleader. Like most cheerleading teams, the Navarro College cheer team had no openly queer or lesbian women.

## "I Do It for the Girls and the Gays, That's It": The Missing Discourse in Cheerleading

Netflix's *Cheer* revealed something to the general public that insiders have long known: Cheerleading at the collegiate level is unique in the world of sports. Not only do men and women train, practice, and compete side by side, but openly gay male cheerleaders and straight-identifying male cheerleaders work with each other daily with little conflict. That is not to suggest that every coed collegiate squad is a safe space for gay athletes. But for many LGBTQ+ men, cheerleading at the collegiate and All Star level has proven to be a less hostile, more welcoming environment than that found in most traditional sports. Further, queerness in cheer has become more prevalent as American society has also become more accepting of identities that fall outside of the heteronorm. Nonetheless, because of cheerleading's deep roots in femininity and sexualization, there continues to be a double standard for who is allowed to be queer in the world of cheerleading.

As noted in chapter 4, cheerleading can and often is a welcoming and inclusive space for gay men. Even as masculinity within cheer is policed, many men—not just queer men—find cheer to be a liberatory space in which femininity can be explored in conjunction with masculinity.[20] This does not mean that straight men are discouraged from joining cheer teams; in fact, it is quite the opposite. Particularly on coed collegiate teams, where gender roles are much more clearly defined, men's successful performance of traditional masculinity (i.e., appearing strong and athletic and refraining from any "feminine" moves, motions, or actions, such as dancing or showing excessive spirit) may help enhance the image of cheerleading as a tough, athletic, and acceptable activity for men.[21] But within the world of All Star cheer, gay men are often praised for their performance of femininity through dancing, animated facial expressions, and exaggerated demonstrations of emotion. Gay men's acceptance in the cheerleading world may be due in part to the sexualization experienced by female cheerleaders.

As Laura Grindstaff and Emily West note, heterosexual male cheerleaders often sexualize their female teammates in order to prove their straightness.[22] For example, to deflect assumptions that only gay men cheer, straight male cheerleaders talk about touching their female teammates' crotches and spending time with the most sexually desirable women, or even hooking up with them. Thus, for female cheerleaders, gay men offer a safe, nonsexualizing alternative.

Traditionally, cheerleading has not been as safe an environment for queer female-presenting cheerleaders. Whether because of cheerleading's history as an activity in which women support men, its continued use of emphasized femininity, or its constant sexualization, female cheerleaders are presumed to be heterosexual.[23] As explained in chapter 9 of this volume, female cheerleaders, unlike female athletes in other sports, do not have their sexual identity constantly questioned. After all, many female athletes in more traditional sports often emphasize their femininity to avoid being labeled as queer, but the "girliness" of cheer allows women to express their (presumably masculine) athleticism without being accused of lesbianism.[24] For straight women, the assumed heterosexuality of cheer has been beneficial, especially during times when the involvement of women and girls in sports was a radical idea. But for queer women, the heteronormativity of cheer has required them to remain in the closet, or it has pushed them away from the sport entirely.

Many queer female cheerleaders report feelings of shame as they begin coming to terms with their sexuality. Some worry that the close bodily contact that cheerleading requires when stunting, or the tendency for cheerleaders to change clothing and get ready for practices, games, and competitions in shared spaces, might lead teammates to feel uncomfortable around them if they reveal their sexuality. Many have struggled with hiding their sexual identity just as they were first beginning to learn about that part of themselves: "As I got older, I started understanding more, and cheering with all women, most of us were in sports bras; I had to shove that feeling deep down," states Kayla A. Former All Star cheerleader Alyssa M. notes that despite support from most people, she lost friends and felt her teammates grow distant after she came out as bisexual. Kristin S. shares that her teammates' homophobic comments caused her to feel uncomfortable in her program and contributed to internalized homophobia: "A large part of me being in the closet for eight years, even with accepting family and friends, was because of shame I internalized at cheer."

Perhaps cheer is slowly becoming more accepting of all queer cheerleaders, including queer women. As Kendall S. states, "When it comes to sexuality, cheerleading is open to anyone." Current All Star cheerleader Raegan G. shares that exposure to the vast and diverse cheerleading community transformed her perspective on herself and others:

> I didn't grow up learning very much about different sexualities and that you should love whoever you want. I honestly thought that there was only one way to love, which led to a lot of confusion towards what love actually was. That was until I joined cheer, which opened my eyes completely. The cheer community is so huge and diverse, and seeing so many different people has really changed my perspective from everything that I knew before. I learned at a young age that there is a lot of hate in the world . . . but cheer taught me to rise above and that if I am not myself, then I am someone else, which is no way to live. Cheer is a huge reason why I am the way I am today and why I'm so certain and proud of the person I've become.

As queer girls and women become more open about their sexuality, and their inclusion on teams becomes as commonplace as their gay male counterparts, their visibility may change the sexist and sexualized perceptions of cheerleading in positive ways. Perhaps naysayers may finally realize that cheerleaders do not participate in their sport because they want to please men. They do not see themselves as secondary to male athletes, nor do they see their uniform and other feminine accouterments as anti-feminist. Their reasons for cheering are much deeper than a simple desire for the male gaze.

### Let's Get Fired Up! What's There to Cheer About in Cheerleading?

Given all the challenges discussed in this chapter, one may rightly ask, Why does anyone choose to cheer? Certainly, many of us have considered quitting for one reason or another: when the practices get tough, when our bodies are exhausted, or when we think we just can't possibly run one more routine or cheer one more game. Some consider it more seriously than others, and of course some do quit, but the idea of quitting cheerleading has become a sort of running joke in the cheer community. Instagram accounts dedicated to all things cheerleading make memes of it every spring, posting some version of "When you said all season you're going to quit, but you show up to next season's tryouts anyways!" Every spring we laugh and forward the memes to our friends, because we know that for all its faults, cheerleading reels us in time and time again.

Cheerleaders, and those closest to them, know the extreme difficulty of the sport—the toll it takes, not just physically but mentally. Grueling practices, injuries, sore muscles, and aching joints only skim the surface of the hardships we endure for the sake of our beloved sport. We must exhibit tremendous mental strength when we convince ourselves not only to perform inhuman feats but also to endure the brunt of society's worst sexism, sexualization, and prejudices. Further, cheerleading's lack of regulation—caused in part by a cheer industry and a pseudo-governing body more interested in generating profits than protecting young, vulnerable athletes—has led to toxic behaviors and environments that are accepted as inherent facts of the sport. These obstacles leave many athletes and parents with conflicting feelings surrounding cheerleading. Some choose to leave the sport behind, but as evidenced by cheerleading's continued popularity, many stay. The reasons why are as diverse as cheerleaders themselves, but there is one commonality among them all. It is the simplest answer to why cheerleaders do what we do: We cheer because we love it.

Most people outside of the relatively small world of cheerleading don't understand the joy the sport brings to its athletes. It is common to be asked why we don't participate in other, seemingly comparable sports, such as gymnastics. After all, gymnastics is afforded more respect (e.g., Olympic status), has its own governing bodies, and offers better career opportunities and financial incentives. We cheerleaders roll our eyes, because we know there is nothing like cheer. Critics think that cheerleaders only cheer to gain the attention of men, to become popular, or to wear cute outfits. While these reasons might draw some to the sport, they are not enough to inspire us to continuously push ourselves to our physical and mental limits. The reasoning must be deeper; there must be something that cheer has to offer that participants can't find anywhere else.

Many cite the community and companionship that cheer offers as the reason they love the sport. Kaitlyn B. says it best: "There's just something special about the community associated with cheerleading." For some, cheerleading offers an escape from tough times at home or school. "Cheerleading has been my home away from home for as long as I can remember. It's where I go when I just need to forget everything else in my life," says Ainsley R. The sense of community and friendship that cheerleading provides is hard to find anywhere else, as Chloe T. expresses: "Cheer gave me some of the best long-lasting friends I could ever ask for. My teammates were my family." Through shared experiences such as tough practices, competitions, victories, and defeats, cheerleaders grow close with their teammates as they witness and share each other's best and worst moments.

Many participants also state that cheerleading has taught them valuable lessons they could not have learned anywhere else, shaping them into the people they are today. "Cheer has gotten me through some of the toughest periods of my life, and I'm grateful for every second and all that it taught me," says Kristin S. Collegiate cheerleader Leah H. concurs: "I love watching myself improve with each rep of a skill or stunt that I do and the feeling of accomplishment when I get a skill that I was working hard to get." Cheerleading, like other sports, teaches the importance of teamwork, grit, and drive, and athletes feel that these values become fundamental to their identity. As current All Star cheerleader Raegan G. states, "I loved the challenges it put upon my mental and physical state, and I can say with full certainty that cheer has made me the person I am today."

Cheerleaders are aware of the sport's sexualized image and the criticisms of others, who often express their contempt publicly. Despite outside negativity and internal and external challenges, cheerleaders claim that their love for cheerleading and for their teammates motivates them to keep going. "The reason I continue to cheer is because I don't know where I'd be without it," says high school cheerleader Avery B. "Cheer has helped me step out of my comfort zone, become a better person, and given me so many friends." Even those whose experiences, for one reason or another, were less favorable look back on their time in cheerleading with appreciation. Savannah S. states, "The coaches were a problem, but the girls never were. I loved being in a predominantly female environment who, despite being pitted against each other, still felt like family to me." Because they love their sport and experience great joy in it, many cheerleaders can brush off negativity from the outside world. Some, such as Kayla A., even express smugness toward cheer critics: "If anyone wants to talk negatively on it, I would like to see you try to do what some of my coaches made me do." Athletes know their worth and know that what they do is difficult. To them, nothing else matters. Collegiate cheerleader Alexis R. states, "Yes, there are negative stereotypes with cheer, but to me, unless you do it, no one will ever know what it's like to have a hard practice at cheer or do multiple full outs in one practice. So let them say what they want to because you know, and your team knows, what they do and how hard it is."

## Notes

1. Emma Jane, "Beyond Antifandom: Cheerleading, Textual Hate and New Media Ethics," *International Journal of Cultural Studies* 17, no. 2 (2014): 175–190, https://doi.org/10.1177/1367877913514330; Natalie G. Adams and Pamela J. Bettis, "Commanding the Room in Short Skirts: Cheering as the Embodiment of Ideal Girlhood," *Gender and Society* 17, no. 1 (2003): 73–91, https://doi.org/10.1177/0891243202238979; Natalie G. Adams and Pamela J. Bettis, *Cheerleader! An American Icon* (Palgrave Macmillan, 2003); Laura Grindstaff and Emily West, "Cheerleading and the Gendered Politics of Sport," *Social Problems* 53, no. 4 (2006): 500–518.

2. Rick Reilly, "Sis! Boom! Bah! Humbug!," *Sports Illustrated*, October 18, 1999, 116.

3. Marty Beckerman, *Death to All Cheerleaders* (Infected Press, 2000).

4. Megan Abbot, "Looking Past the Smile and the Sheen," *New York Times*, July 26, 2012.

5. Jessica S. Gullion, "Cheerleader: A Feminist Mom, Her Pre-Teen Daughter, and the Spaces for Girls in American Football," *Continuum* 30, no. 5 (2016): 542–546, https://doi.org/10.1080/10304312.2016.1210755; A. Patrice Oppliger, *Girls Gone Skank: The Sexualization of Girls in American Culture* (McFarland, 2008).

6. Oppliger, *Girls Gone Skank*; Adams and Bettis, *Cheerleader!*

7. Jane, "Beyond Antifandom"; Adams and Bettis, *Cheerleader!*; Pamela J. Bettis and Natalie G. Adams, "Short Skirts and Breast Juts: Cheerleading, Eroticism and Schools," *Sex Education* 6, no. 2 (2006): 121–133; Oppliger, *Girls Gone Skank*.

8. Grindstaff and West, "Cheerleading and the Gendered Politics of Sport"; Adams and Bettis, *Cheerleader!*

9. Gullion, "Cheerleader."

10. All names from my interviews, conducted in December 2024, are pseudonyms.

11. Emma Tom, "Flip Skirt Fatales: How Media Fetish Sidelines Cheerleaders," *Platform: Journal of Media and Communication* 1 (2010): 52–70.

12. Jane, "Beyond Antifandom."

13. Tom, "Flip Skirt Fatales."

14. Jane, "Beyond Antifandom."

15. Jane, "Beyond Antifandom."

16. Jane, "Beyond Antifandom."

17. For example, see Amanda Mull, "Cheer Is Built on a Pyramid of Broken Bodies," *The Atlantic*, January 22, 2020, https://www.theatlantic.com/health/archive/2020/01/athletes-cheer-deservebetter/605326/; Jia Tolentino, "The Pathos of 'Cheer' and the Wild Deception of Cheerleading," *New Yorker*, January 16, 2020, https://www.newyorker.com/culture/cultural-comment/the-pathos-ofcheer-and-the-wild-deceptions-of-cheerleading.

18. Jane, "Beyond Antifandom."

19. Mary Anderson, "Today's All-American Cheerleaders Are Proud Black LGBTQ Men," *MIC*, January 22, 2020, https://www.mic.com/p/netflixs-new-docu-series-cheer-celebrates-black-queer-athletes-21738537.

20. Eric Anderson, "Orthodox and Inclusive Masculinity: Competing Masculinities Among Heterosexual Men in a Feminized Terrain," *Sociological Perspectives* 48, no. 3 (2005): 337–355; Eric Anderson, "'Being Masculine Is Not About Who You Sleep With . . .': Heterosexual Athletes Contesting Masculinity and the One-Time Rule of Homosexuality," *Sex Roles* 58 (2008): 104–115.

21. Grindstaff and West, "Cheerleading and the Gendered Politics of Sport."

22. Grindstaff and West, "Cheerleading and the Gendered Politics of Sport."

23. Adams and Bettis, *Cheerleader!*

24. Adams and Bettis, *Cheerleader!*; Grindstaff and West, "Cheerleading and the Gendered Politics of Sport."

# PART IV

# Cheer Trouble

CHAPTER 12

# Gimme an *F*

## CHEERLEADING GOES TO THE SUPREME COURT

*Zoie Comer and Stanley J. Murphy*

### Brandi Snaps

On May 28, 2017, a date that will live as a beacon illuminating freedom of expression for all Americans, outshining those Friday night lights that too often confine our image of cheer as a national phenomenon—a shared and profoundly mistaken image of superficiality, distilled into a stereotyped world of pom-poms and somersaults—young Brandi Levy Snapped. She didn't break. No, she just sent a Snap to a couple hundred of her fellow Snapchatters. Unjustly denied her spot on the varsity cheer team—for which she had striven to the last ounce of her physical energies and spiritual focus, all the while with a perfect, varsity-level smile—she was passed over for someone who hadn't even been on the JV team! A freshman at that! Brandi, with a passionate intensity known only to those sixteen-year-olds for whom life is effectively over, with a prospect of a slow but certain descent into a matronly life of quiet desperation, put her anger and shame into words. While off school grounds shopping at the Cocoa Hut, a local convenience store, emotion conquered prudence, and Brandi Snapped. Knowing that brevity is indeed the soul of wit, and that Snapchat enforces Polonius's wisdom with a strict character limit, she wrote, "Fuck school fuck softball fuck cheer fuck everything."[1] If any clarification was needed, she accompanied her words with a selfie sporting the universal finger signal expressing the same sentiment (fig. 12.1).

Inevitably, her Snap leaked from her so-called friends. School authori-

FIGURE 12.1. *Screenshot of Brandi Levy's 2017 Snapchat. Exhibit D-1 in* Mahanoy Area School District v. B.L. *(2021).*

ties found out. Sensing either a teachable moment or venting their own anger, they disciplined Brandi. She was disqualified from the JV cheer team for a year for violating Mahanoy Area High School's cheerleading rules, which prohibited cheerleaders from posting any "negative information" about cheerleading online. Brandi and her parents sought and received legal help from the ACLU of Pennsylvania, which filed a federal lawsuit on her behalf. Four years later, her case challenging the school board's discipline on First Amendment grounds made its way to the US Supreme Court in *Mahanoy Area School District v. B.L.* (2021).[2]

## The First Amendment and the Schoolhouse Gates

The First Amendment protects many forms of expression. From soapbox rants, to campaign leaflets, airplane banners, and bumper stickers, to armbands worn in silent protest, the speech that is protected can be symbolic, artistic, or political. It can be deliberately provocative, a literary masterpiece, or inane and senseless ramblings. The protection applies to new and old technologies alike. It protects both adults and children, the sacred and the profane. But "free speech" has never meant "all speech." Governments and leaders can impose some limitations, depending on both the nature of the speech and the context in which it is made. When the leader is a public school board and the speaker is one of its students, the courts frequently get involved.

One of the Supreme Court's first efforts to explain that students were citizens and were no longer to be treated or viewed as custodial wards of their schools came in *Tinker v. Des Moines Independent Community School District* (1969).[3] In December 1965, students at a public school in Iowa wore black armbands to school as a silent protest against the Vietnam War. Mary Beth Tinker was a thirteen-year-old junior high student at the time. Reflecting on the decision to wear the armbands, she explains, "For me it was all about the emotions, the feelings about the war being so sad watching the news. . . . We would see horrific stories of children running from their burning huts and the world looked like it was on fire. The soldiers in their body bags and they would give this body count and it's just horrible."[4] The students were suspended, and their parents sued the school for violation of their children's right to free speech. The school argued that wearing the armbands could disrupt learning, but the Supreme Court disagreed. It decided that passive, nondisruptive political speech in public schools (e.g., wearing armbands to protest war) is protected by the First Amendment. The court explained that such forms of expression do not and cannot justify disciplinary action unless the expression materially or substantially disrupts the work of the school or interferes with the rights of others. The decision enforced the idea that state-operated public schools cannot serve as enclaves of totalitarianism, and that school officials have no right to exercise absolute authority over their students. While *Tinker* was an important decision in the protection of students' free speech rights, it also explained that these rights have limits. Schools, the court ruled, may limit student speech when it materially or substantially interferes with a school's mission of teaching students.

Another student free speech case came to the court nearly forty years later in *Morse v. Frederick* (2007).[5] Joseph Frederick, a senior high schooler in Juneau, Alaska, attended an Olympic torch relay in downtown Juneau as part of a school-supervised activity. While there, Frederick held up a banner with a seemingly important yet enigmatic message: "Bong Hits 4 Jesus." When school officials told him to put away the banner in fear that it might advocate illegal drug activity, Frederick refused. He was then suspended for violating a school policy that forbade advocating for the use of illegal drugs. The Supreme Court sided with the school, holding that the First Amendment does not prevent school administrators from restricting student expression reasonably viewed as promoting drug activity. The court contrasted this case with *Tinker*, explaining that the use of armbands there was considered political speech, only to be prohibited if it substantially disrupted the educational process. It held that the Constitution and its First Amendment affords lesser protections to certain types of speech at school or school-sponsored events. Thus the phrase "Bong Hits 4 Jesus" at a school event would not be afforded the same protection as armbands worn in an antiwar protest. The Supreme Court found that the special characteristics of the school environment, along with the governmental interest in preventing student drug abuse, would allow schools to restrict student expression reasonably related to promoting such abuse.

The Supreme Court has heard and decided a myriad of cases that discuss students' First Amendment rights. In 1986, it ruled in *Bethel School District v. Fraser* that there is no First Amendment violation when a school punishes a student for lewd, vulgar, indecent, and plainly offensive speech during classes, assemblies, or other times when students are forced to listen.[6] In 1988, the court upheld in *Hazelwood School District v. Kuhlmeier* a school principal's decision to delete stories from a school newspaper that discussed birth control and sexual activity, reasoning that educators may exercise editorial control over the style and content of student speech in school-sponsored expressive activities, so long as their actions are reasonably related to legitimate pedagogical concerns.[7]

## Brandi's Trip to the Supreme Court

Brandi Levy's legal trek to the nation's highest court began when the ACLU of Pennsylvania agreed to take her case. Upset that their daughter was punished for speaking out on social media on her own time and off school grounds, and before seeking legal help, the Levy family initially approached the coaches who had decided to suspend Brandi from the JV team. When the coaches held their line, the Levy family decided legal action was necessary. Confident the school's decision was wrong, the family believed that the school was acting more like a parent by imposing punishment for off-campus activity. While the ACLU of Pennsylvania takes only a handful of the thousands of cases presented to them each year, there was something special about Brandi's case. Molly Tack-Hooper, an ACLU of Pennsylvania attorney when Brandi's case came in, was instrumental in the decision to take the case. Tack-Hooper explains that she fought hard to take Brandi's case and expected the school to argue that cheerleaders are emblematic of positivity and can be punished for swearing on the weekends (unlike their male peers on the football team, for whom Saturdays are a chance to practice whole new combinations of profanity learned from their coaches the night before). When they agreed to represent her, the ACLU thought that Brandi's case would be an easy win. The legal team at the ACLU believed that Brandi's problem would be resolved with a simple letter asking school authorities to reverse their decision, resulting in her reinstatement on the team. Brandi would now be free to Snap, unfettered by the constraints of positivity. Though the ACLU predicted an easy vindication for Brandi, the school authorities and cheer coaches fought back, holding firm in their position that cheerleaders essentially exist as an exception to students' free speech.[8]

Once the school board dug in and maintained its absolutist position that Brandi should be punished for her off-campus Snap, the ACLU, disappointed but undeterred from its commitment to Brandi and her family, filed suit in federal court in 2019.[9] They urged the court to recognize that young people's ability to express themselves, whether in the lunch line at school or in the checkout line at the convenience store, was worthy of constitutional protection. And more broadly, the ACLU was committed to the proposition that public schools should not have the authority to run a student's life both inside and outside the schoolyard gates. The federal judge agreed and ruled for Brandi. In most cases that would have ended the matter, but the school board's feet were firmly planted. The school board appealed to the next higher court and lost again. At this point, the federal court system offers slim prospects for the losing side. Most take their lumps, shake hands with the winners, and live with the result. Not this school board. Embodying the never-quit spirit that makes fourth quarters worth hanging around for, the school board asked the US Supreme Court for two things: to grant certiorari (i.e., to take the case), which against all statistical odds it did; and to reverse the decisions of the two lower courts, which it didn't. In an 8–1 decision, the Supreme Court ruled in *Mahanoy Area School District v. B.L.* (2021) that Brandi's Snap was protected by the First Amendment. The cursing cheerleader had prevailed!

But why did the Supreme Court take on this case? The court is asked to review thousands of cases a year, many with profound, sometimes life-or-death implications and significance for the boundaries of constitutional protection. The great majority of those cases, even those involving death, crippling injury, or loss—for example, from a police officer's excessive force, abuse in a state-owned mental institution, or loss of a home to the powers of a state—never have a chance to be considered by the highest court. To some observers, it might appear that the Supreme Court, in taking on a case about a profane Snapchat, indulged in idle triviality at the expense of vastly more consequential matters. One could argue that this case, on its surface, is only about a teenager who had a burst of anger over what appears to be an insignificant injury. The case of a teenager deprived of her place on the JV cheer team and her right to spew expletives on social media might seem unworthy among a sea of cases of great and broad consequence. To many observers, perhaps, there could not be anything less significant than the right to be on the cheer team. But the court recognized, as had the ACLU of Pennsylvania, that much more was at stake. Brandi's Snap stands fully within the court's precedent that "the vigilant protection of constitutional freedom is nowhere more vital than in the community of American schools."[10]

Brandi's rant, the discipline meted out to her, the school's intransigence, and the ACLU's stalwart dedication to the First Amendment now mark a waypoint in the evolution of American law. The ruling in Brandi's case reinforced and extended the proposition that "it can hardly be argued that either students or teachers shed their constitutional rights to freedom of speech or expression at the schoolhouse gate."[11] Although superficially about cheer and Snaps, Brandi's case also gave the court an opportunity to examine and explain its consistent cautionary acknowledgment that protection of students' First Amendment rights in the context of schools is not always simple: "The Court has repeatedly emphasized the need for affirming comprehensive authority of the States and of school officials, consistent with fundamental constitutional safeguards, to prescribe and control the conduct of schools."[12] Although Brandi stood at the doors of the Cocoa Hut rather than the schoolhouse gate, her right to cheer and her right to express her frustration were taken from her. And just as Brandi was frustrated with her failure to make the varsity cheer team, so too was the school administration frustrated (rather, they were "visibly upset") with Brandi's Snapchat and the feared resulting inability to "avoid chaos."[13] But Brandi won her case, the First Amendment gained some ground, and the law of the land recognized that cheer is not just about pom-poms anymore.

To the extent that cheer is a metaphor, perhaps this case offers a way to look deeper into the rituals embedded in the American identity—as important as Fourth of July fireworks shows and Thanksgiving turkey carvings. While it would be easy to brush off Brandi's case as unworthy of Supreme

Court precedent or even as a lark, it stands as a pinnacle of rights that transcend cheer and Snap. At stake among the principles of American law and pedagogy is the ability of students to speak their minds without retribution. This case combines the perennially recurring issues of free speech and school powers, within a new age of expressive activity. While conflicts between government authority and free expression were once exemplified by Socrates's disquieting observations to the youth of Athens, and later by the incendiary works of Revolutionary War–era pamphleteers, they now come in the form of Instagram Stories, Snapchats, and TikToks. And even though being kicked off the JV cheer team is hardly a cup of hemlock, Brandi's Snap allowed the court to deal with substantively important legal issues in a contemporary context, in new media, and for once, outside the realm of politics or religion. In accepting Brandi's case, the court made a point that for First Amendment violations, the significance of the underlying issue does not matter. Whether one is protesting war or protesting an unfair assessment of cheerleading skills, the First Amendment protects the monumental and the trivial, the sacred and the profane, alike.

### Protection of the Profane: Something to Cheer About

Why, then, does a profanity-laced Snapchat meet the court's standard of protection? Brandi's terse message was more in line with Frederick's banner than Tinker's armband. Brandi did not make a political statement or call for an end to injustice but instead issued a vulgar rant on social media. As a result, it would have been easy for the Supreme Court to side with the school authorities, holding that Brandi's speech promoted a negative attitude toward her school and her cheer team. It could have issued a majority opinion similar to that of Justice Clarence Thomas's dissent in the case.[14] As the only justice to dissent, Thomas criticized Brandi's "profanity-laced message," arguing that history calls for a public school's ability to "discipline students for off-campus speech or conduct that had a proximate tendency to harm the school environment."[15] For a dedicated "textualist,"[16] however, Justice Thomas, unlike Justice Stephen Breyer writing for the rest of the justices, does not accurately quote Brandi's Snap in his dissent. Instead, he writes "F***" in place of the original "Fuck."[17] This bowdlerized version of the evidence will be a mystery to future scholars who wonder just what was so objectionable about the Snap. The First Amendment protects words, not asterisks.

Further, unlike Justice Breyer (and all the other justices), Justice Thomas believed that "the purpose of B. L.'s speech was to 'degrade the [program and cheerleading staff]' in front of 'other pupils,' thus having 'a direct and immediate tendency to . . . subvert the [cheerleading coach's] authority.'"[18] The court could have easily ruled that Brandi's rant only degraded the cheer program and thus was unworthy of constitutional protection. This case did not arise amid social or political unrest or involve a student's political statement (like the facts in *Tinker*). Why was a varsity-deprived student worthy of being singled out for constitutional protection by the nation's highest court?

Brandi's case offered a way for the Supreme Court to recognize the importance of the phenomenon of cheer as a marker of American society. Not so idiosyncratic as to be inapplicable when future cases arise in different contexts, cheer is a metaphor easily applied to other circumstances. In the service of the court's hope to create broad legal rulings applicable throughout a larger array of cases before the lower courts, it's hard to beat cheer litigation as the O-negative of legal principles. Like the universal donor blood type, the rules from this decision can infuse and inform any number of cases without causing a reaction. It can be applied in free speech, student speech, school discipline, and profanity cases that reach lower courts regularly. Its vanilla factual circumstances, arising from a part of American society too often discounted as insignificant, make it all the more powerful as legal precedent.

Against the backdrop of free speech cases (and there have been many), this case did not break any new ground by holding that students have constitutional rights. Nor did it establish new First Amendment law by ruling that social media is a constitutionally protected form of expression. And while the Supreme Court has long dealt with on-campus versus off-campus speech, this case brought together the issues of students' constitutional rights, social media posts, and off-campus expression in one package, presented as neatly as a bow on a cheerleader's ponytail. This case of a wannabe varsity cheerleader is perhaps most notable for the company it keeps in the history of First Amendment law. The cases that have made it to the Supreme Court have consistently concerned speech about the most serious and contentious social and political matters: war, civil rights, and religion. Many adults will shrug off Brandi's case, believing that protesting denial to the varsity cheer team is a triviality unworthy of the court's time. By taking this case and treating it as worthy of serious examination, however, the court buttressed and reaffirmed the constitutional protections of student speech. By choosing this particular case to advance the contours of constitutional protection, the Supreme Court recognized that the culture and tradition of cheer is so deeply woven into the fabric of America that it can serve as an ideal example of the reach, power, and universality of the First Amendment.

## Notes

1. William Shakespeare, *Hamlet*, act 2, scene 2. Adding salt to her open wound, Brandi also did not make the softball team in her desired position. Brandi also did not make the softball team in her desired position, adding salt to her open wound. It was just too much.
2. Mahanoy Area School District v. B.L., 594 U.S. 180 (2021).
3. Tinker v. Des Moines Independent Community School District, 393 U.S. 503 (1969).
4. Allison E. Hayes, "From Armbands to Douchebags: How *Doninger v. Niehoff* Shows the Supreme Court Needs to Address Student Speech in the Cyber Age," *Akron Law Review* 43 (2010): 247–290; "Mary Beth Tinker Describes Her Experiences Participating in a Student Protest in 1965," Iowa PBS, February 21, 2019, https://www.iowapbs.org/iowapathways/artifact/1423/mary-beth-tinker-describes-her-experiences-participating-student-protest.
5. Morse v. Frederick, 551 U.S. 393 (2007).
6. Bethel School District v. Fraser, 478 U.S. 675 (1986).
7. Hazelwood School District v. Kuhlmeier, 484 U.S. 260 (1988).
8. Molly Tack-Hooper, interview by Zoie Comer, September 20, 2024.
9. B.L. v. Mahanoy Area School District, 376 F. Supp. 3d 429 (M.D. Pa. 2019).
10. Shelton v. Tucker, 364 U.S. 479, 487 (1960).
11. *Tinker*, 393 U.S. at 506.
12. *Id.* at 506–507.
13. *B.L.*, 376 F. Supp. 3d at 433, *aff'd*, 964 F.3d 170.
14. *Mahanoy*, 594 U.S. at 211–219 (Thomas, J., dissenting).
15. *Id.* at 212.
16. Legal scholars are divided on how to best interpret legal documents. On one side of the interpretative war are textualists, who believe that it is best to focus on the plain meaning of the text of the legal document.
17. *Mahanoy*, 594 U.S. at 211 (Thomas, J., dissenting).
18. *Id.* at 215.

CHEER NOTE #8

# Famous Cheerleaders

As its history highlights, cheerleading has, from its beginnings, been touted as excellent preparation for professional life. Cheerleaders learn teamwork, cooperation, confidence, leadership, conflict resolution, and interpersonal communication—skills easily transferrable to the workplace. How well do you know some of our most famous former cheerleaders?

1. Which of the following US presidents was not a cheerleader?
   A. George W. Bush
   B. Bill Clinton
   C. Dwight Eisenhower
   D. Franklin Roosevelt
   E. Ronald Reagan

2. Which of the following members of the US Congress was a cheerleader?
   A. Senator Katie Britt
   B. Representative Marjorie Taylor Greene
   C. Senator Kirsten Gillibrand
   D. Senator Tommy Tuberville

3. Which of the following Supreme Court justices was a cheerleader?
   A. Ruth Bader Ginsburg
   B. Brett Kavanaugh
   C. Sandra Day O'Connor
   D. John Roberts

4. Which of the following actors was not a cheerleader? (Hint: There are two.)
   A. Kirk Douglas
   B. Will Ferrell
   C. Samuel L. Jackson
   D. Matthew McConaughey
   E. Steve Martin

5. Which of the following TV morning show hosts was a cheerleader?
   A. Jenna Bush Hager
   B. Katie Couric
   C. Gayle King
   D. Hoda Kotb

   (Answers found on page 283.)

CHAPTER 13

# Monopolizing Spirit

## VARSITY AND THE BUILDING OF A CHEEROCRACY

*Natalie G. Adams*

Torrance: Courtney, this is not a democracy; it's a cheerocracy. I'm sorry, but I'm overruling you.
Courtney: You are being a cheertator, Torrance, and a pain in my ass!

*Bring It On*

In the world of cheerleading, there is one "cheertator": Varsity Brands. Its leader for the last forty years was Jeff Webb, former cheerleader turned serial entrepreneur and the global face of cheerleading, who died, sadly, shortly before this book went to press. Webb sold Varsity to Charlesbank Capital Partners in 2014 for $1.5 billion but remained its CEO until 2017 and its chairman until December 2020. In 2018, Charlesbank sold Varsity to private equity giant Bain Capital for $2.5 billion. At the time of the acquisition, CNBC described Varsity as "one of the few retail businesses of scale that may have an Amazon defense."[1] And in 2024, Kohlberg Kravis Roberts (KKR), another private equity firm, bought Varsity for $4.75 billion.[2] Cheerleading itself exemplifies optimism, positivity, and encouragement, but the business of cheer has not been so friendly. Cheer czar Jeff Webb explained his approach to building a multi-billion-dollar business: "We knew we wouldn't grow and succeed by playing soft and easy. We were going to have to throw elbows. . . . We did what we had to do to get things done. Always ethically, never timidly."[3]

In this chapter, I examine the history of the cheer industry and how two former cheerleaders recognized the market power of cheerleading and built an industry that has become Amazon-proof. I detail Varsity's rise from a small company run from the back seat of Webb's car to a multi-billion-dollar business that many consider a monopoly. The history of the cheer industry is a story of intrigue, capitalism, competition, familial ties and breakups, corporate takeovers, greed, jealousy, power, and money. Think *Succession* and *Yellowstone* meet *Bring It On* and *Cheer*. But before we delve into the underbelly of the spirit industry, a quick note about methodology.

### There's No Business Like Cheer Business: A Research Note

I began researching cheerleading in 1998 as part of a research group conducting an ethnographic study of girls and leadership in a diverse middle school in rural Oklahoma. What was supposed to be a year-long study turned into a twenty-five-year research project. Data for this chapter on the history of the cheer industry comes from the archival research (e.g., newspaper, journal, and magazine articles dating back to the early 1900s) and traditional qualitative research (interviews and fieldwork) conducted over this twenty-five-year period. Like most people, I didn't give much thought in those early years to who designed and marketed the uniforms, delivered the training, sold the pom-poms, or sponsored the competitions. I was more interested in why cheerleading remained so popular despite feminist movements, girl power, and an unprecedented focus on the academic and athletic achievements of girls and young women. But a friend who worked at Varsity suggested that I delve into Jeff Webb's journey from being a University of Oklahoma cheerleader to founding the world's largest cheerleading company. In June 2002, I was fortunate to spend a week roaming freely throughout Varsity's headquarters in Memphis, Tennessee, interviewing most of the company's top brass at the time, including Jeff Webb. Webb, his brother Greg Webb, Jim Lord, Kline Boyd, Robert Tisdale, Kris Shepherd, Marlene Cota, Kavin Finley, Chris Darby, Mike Fultz, Sean Ellis, Ray Arnold, and Bill Seely were incredibly open and honest in answering my questions.[4] They provided invaluable insight into the origins of Varsity, its culture, its changing goals, and its future aspirations. I also analyzed numerous Varsity documents (e.g., coaches' manuals, injury protocols, and handbooks for camp instructors and attendees) as well as internal documents that Varsity employees and members of the Varsity cheer community provided to me. When I hung out at Varsity over twenty years ago, it felt like one big, happy, fun cheerleading camp. No lawyers followed me around. I didn't have to jump through a bunch of hoops to interview folks, and everyone was really, really nice and smiled a lot. Almost all of them were former cheerleaders and, for the most part, still exuded that cheerleader vibe.

Varsity has since become much more cautious about sharing information with scholars, journalists, and roaming outsiders, so researching the contemporary history of Varsity proved much more difficult. Further, because cheerleading remains an underresearched topic of academic study and few journalists have written lengthy, nuanced stories about cheerleading—choosing instead to focus on sensationalizing, sexualizing, or satirizing cheer—this research has required me to employ multiple research strategies and analytical tools. I had to piece together Varsity's contemporary legal woes through a variety of sources, including legal documents (e.g., antitrust lawsuits), court transcripts, blogs, websites, and investigative stories by several journalists (e.g., Daniel Libit of *Sportico*) who have deemed cheerleading worthy of serious reporting.

With that methodology in mind, we can now turn to our discussion of cheerleading's role in monopolies, mergers, markets, innovation, regulation, price fixing, branding, acquisitions, supply and demand, and absentee ownership—terms typically associated with capitalism, not cheer. To understand the infrastructure of cheerleading, and the industry developed over the years to support it, we begin in the late 1940s.

## The Origins of the Spirit Industry

In 1948, as cheerleading transformed from a predominantly male to a predominantly female activity, Lawrence Herkimer (aka Herkie) formed the National Cheerleaders Association (NCA). A former high school and collegiate cheerleader and a World War II veteran, this Texas entrepreneur quickly dominated the production and distribution of cheerleading products and services. Herkimer and his NCA team wrote cheerleading books and manuals. They published *The Megaphone* (the first cheerleading magazine) and delivered cheerleading training to high school and collegiate cheerleaders. In 1951, Herkimer and his wife, Dorothy, opened a cheerleading apparel business called the Cheerleader Supply Company and began aggressively marketing their products to cheerleading squads across the country.[5] Herkimer also invented three of cheerleading's most iconic symbols: the Herkie jump (still performed by thousands of cheerleaders across the world),[6] the pom-pom,[7] and the spirit stick.[8] For over twenty-five years, Herkimer was the undisputed king of cheerleading and the cheer industry. As he told *The New York Times*, "We like to say we're the Christian Dior and the Neiman Marcus of the cheerleading business."[9] In 1986, Herkimer sold his cheerleading company for an estimated $20 million. By that time, he had a fierce competitor knocking on his back door, someone he knew very well—Jeff Webb.

## The Birth of an Empire

Herkimer's NCA cheerleading camps were the industry standard and were copied by dozens of competitors over the years. Held on college campuses during the summer, the camps were primarily taught by collegiate cheerleaders. One of those NCA summer camp instructors was University of Oklahoma cheerleader Jeff Webb. In 1972, Webb began working full-time for NCA as its director of external programs. Within six months, he was promoted to vice president.[10]

Herkimer was twenty-five years older than Webb, and their personalities and vision for cheerleading's future clashed. According to Webb, Herkimer refused to innovate: "There was real resistance to bringing that organization into [modern times]. I was out there among the cheerleaders, and I knew that kids had changed and that we really weren't providing what they needed. So I decided to do it myself."[11] In 1974, Webb left Herkimer's business to form his own company, the Universal Cheerleaders Association (UCA), using $5,000 of his own money and $80,000 borrowed from friends and relatives. Webb hired twelve NCA instructors, and they all moved to Memphis, the headquarters of his new company. Kline Boyd was one of them. Boyd explains why he decided to leave the NCA:

> We thought it could be more than what it was—more athletic, more gymnastics, bring the crowd more into it. We thought we had a better way of doing it. Not that anything was wrong with the other place [NCA] but they weren't ready to be as progressive. Jeff had this great energy—that kind of driving force and the kind of talent he brought with him, it attracted a lot of people.[12]

One year later, Webb introduced his own cheerleading camps.[13]

Webb recognized that the times demanded a reinvention of cheerleading. Congress had recently passed Title IX, a feminist movement was reshaping how girls and women engaged in athletics, and the student and antiwar movements of the late 1960s and early 1970s had revealed deep generational divisions between young adults and their parents. Herkimer's NCA, birthed in the postwar 1940s, seemed out of touch with the new generation of high school and collegiate students. Webb and his entourage introduced a much more athletic, more daring, and more entertaining form of cheerleading. In 1979, Webb and eight investors, each contributing $25,000, formed a second cheerleading company, Varsity Spirit Fashion and Supplies, which specialized in cheer uniforms with sharper and more athletic-looking designs, made with fabric that easily stretched when cheerleaders tumbled, jumped, and flew off pyramids.[14] In 2017, the Supreme Court ruled that Varsity's uniform designs were so unique that they were eligible for copyright protection as an artistic work.[15]

In 1980, Varsity began organizing national cheerleading championships to showcase the new form of cheerleading that allowed its participants to compete for the types of awards and titles long offered in other sports. In 1983, Webb convinced ESPN, a fledgling new sports network, to televise these national competitions, thus bringing cheerleading into the homes of people all over the United States and, later, the world. By the mid-1980s, Webb was the new giant of the cheer industry—the one credited with transforming cheerleading from a sideline activity to an athletic spectacle worthy of attracting its own audience.[16]

Over the years, Varsity dabbled in other ventures—football equipment through Riddell and soccer apparel and equipment through the acquisition of the Umbro license. But its bread and butter has always been cheerleading.[17] In 1994, Varsity acquired one of its leading cheer camp competitors, the United Spirit Association (USA), popular on the West Coast. In 1996, it bought another cheer camp competitor, the California-based United Special Events. But its most consequential acquisition came in 2004, when Varsity acquired the National Spirit Group, the parent company of the NCA, which Webb's mentor, Larry Herkimer, had founded fifty years earlier.[18] Before his death in 2015, Herkimer quipped of Webb's success: "Jeff ought to be thrilled he ever knew me."[19]

If Herkimer is the so-called father of modern cheerleading, Webb is either the ungrateful stepson or the shrewd cousin whose business sense saved cheerleading from possible extinction. For the last forty-five years, Webb has been the face of cheerleading and has been personally involved in every aspect of the cheer industry. Years ago, Herkimer declared, "Once

I have a cheerleader; she's mine for life."[20] Webb took over this adage and built a cheerleading empire that seems impervious to any serious competition.

### "That's Alright, That's OK; You're Going to Work for Me Someday": The Empire Expands

After the acquisition of the National Spirit Group, Varsity Brands went on an aggressive buying spree. From 2012 to 2018, it acquired almost every rival company that hosted cheerleading competitions and events: CHEERSPORT, Cheer Limited, JAM Brands, Spirit Celebration, and Team Epic Brands. It bought a competing apparel company called Just Briefs in 2010 and subsequently closed the business. In 2012, it also acquired two important media outlets: the magazine *American Cheerleader* and Cheersport TV. Eventually, Varsity created its own live-streaming business, which requires a subscription to watch its national cheerleading and dance championships.[21]

Varsity's tight hold on cheerleading extends beyond purchasing most of its rival cheerleading camp, event, and supply companies. It also controls the governance and regulatory arm of cheerleading both in the US and globally. In 1987, it created the American Association of Cheerleading Coaches and Advising (AACCA) to promote safety certification in cheerleading. In 2003, Varsity created the US All Star Federation (USASF) in partnership with several other cheerleading organizations to regulate All Star cheerleading. Varsity gave USASF a $1.8 million interest-free loan. That same year, Varsity formed the International All-Star Federation (IASF), which was governed by USASF. In 2004, Varsity helped form the International Cheer Union (ICU) to regulate cheerleading internationally, with Jeff Webb as the president. In 2007, Varsity formed USA Federation for Sport Cheering (known as USA Cheer) and declared itself the "National Governing Body for Sport Cheering." The AACCA was disbanded and its operations moved to USA Cheer. Varsity, its executives, and its subsidiaries hold most of the board positions of each of these organizations, and, until recently, paid the salaries of most of their employees. Varsity's role in creating these organizations gives the company immense control and power over all aspects of cheerleading: USASF and IASF (All-Star), ICU (international), and USA Cheer (high school and college). Additionally, in 2003, Varsity formed an alliance with the National Federation of State and High School

Associations (NFHSA), the governing body for high school sports, and paid them $3 million in exchange for endorsing Varsity-owned cheerleading competitions.[22]

As Varsity grew into the mega-giant of cheerleading, murmurs of unfair competition, monopoly power, and unsavory business practices began to rumble through the cheer world. At the helm of this growing anti-Varsity sentiment was the founder of a new rival cheerleading apparel company.

### A Rebel Sows Seeds of Discontent

When the Navarro College cheerleaders made a splash in 2020 in the Netflix hit *Cheer*, cheer insiders took notice of their uniforms. To the untrained eye, the uniforms' midriffs, short skirts, and glittery sequins were nothing new, but to insiders, the uniforms stood out. Navarro was not wearing Varsity. They were wearing Rebel Athletic. And its founder, Karen Noseff Aldridge, had done something that many in the cheer business had been afraid to do: She had publicly challenged Varsity.

Unlike Jeff Webb, who split from his mentor to form a rival company, Aldridge was not a former Varsity employee gone rogue. In 2007, she and a classmate quit Southern Methodist University Law School to start a business called Fortune Denim, a premium jeans company. After the business folded, Aldridge began teaching dance in the Dallas, Texas, area, which led her to connect with Billy Smith, owner of Spirit Celebration.[23] Smith told Aldridge he needed two thousand customized jackets for an upcoming cheer and dance competition. Aldridge delivered the goods, and shortly thereafter, she formed Rebel Athletic, specializing in "couture fashion" for cheerleaders.[24]

Aldridge's uniforms quickly became a hit in the Dallas area. Rebel wooed several large All Star gyms away from Varsity. According to Aldridge, Webb's company responded with a vigorous pressure campaign to deter cheer teams from buying Rebel uniforms.[25] In 2013, Aldridge joined six other cheerleading companies to form GrowCheer.org to curtail Varsity's growing control over every aspect of cheerleading. They submitted a proposal to the USASF, stating, "We believe that the first (and most important) step in fostering future growth in our sport is a FREE and INDEPENDENT United States All Star Federation." Their manifesto called for Varsity to relinquish its control of the USASF and allow for a more representative board of directors.[26] Varsity did not respond to these demands.

Aldridge challenged Varsity's power in other ways. In 2014, she created Rebel Alliance to strengthen relationships among non-Varsity cheerleading associations. She formed partnerships with independent, small cheer businesses and offered her consulting services to them. She explains, "Anything we can do to help make their event better, their gym better, their business better or stronger to compete against Varsity, we will do it."[27] These alliances helped Rebel Athletic secure important contracts with independent cheerleading companies—the most significant being an exclusive deal with JAM Brands, then Varsity's biggest competitor for cheerleading and dance events. Rebel would be the only company selling its uniforms at JAM events, an important negotiation since Varsity prohibits competitors from selling their merchandise at its events. In 2015, Varsity bought JAM Brands and then retracted its agreement with Rebel.

In 2016, Rebel posted a thirty-seven-second video called "Rebels Take the Mat: Take Back Your Freedom to Choose." While Varsity was not explicitly named in the text of the post, cheer insiders knew exactly the subject of Aldridge's accusations:

> Across the nation, insinuation is being made to gym owners and coaches that winning teams are usually wearing a certain brand. A seed is being planted by representatives of this brand that, to win, you should be in a uniform made by them. We have been hearing this from our customers since we entered the Allstar Industry, and we will no longer stand by in silence accepting that this behavior is ok. Intimidation tactics are never ok. Don't fall for the lie used by them to keep you in a state of fear.[28]

Today, Rebel Athletic is a strong competitor in the cheerleading uniform business, and Aldridge is no longer waging a public battle against Varsity. Nevertheless, the seeds of discontent had been sown, and others stood ready to continue the fight against the cheerleading giant.

## Taking Varsity to Court

In 2020, four class action lawsuits were filed against Varsity Brands for violating the Sherman Antitrust Act, which prohibits businesses from creating a monopoly.[29] The first step a court takes in an antitrust complaint or lawsuit is to ask if the company has "monopoly power" over products and services sold, and the prices charged for such. The answer is a resounding "yes," according to the All Star gym owners, All Star cheerleaders and their parents, and several small cheerleading businesses who filed the lawsuits.

The plaintiffs claimed that Varsity controls 90 percent of the All Star competition market and 80 percent of the All Star apparel market. Further, they argued, Varsity's control over all the governing and regulatory bodies of the cheerleading industry is a conflict of interest and gives Varsity an unfair business advantage. As one example of Varsity's dominance, they cited its control of the USASF board, maintained through bylaws stating that board members will be appointed from the UCA, CHEERSPORT, the NCA, the American Cheerleaders Association, the Universal Dance Association, and JAMfest. Varsity is the parent company of all of these organizations.[30] The plaintiffs accused Varsity of using coercive and exclusionary contracts to ensure that All Star gyms only use their services. They contended that Varsity representatives intimidated All Star gyms into multiyear contracts that incentivized the sole purchasing of Varsity products. The suits argued, for example, that Varsity issues gym owners cash rebates (i.e., Varsity Fashion Dollars) if their teams compete in Varsity competitions and buy Varsity products. The lawsuits also claimed that Varsity uses its power to coerce collegiate coaches to compete only in Varsity-sponsored competitions.[31]

Varsity dismissed the lawsuits as baseless, and as emanating from disgruntled business owners jealous of Varsity's success. Webb himself was unapologetic about how he built his business from a small company to an empire that now controls all aspects of the spirit industry. As he explained in *Chief Executive*, a demand for innovation in cheerleading existed,[32] and he supplied it by responding quickly to new trends, new technology, cultural and social changes, and shifting economic forces: "We were really creating an industry as we went along and it became an ecosystem in that we were creating the concept, we were creating the industry, and then we were positioning ourselves to provide all the products and services that that affinity group utilized."[33] What Webb calls an ecosystem, his critics call a monopoly.

These lawsuits never made it to court. A judge dismissed two of them because of procedural violations by the plaintiffs' attorneys. In January 2023, the plaintiffs in the *Fusion Elite All Stars et al.* lawsuit agreed to a $43.5 million settlement. While admitting no wrong, Varsity agreed to the following stipulations limiting their control over the USASF:

- Varsity board members could not also serve on the board of the USASF.
- Varsity could not pay the salaries or benefits of USASF employees or executives.
- No single cheerleading event producer could occupy more than a third of the voting seats on the USASF's board or comprise more than 40 percent of the USASF's sanctioning committee.[34]

In May 2024, Varsity settled *Jones et al. v. Varsity Brands* before its scheduled court date, agreeing to pay the plaintiffs $82.5 million.[35]

In 1982, amid an economic downturn, Herkimer told *Forbes* that cheerleading is "Depression-proof. No matter how bad times are, are you going to tell your little girl she can't have her sweater and skirt and pom-poms? Hell, you'll sell the boat before you have to tell her that."[36] Thus far, Herkimer has been right. Cheerleading has proven to be depression and recession proof, and according to Varsity CEO Adam Blumenfeld, it is also pandemic proof.[37] In June 2020, amid the COVID-19 lockdowns, Varsity raised $185 million in new capital in less than ten days. This was four times their expected goal.[38]

### More Lawsuits Threaten Varsity's Future as a Cheerocracy

At the time of this writing in 2025, the future of Varsity is unclear. By the time KKR acquired Varsity in June 2024, the leader of the spirit industry had been mired in controversy since 2020.[39] Accusations about monopolistic power, unfair business practices, and aggressive attempts to disrupt cheer's recognition as a sanctioned sport are but a few of its problems. In 2023, the company paid over $125 million to settle the antitrust lawsuits. It is now in a vitriolic dispute with its insurance companies about who is legally responsible for paying these settlements and accompanying legal fees.[40] But even more troubling is that Varsity has been named in a string of lawsuits claiming it fosters a culture of sexual abuse in All Star cheer.[41]

On September 14, 2020, *USA Today* published a story about Jerry Harris, one of the most beloved stars of *Cheer*. Harris was accused of soliciting nude photos and sex from two teenage boys. The boys and their mother filed a lawsuit against Harris, Varsity, the USASF, and Cheer Athletics (the All Star gym where Harris and the boys cheered).[42] Four days later, *USA Today* followed up with an incriminating investigative report about the cheerleading industry's failure to protect athletes in its care from sexual predators.[43] According to the article, 140 individuals accused of sex abuse or sexual misconduct and 74 registered sex offenders were working directly with underage cheerleaders in All Star gyms. The article claimed that the USASF—founded and controlled by Varsity—had failed to adequately investigate complaints of sexual abuse and exploitation. *USA Today* continued to publish stories about the cheer industry's complicity in creating unsafe environments for young athletes, and more lawsuits were filed against individual All Star gym owners and coaches. Varsity, Bain Capital, Jeff Webb, USA Cheer, and the USASF were also named in several lawsuits for "creating, organizing and propagating a system of young-athlete abuse against innocent victims."[44] In 2022, Harris was indicted on sex charges and sentenced to twelve years in prison. The lawsuit filed against Varsity by Harris's accusers and their mother was settled out of court.[45]

These allegations about Varsity's negligence in protecting its cheerleaders from sex offenders are potentially damaging to the future of cheerleading. One need only look at the recent sexual abuse scandal in gymnastics to understand the power of lawsuits and good investigative journalism to force an industry and its leaders to a day of reckoning. One of the lead reporters of the *USA Today* cheerleading exposés is Marisa Kwiatkowski. She was one of the *Indianapolis Star* reporters, along with Tim Evans and Mark Alesia, who broke the 2016 story of sexual abuse in gymnastics.[46] That story eventually led to the indictment of USA Gymnastics team physician Larry Nassar for sexually assaulting five hundred girls and young women over a twenty-year period. In January 2018, Nassar was sentenced to up to 175 years in prison. USA Gymnastics filed for bankruptcy, and many of the top brass at USA Gymnastics and Michigan State University (where Nassar had worked) were removed. Gymnastics as a sport is still reeling from the fallout of that scandal.[47]

In 2024, Varsity settled with twenty-one plaintiffs for an undisclosed amount in several of these sex abuse lawsuits.[48] But Varsity's financial, legal, and reputational woes have turned this once shining example of entrepreneurship and innovation into a tainted and controversial company. In December 2020, amid these lawsuits, Webb stepped down from his position as chairman of Varsity's cheer division. According to Reuters and *Sportico*, Varsity's owner, Bain Capital, began seeking opportunities to either sell Varsity or go public with it.[49] When the company sold to KKR, Varsity's credit rating had dropped, and according to *Sportico*, "Moody considers Varsity Brands a 'high risk' issuer with debt that is not investment grade—otherwise known as junk bonds."[50] Varsity's tenuous position as the global representative of all things cheer portends potential problems for the quest to gain sports status in the United States and for cheer's expansion and growth globally. Will these allegations strengthen the resolve of an already-hesitant National Collegiate Athletic Association (NCAA) to deny cheerleading formal entrance into the world of US sports? Will student athletes continue to flock to the sport if cheerleading coaches, gym owners, and the cheer industry are found to be complicit in perpetuating sexual misconduct and abuse? Will the International Olympic Committee (IOC) admit cheerleading into the Olympics if the sport is shrouded in accusations of a pervasive toxic culture? Can Varsity survive this reputational smearing?[51]

### Beyond the Mat: Taking Cheer Lessons to Politics

Matt Stoller, author of *Goliath: The 100-Year War Between Monopoly Power and Democracy*, knew nothing about Varsity when he wrote his six-hundred-page tome about the rise of monopolies and their threat to democracy in the United States.[52] After hearing a reference in *Cheer* to Varsity's monopolistic practices, he began researching the company and discovered a classic American rags-to-riches business story. Stoller writes, "As unlikely as you may find cheerleading to be as a useful model for how the American economy functions, it actually works quite well as a case study. It's got private equity, monopoly, small business, and American culture, all wrapped up into one nice package."[53] Critics of Varsity contend that its control of the cheer market is similar to the dominance of Amazon, Meta, Apple, and Google, which have all been sued by the US Department of Justice for violating antitrust laws. Yet Varsity has escaped serious scrutiny, outside of a small group of reporters, lawyers, cheer insiders, and one sole economist. Stoller contends that this lack of attention reflects the trivialization of cheerleading itself: "There are no advanced technologies in cheer, no economies of scale, and no fancy business jargon to demystify." He notes that people tend to think of cheerleading as "just a team of (mostly) girls doing gymnastics together, trained at a common gym, with the equipment, training and travel paid by parents."[54] But it would be a mistake, he argues, to dismiss the importance of cheerleading. Not only can we learn much about the common tactics used to build monopolies in a variety of industries, but also we can look to Varsity as an example of the dangers of a certain type of "absentee ownership" in which a company is not involved in the day-to-day operations of a business but wields significant power over it. In 1912, Supreme Court Justice Louis Brandeis argued that "absentee capitalist control" (as exemplified then in the steel industry) allows a few men to accrue great wealth while releasing them and their companies from any responsibility, accountability, or liability. To Justice Brandeis, this economic arrangement is an attack on the basic values of free enterprise in a functioning democracy.[55] Applying the economic principle of "absentee capitalist control" to Varsity, Stoller notes that the company and its owners have been protected from legal repercussions of its negligent behavior through a complex system of "laws and rules that immunize them from liability."[56] Varsity's defense in the sexual abuse lawsuits is that the abuses occurred at All Star gyms, which are privately owned and run businesses. Further, Varsity contends it has no "real" governing or regulatory power over these private enterprises, since the USASF and USA Cheer are not formally or legally recognized as such. They argue that they should not be held responsible for sexual misconduct at businesses they do not own or control.

Stoller predicted in 2020 that we were about to witness the "coming collapse" of Varsity.[57] That remains to be seen. Webb stepped away from Varsity to enter a new sphere of influence: politics. He founded the American Populists, a political advocacy group, and was the publisher and senior editor of Human Events, a conservative political news and analysis website. In 2020, he published *American Restoration: How to Unshackle the Great Middle Class*, in which he set forth a plan to rebrand the Republican Party, using some of the same techniques he employed to reshape cheerleading and an industry to support it.[58] Webb's vision of how to bring Americans together utilizes language found in any high school or collegiate cheerleading constitution in the United States: "Focus on the positive, concentrate on what we can do together, and concentrate on remaking a country built on the best."[59] In other words, Go! Fight! Win!

## Notes

1. Lauren Hirsch, "Bain to Acquire Varsity Brands, a Top Maker of Cheerleader Uniforms and School Spirit Items, for Roughly $2.5 Billion," CNBC, June 19, 2018, https://www.cnbc.com/2018/06/19/bain-nears-2-point-5-billion-deal-for-cheer-uniform-leader-varsity-brands.html.

2. "KKR Completes Acquisition of Varsity Brands from Bain Capital and Charlesbank," Varsity Brands, June 26, 2024, https://www.varsitybrands.com/news/kkr-completes-acquistion-of-Varsity-Brands-from-Bain-Capital-and-Charlesbank/.

3. Jeff Webb, *American Restoration: How to Unshackle the Great Middle Class* (Post Hill Press, 2020), x.

4. These interviews conducted in 2002 helped form the author's discussion of Varsity's origins. See Natalie G. Adams and Pamela J. Bettis, *Cheerleader! An American Icon* (Palgrave Macmillan, 2003), 111–128.

5. "Cheerleading Pioneer and SMU Alumnus Lawrence Herkimer Dies," SMU News, July 3, 2015, https://www.smu.edu/news/archives/2015/lawrence-herkimer-dies-03july2015.

6. Joe Nick Patoski, "Texas Primer: The Herkie Jump," *Texas Monthly*, October 1989, https://www.texasmonthly.com/being-texan/texas-primer-the-herkie-jump/.

7. Herkimer changed the name of his iconic patented invention from "pom-pom" to "pom-pon" after conducting a camp in Hawaii, where he discovered that US Army troops stationed in the Pacific used "pom-pom" as a slang term for sexual intercourse. The term "pom-pon" never caught on. See Harold Wentworth and Stuart Flexner, *Dictionary of American Slang* (Thomas Y. Crowell, 1975), under "pom-pom."

8. Adams and Bettis, *Cheerleader!*, 112–114.

9. Peter Applebome, "A Texan Turns Cheerleading into Big Business," *New York Times*, January 6, 1984.

10. Erik Brady, "From Megaphones to Mega-Profits," *USA Today*, April 26–28, 2002.

11. Sonja Steptoe, "The Pom-Pom Chronicles," *Sports Illustrated*, December 30, 1991, 38–44, 46.

12. Kline Boyd, executive vice president and general manager of UCA, interview by Natalie Adams, Memphis, Tennessee, June 24, 2002, cited in Adams and Bettis, *Cheerleader!*, 114–115.

13. Kline Boyd interview; Greg Webb, senior vice president and general manager of UCA, interview by Natalie Adams, Memphis, Tennessee, June 24, 2002, cited in Adams and Bettis, *Cheerleader!*, 114–115.

14. Ken Woodmansee, "Cheers: Jeff Webb's Multicolored World Wide Spirit Machine," *Memphis Business* 3, no. 3 (1993): 14–19.

15. This case, *Star Athletica v. Varsity Brands*, was heralded by the fashion industry.

16. Laura Grindstaff, "Hold That (Gender) Line! Cheerleading on ESPN, *Contexts* 4, no. 3 (2005): 71–73; Adams and Bettis, *Cheerleader*!, 114–115.

17. Kavin Finley, controller, Varsity Brands Apparel Division, interview by Natalie Adams, Memphis, Tennessee, June 25, 2002, cited in Adams and Bettis, *Cheerleader!*, 115.

18. Jeff Webb and Jerry Dilettuso, memorandum to Varsity Brands employees,

February 23, 2004, private collection of Natalie Adams. In this internal memo, Varsity announced the acquisition as a "merger."

19. R. Lee Sullivan, "School for Cheerleaders," *Forbes*, October 25, 1993, 118–119.

20. Ann Bagamery, "Go! Fight! Win!," *Forbes*, September 27, 1982, 140.

21. *Fusion Elite All Stars v. Varsity Brands.* In *Cheerleader!*, we list the following smaller cheerleading associations that offered cheerleading camps and training in the early 2000s: Cheerleaders of America (COA), the Fellowship of Christian Cheerleaders, Christian Cheerleaders of America, Americheer, Atlantic Cheer and Dance, and American Cheer Power. See Adams and Bettis, *Cheerleader!*, 119. Varsity acquired COA in 2004, and Varsity is now the parent company of American Cheer Power.

22. Daniel Connolly, "Cheer Empire: A For-Profit Company Built Competitive Cheer, Pays People Who Make Its Rules," *USA Today*, September 18, 2020, https://www.commercialappeal.com/in-depth/news/2020/09/18/cheer-empire-profit-company-created-cheerleading-regulators-pays-salaries/3468551001/; Leif Reigstad, "Varsity Brands Owns Cheerleading and Fights to Keep It from Becoming an Official Sport," *Houston Press*, July 21, 2015, https://www.houstonpress.com/news/varsity-brands-owns-cheerleading-and-fights-to-keep-it-from-becoming-an-official-sport-7606297.

23. At the time, Spirit Celebration was an independent cheerleading and dance company. Smith sold his company to Varsity in 2017.

24. Sooha Ahn, "Fresh from Netflix, This *Cheer* Gear Company Calls Dallas Home," *D Magazine*, December 2020, https://www.dmagazine.com/publications/d-ceo/2020/june-july/fresh-from-netflix-this-cheer-gear-company-calls-dallas-home/; Leigh Buchanan, "Meet Rebel, the $20 Million Cheerleading Startup Living Up to Its Name," *Inc.*, February 21, 2020, https://www.inc.com/magazine/201603/leigh-buchanan/rebel-athletic-custom-cheerleading-uniforms-startup.html.

25. Buchanan, "Meet Rebel."

26. "GrowCheer.org Proposal to the United States All Star Federation," *Spirit Post*, February 15, 2013, https://spiritpost.com/2013/02/growcheer-org-proposal-to-the-united-states-All-Star-federation/.

27. Buchanan, "Meet Rebel."

28. Rebel Athletic Cheer (@RebelAthleticCheer), "Rebels Take the Mat," Facebook, May 19, 2017, https://www.facebook.com/RebelAthleticCheer/videos/2235825629791121/?locale=sv_SE.

29. *Fusion Elite All Stars v. Varsity Brands*; *Jones v. Varsity Brands*; *Radek et al. v. Varsity Brands* (later merged with the Fusion Elite case); and *American Spirit and Cheer Essential et al. v. Varsity Brands.*

30. *Fusion Elite All Stars v. Varsity Brands.*

31. *Fusion Elite All Stars v. Varsity Brands.*

32. See Clifford Cobb's explanation of how innovation and creative destruction became key concepts in the 1980s (replacing production and competition) that allowed the propagation of monopolies. Clifford W. Cobb, "The Social Problem

of Monopoly," *American Journal of Economics and Sociology* 78, no. 5 (2019): 1048–1049.

33. Gabriel Perna, "Varsity Brands Founder on the Big Business of Cheerleading," *Chief Executive*, October 29, 2018, https://chiefexecutive.net/varsity-brands-big-business-cheerleading.

34. Daniel Libit, "Varsity Strikes $43 Million Settlement with Antitrust Accusers," *Sportico*, March 27, 2023, https://www.sportico.com/law/news/2023/varsity-antitrust-cheer-settlement-1234717352/.

35. Mike Scarcella, "Varsity Spirit, Bain to Pay $82 Million in Cheerleading Antitrust Settlement," Reuters, May 14, 2024, https://www.reuters.com/legal/litigation/varsity-spirit-bain-pay-82-million-cheerleading-antitrust-settlement-2024-05-14/.

36. Bagamery, "Go! Fight! Win!," 140.

37. Varsity Brands is split into two divisions: Varsity Spirit and BSN Sports. Blumenfeld's father was the founder of BSN Sports.

38. Natalie Walters, "Cheerleading Giant Varsity Brands Gets $185 Million in New Capital to Power Through Pandemic," *Dallas Morning News*, June 22, 2020, https://www.dallasnews.com/business/local-companies/2020/06/22/cheerleading-giant-varsity-brands-gets-185-million-in-new-capital-to-power-through-pandemic/.

39. Abigail Summerville, "Bain Eyes Varsity Brands Cash-Out at $6 Billion-Plus Valuation," Reuters, November 13, 2023, https://www.reuters.com/markets/deals/bain-eyes-varsity-brands-cash-out-6-bln-plus-valuation-sources-2023-11-13/.

40. Daniel Libit, "Varsity, Bain Keep Settling Cheer Suits as Possible Sale Looms," *Sportico*, April 27, 2024, https://www.sportico.com/leagues/other-sports/2024/varsity-bain-settling-second-antitrust-cheerleading-lawsuit-1234777001/.

41. Daniel Libit, "Varsity Must Face Negligence Claims in Cheerleading Sex Abuse Suit," *Sportico*, June 21, 2023, https://www.sportico.com/law/news/2023/cheerleading-sex-abuse-lawsuit-varsity-bain-capital-1234726822/; *Doe 1 et al. v. Varsity Brands et al.*

42. Marisa Kwiatkowski and Tricia Nadolny, "Jerry Harris from 'Cheer' Under FBI Investigation for Allegedly Soliciting Sex from Minor," *USA Today*, September 14, 2020, https://www.usatoday.com/in-depth/news/investigations/2020/09/14/jerry-harris-cheerleader-netflix-cheer-fbi-investigation-search-warrant-alleged-sexual-misconduct/5741805002/; Sarah Bahr, "Jerry Harris of 'Cheer' Accused of Sex Abuse in Teenagers' Lawsuit, *New York Times*, September 16, 2020, https://www.nytimes.com/2020/09/16/arts/television/jerry-harris-cheer.html.

43. Marisa Kwiatkowski and Tricia L. Nadolny, "Cheerleading's List of People Banned from the Sport: It Was Missing 74 Convicted Sex Offenders," *USA Today*, September 18, 2020, https://www.usatoday.com/story/news/2020/09/18/cheerleading-investigation-into-sexual-misconduct-sex-offenders-banned-list/3491411001/.

44. Kathryn Casteel, "Settlement Reached in Federal Lawsuit Alleging Sex Abuse at Rockstar Cheer," *Greenville News*, April 15, 2024, https://www.greenvilleonline.com/story/news/local/south-carolina/2024/04/15/settlement

-reached-in-federal-sex-abuse-case-against-rockstar-cheer/73323602007/.

45. Daniel Libit, "Sex Abuse Suit Against 'Cheer' Star, Varsity Quietly Settled Last Year," *Sportico*, March 10, 2023, https://www.sportico.com/law/news/2023/jerry-harris-cheer-varsity-lawsuit-settled-1234711935/.

46. Marisa Kwiatkowski, Mark Alesia, and Tim Evans, "A Blind Eye to Sex Abuse: How USA Gymnastics Failed to Report Cases," *Indianapolis Star*, August 4, 2016, https://www.indystar.com/story/news/investigations/2016/08/04/usa-gymnastics-sex-abuse-protected-coaches/85829732/.

47. Georgia Cervin, *Degrees of Difficulty: How Women's Gymnastics Rose to Prominence and Fell from Grace* (University of Illinois Press, 2021); Juan Martinez, "Sexual Abuse and Bankruptcy: How Organizations Abuse Chapter 11 to Avoid Victims' Demands for Answers," *Emory Bankruptcy Developments Journal* 37, no. 1 (2020): 213–253; Becky Sullivan, "Tracing USA Gymnastics' Journey from Rock Bottom to Olympic Dominance," NPR, July 16, 2024, https://www.npr.org/2024/07/16/nx-s1-5040629/usa-gymnastics-from-rock-bottom-back-to-olympic-dominance; Alice Park, "Can Anyone Save USA Gymnastics at This Point?," *Time*, June 24, 2019, 14–15.

48. Ronald V. Miller Jr., "Cheerleader Sex Abuse Class Action Lawsuit," Lawsuit Information Center, March 22, 2024, https://www.lawsuit-information-center.com/cheerleader-sex-abuse-class-action-lawsuit.html.

49. Libit, "Varsity, Bain Keep Settling."

50. Brendan Coffee and Daniel Libit, "Varsity Brands Taking on $2.4B Debt to Fund KKR Takeover from Bain," *Sportico*, July 19, 2024, https://www.sportico.com/leagues/other-sports/2024/varsity-brands-kkr-bain-capital-private-equity-1234790097/.

51. For more details about the inner conflict between Varsity and its former employees, see David Herbert, "How Cheerleading Became So Acrobatic, Dangerous, and Popular," *New York Times*, October 22, 2024, https://www.nytimes.com/2024/10/22/magazine/cheerleading-jeff-webb.html.

52. Matt Stoller, *Goliath: The 100-Year War Between Monopoly Power and Democracy* (Simon and Schuster, 2019).

53. Matt Stoller, "The Coming Collapse of a Cheerleading Monopolist," *BIG*, May 27, 2020, https://www.thebignewsletter.com/p/the-coming-collapse-of-a-cheerleading.

54. Stoller, "Coming Collapse."

55. Cited in Cobb, "Social Problem of Monopoly," 1048–1049.

56. Matt Stoller, "Cheerleading, Monopolies and Sexual Predators," *BIG*, September 27, 2020, https://www.thebignewsletter.com/p/cheerleading-monopolies-and-sexual.

57. Stoller, "Coming Collapse."

58. Webb, *American Restoration*.

59. Jeff Webb, "Stepping into a New Role in the Most Challenging of Times," Human Events, January 22, 2021.

CONCLUSION

# Cheer Matters

## NOW AND IN THE FUTURE

*Natalie G. Adams*

Save the cheerleader, save the world.
*Heroes*

If we think of the Supreme Court as the place where the nation's most pressing issues are debated, with some of the smartest legal scholars in the world weighing in, then the case of the cursing cheerleader, *Mahanoy Area School District v. B.L.* (2021), is a clear indication of the importance of taking cheerleading seriously. In deciding to hear the case, the justices recognized two essential components of cheer that made it the perfect choice for a contemporary case about free speech: (1) its ordinariness and ubiquitousness in American culture and (2) its enduring appeal. Cheerleading is ingrained in American culture; thus it serves as an excellent backdrop for examining other issues relevant to social and cultural life. The authors in this volume, using various methodologies, theoretical frameworks, and disciplinary knowledges, demonstrate the reach of cheerleading in so many facets of American life. In other words, they convincingly argue that cheer matters. In this final chapter, I revisit some of the book's central themes and look to the future of cheer to predict that cheer does, indeed, have a cheery future.

## Gender and Sexuality Matters

Gender is the primary category for organizing and understanding our social life. Its importance precedes birth, as evident in the popularity of gender reveal parties. From day one of our lives, gender matters. Newborn baby boys are dressed in blue, girls in pink. We are socialized to speak, act, and dress in ways that reflect conventional gender norms associated with the sex we were assigned at birth. Big boys don't cry. Girls don't hit. This gendered socialization occurs through the ordinary doing of everyday things in our lives. Girls play with dolls; boys play with guns. Girls take ballet; boys take karate. Boys can't sit still; girls color and entertain themselves. The meanings we ascribe to gender are not biologically determined. Rather, they are socially and culturally determined, but the social construction of gender has a powerful influence on how we live our lives individually and collectively. The institutions that define our social life (e.g., family, church, and school) reflect, reproduce, and reify these gender norms. And they sometimes present opportunities to resist or rethink these gendered norms.

Cheerleading is one such institution. Its history is unusual in the annals of American institutions because of its evolution from a male activity signifying normative masculinity to a female activity symbolizing ideal femininity. Birthed on Ivy League campuses, cheerleading was initially an activity for men only. Its close association with football from its beginnings made it a desirable activity for collegiate men. In fact, many of the earliest cheerleaders were baseball and basketball players. While college presidents like Harvard's A. Lawrence Lowell decried cheerleading as the "worst means of expressing emotion ever invented," college men in the late industrial era viewed it differently: "The reputation of having been a valiant 'cheer leader' is one of the most valuable things a boy can take away from college. As a title to promotion in professional or public life, it ranks hardly second to that of being a quarterback."[1] The male cheerleaders who dominated the activity for its first sixty years were considered manly men who were campus leaders participating in a high-status activity integral to sporting culture. In other words, the activity of cheerleading and its performance of gender norms (here masculinity) were congruent.

Women began dominating cheerleading during World War II, when men left college campuses to fight in the war. By the 1950s, the activity itself had changed significantly in its composition and the gender norms it embodied. Cheerleading squads were now comprised primarily of girls and women. Like their earlier male counterparts, cheerleaders in the 1950s were considered popular leaders at their schools. But the activity itself changed to align with norms about the role of women. Cheerleaders were supporters of the men on the field; they were subordinate to the male athletes. Their position was incumbent upon their ability to represent conventional norms of femininity, as illustrated in this 1955 list of the desirable traits for cheerleaders: "manners, cheerfulness, good disposition, character of high standing, leadership ability, scholarship of high standing, good personal appearance, citizen of high standing, and good coordination and voice."[2]

By the 1960s, the cheerleader had become a cultural icon representing the highest form of American femininity. Cheerleaders were "expected not simply to master routines but to project a 'look,' a combination of clothing, hairstyle, figure and enthusiastic charm considered to embody the ideals of youthful womanhood."[3] As the all-American girl next door, the cheerleader was the standard by which all other girls were judged. The writer Maxine Paetro explains, "We really, really wanted to be good. This is why we looked up to cheerleaders. They were athletic in a ladylike way. They got good grades, but they weren't considered 'brainy.' They observed the rules. They always had Saturday night dates. And they were very, very nice. They were our moral standard-bearers; the best that girls could be."[4]

A set of informal but understood rules emerged that not only enshrined cheerleaders' secondary status but also concretized the close association between ideal femininity and cheerleading. I call these rules the "cheerleader handbook." These rules are not recorded anywhere officially, but as any girl or guy who has ever tried out for their high school or college team knows, these cheer rules still rule. They determine who gets in and who does not, who belongs and who is excluded.

*Rule #1: Boost others.* Cheerleaders affiliated with schools, universities, and professional sports franchises are expected to be first and foremost demonstrably enthusiastic supporters of others, most often male athletes. Cheerleaders, like women in other spaces, are expected to put the needs of others before themselves and to do the emotional work needed to help the athletes (typically men) experience success.

*Rule #2: Serve your school.* Cheerleaders are expected to be extensions of their school or franchise; their behavior and appearance are to reflect the values of that institution. At secondary schools and colleges, this ambassador role is often formally detailed in a cheerleading constitution, with some semblance of this description: "Cheerleaders are to uphold, reflect and project the goals and ideals of the school community; they are to represent the school by acting as positive role models and demonstrating good leadership; they shall promote a positive school climate." The athletes on the field and the fans in the stands can curse, taunt, heckle, argue, and fight. But as representatives of the school and the embodiment of traditional femininity, cheerleaders cannot. They are expected to demonstrate impeccable manners, to always be nice, and to serve as role models in civility and decorum.

*Rule #3: Be conventionally pretty and fit.* Most official documents detailing the cheerleading selection process never explicitly state the rules about physical appearance. In fact, many cheerleading programs make public statements like "We welcome all body types" or "We don't require weigh-ins or body fat measurements." But everyone knows that appearance counts. In 2016, the University of Washington made this explicit in an infographic entitled "W: Cheer and Dance Tryout Look." Pictured was a petite, blond, young white woman wearing a black sports bra and Nike shorts. Next to this image of the "perfect" American girl was a list of rules:

> Do wear:
>
> Hair down, curled or straight, and partially off face
> False lashes
> "Girl about town" lipstick
> Solid black sports bra and mid-rise black shorts
>
> Don't have:
>
> Visible tattoos
> Trendy hair color
> Dark smoky eyes
> Tops that cover the midriff
> Distracting fingernail polish[5]

These rules, and the first three rules more generally, pertain primarily to female cheerleaders. Male cheerleaders have always had much more latitude, particularly in physical appearance. As the photographs in chapter 1 of the early cheerleaders at Oregon State University illustrate, being short or not conventionally handsome did not preclude men from participation. What was most important was their leadership, particularly their skill in rallying, directing, and controlling spectators. Their uniforms, which mirrored the everyday clothing of men at the time, accommodated diverse body types. This is still largely true in contemporary cheerleading, in which a chubby young man vying for a spot on the mat is far more likely to make the team than a slightly overweight girl.

*Rule #4: Be good and wholesome at all times.* This rule demonstrates how gender and sexuality are inextricably bound together in cheer. While "wholesome" is not a word used much today, it is prevalent in many cheerleading constitutions, such as this one from St. Clair County Schools that defines the desirable cheer look: "No excessive makeup will be worn. A natural, wholesome look is desired."[6] And this one from Ware Shoals High School: "Cheerleaders exist to promote good sportsmanship, good citizenship, and wholesome and enthusiastic school spirit."[7] *Merriam-Webster* defines "wholesome" as "promoting mental or moral health or well-being."[8] In common usage, it implies sexual morality. The Dallas Cowboys Cheerleaders organization has built an entire industry around this image of cheerleaders as sexual in the abstract but wholesome in real life. Suzette, Stephanie, and Sheri Scholz, sisters and former Dallas Cowboys Cheerleaders, explain this strategy: "Barrage the fans with the girl-next-door rhetoric while you tease, tease, tease. Tell them they're not seeing what they're seeing. . . . Get them hot over these girls, then tell the fans that they can't have them. They're sweet and untouchable. Oh, it's the stuff obsessions are forged from."[9]

The sexualization of female cheerleaders began long before the Dallas Cowboys Cheerleaders. In his 1956 history of cheerleading, Arturo Gonzales describes the typical male cheerleader in terms of his leadership and popularity: He was the "Big Man on Campus." In sharp contrast, Gonzales's depiction of female cheerleaders is filled with sexual innuendo: "No report on cheerleaders over the past three decades could be complete, of course, without reference to the coeds. Pretty young things in vestigial skirts, amply filled sweaters, and wearing baby shakos, they've burbled and twirled to the intense enjoyment of those fans easily distracted from the male carnage at the midfield by a few well-placed curves."[10]

Sexuality creeps into the language, uniforms, and expectations of all cheerleaders. My colleague Pam Bettis and I experienced this firsthand at a workshop that prepared middle school girls for upcoming cheerleading tryouts. The cheer coach instructed the girls, "When you make that turn, give the judges a sexy look. You should be oozing out cheerleading stuff. Dazzle me, smile, give me goosebumps. I want to be dazzled." She then ended her instructions with, "Put Vaseline on your teeth and put on a little extra makeup but not too much. Don't come looking like someone who could stand on the street."[11] Sexuality finds its way into dances and cheer moves; it pronounces itself in cheerleading uniforms; it is embodied in the glitter, big bows, makeup, and hairstyles on full display at any cheerleading competition—even those for six-year-old girls.

What does it mean to be wholesome or to have wholesome spirit? To look sexy but not be sexual? To be a booster, ambassador, and athlete while performing booty bumps in a short skirt? On one hand, it means cheerleaders must carefully navigate rules and expectations about personal sexual behavior while participating in an activity enveloped in sexuality. It means that cheer's close association with femininity and sexuality has led to its trivialization and is the primary obstacle to it ever being recognized as a "real" sport. This is the criticism feminists typically aim at cheerleading, and yet cheerleading continues to flourish despite continuous critique. On the other hand, as chapter 11 highlights, cheerleaders themselves may offer a quite different interpretation of the sexualization inherent in cheer. "It's just part of the game," some say, while others say they like being the center of attention: "I like people looking at me, wishing they were me." These types of comments align with the assessment of Jane Kenway, Susan Willis, Jill Blackmore, and Leonie Rennie, which holds that "femininity can become a source of power and pleasure rather than a source of control."[12] Or put another way, as Naomi Wolf declared in her 1993 critique of second-wave feminists, "I am sick of the opposition trying to make me choose between being sexual and serious; and I am sick of being split the same way by victim feminism. I want to be a serious thinker and not have to hide the fact that I have breasts; I want female sexuality to accompany, rather than undermine, female political power."[13] As demonstrated throughout this volume, cheerleading is rife with contradictions, which, along with its ubiquity in American culture, situates it as an essential site to study social and cultural life in the United States.

To understand these two different interpretations of the close association between gender and sexuality in women's cheerleading, it is important to understand another concept about gender ideology. Gendered norms and ideals are not fixed or static. They morph in response to larger macro forces. The fluidity of gender norms and their embeddedness in our institutions can be viewed in how cheerleading changed during second-wave feminism in concert with other societal changes about women's place in the public sphere. After the passage of Title IX in 1972, girls had more choices about how to spend their free time. Cheerleading was not the only game in town, so it reinvented itself, becoming more athletic, more competitive, and more exciting. As the twentieth century came to an end, these larger societal changes were reflected in a new gendered discourse that sought to separate itself from what Wolf calls "victim feminism." This change was captured in the opening poem of the 1999 Varsity cheerleading catalog:

> I am not arrogant.
> I am confident.
> I am not a daredevil.
> I am daring.
> I am not a beauty queen.
> I am an athlete.
> I am not a stereotype.
> I am my own person.
> I am not interested in living in the past.
> I am living for the future.
> I am not afraid of success.
> I am afraid of nothing.
> I am not another face in the crowd.
> I am the one others wish they could be.

Referred to, in various ways, as third-wave feminism, superwoman syndrome, and alpha, gamma, or can-do girls, this new feminine discourse encompassed a hybridity of masculine and feminine traits.[14] The superwoman and the alpha girl are confident, athletic, assertive, competitive, and future oriented. They expect lucrative careers and fulfilling lives outside of marriage and child-rearing. They are someone to be reckoned with, living "lives lightly inflected but by no means driven by feminism, influenced by the philosophy of DIY, and assuming they can have (or at least buy) it all."[15] They also are not willing to choose between being pretty and desirable or athletic and confident—between empowerment and objectification.

This changing gendered discourse about normative femininity can be found in myriad cultural spaces and practices, including cheerleading. In the 1980s, All Star cheer developed. Disassociated with any type of support role, All Star cheer is strictly about athleticism, competition, and aspirations for national and international championships. Nevertheless, conventionally feminine signifiers of big hair, makeup, glitter, smiles, and tight skirts are expected on competition day. This new form of competitive cheer reflected the values of third-wave feminism.[16] In *Manifesta: Young Women, Feminism, and the Future*, Jennifer Baumgardner and Amy Richards explain this new gendered discourse that celebrates not only traditional markers of femininity like girliness but also female empowerment: "Girlie says we're not broken, that our desires aren't simply booby traps set by the patriarchy. Girlie encompasses the tabooed symbols of women's feminine enculturation . . . Barbie dolls, makeup, fashion magazines, high heels"—and, I would add, *cheer*—"and using them isn't shorthand for 'we've been duped.'"[17] While outsiders to the sport may see cheerleading as a continuation of the sexual objectification of women, most cheerleaders do not. Performing a harrowing descent from a fifteen-foot pyramid and wearing a short skirt and a bow are not incongruent.

Alpha girls flocked to All Star cheer during the girl power movement of the 1990s. Here they could embody all the traits of third-wave feminism: athleticism, confidence, individuality, self-determination, risk-taking, and girliness. They were joined by young men, who returned to cheerleading in unprecedented numbers. Many were former football and baseball players who were recruited to coed teams, which quickly became the most elite form of cheerleading. When men returned to cheer in the 1990s, they entered a vastly different territory than that of their yell-leading brothers from an earlier era. This was a feminine terrain shaped by a new form of feminism, where aesthetics was prized as much as athleticism, and spirit, perkiness, and the bubbly cheerleader smile were as important as throwing a back tuck. Men's reentry into cheerleading did not destabilize traditional gender norms and relations. Coed teams tended to reproduce a gendered division of labor. As one cheerleader explained, "The guy is the frame. The girl's a piece of art."[18]

Behind the scenes, male and female cheerleaders practice, sweat, and train side by side. In this way, coed (also known as mixed gender) competitive cheerleading is different from most sports. But in the public sphere—on the sidelines of a college football game or at a national competition—their roles are very different. Men are the bases and spotters (i.e., the "frame"). The women are the flyers. The men provide the strength needed to hold a 100-pound girl in a liberty or toss her eighteen feet into the air. They are also the protectors, safely catching the flyers as they spiral downward. Their role is to lift the weight of the team and blend into the background. The girls at the top of the pyramid are the objects of the gaze.

Laurel Davis suggests that in its beginnings, coed cheer had the potential to disrupt conventional gender norms. What if the guy was the piece of art and the girl was the frame? What if guys and girls both danced and wore similar sequined uniforms? That transformation did not occur, as Davis laments:

> Any feminist transformative potential that could have been enhanced when males reentered cheerleading in recent times has seemingly been lost by the construction of a sexual division of labor. The male cheerleader has become increasingly accepted because the image he has constructed and continues to construct does not challenge traditional gender notions of power relations, but rather reinforces them. Cheerleading, as a feminine preserve, remains to be seriously challenged.[19]

In the United States, all-male cheer teams are virtually nonexistent, but some changes have occurred in coed cheer. Male tumblers are often center stage and a crowd favorite. Male cheerleaders dance, some wear makeup, and their uniforms sometimes have a sparkle or two. The range of masculinities accepted and performed in cheerleading is more robust and inclusive than in most traditional sports.[20] And all-male cheer teams do compete globally. Yet because of the association of cheerleading with heterosexualized femininity, and because femininity in men is conflated with homosexuality, male cheerleaders are governed by a different set of cheerleading rules that prove their masculinity and, for straight cheerleaders, their heterosexuality.

According to a 2018 Sports and Fitness Industry Association report, male cheerleaders now comprise over 21 percent of all cheerleaders and 50 percent of all collegiate cheerleaders.[21] How do the four cheer rules discussed above apply to men and boys? If they cheer for a high school or collegiate team, they are expected to be spirit leaders (Rule #1) and, perhaps, school ambassadors (Rule #2). Male cheerleaders, however, are not governed as strictly as women by Rule #3 and Rule #4. Male cheerleaders do not have to be thin or conventionally handsome; they aren't expected to be "wholesome" or "good." But rules do exist for male cheerleaders, and they reflect pervasive and persistent norms about appropriate male gendered behavior.

*Rule #1 for Guys: If you're straight, be übermasculine and hyperheterosexual.* As Eric Anderson, Michelle Bemiller, and others have noted, male cheerleaders are regularly harassed, and their masculinity and sexuality are often questioned.[22] Faced with taunts about being a "fag," a "fairy," or "gay," straight male cheerleaders employ two common strategies to justify their participation in a highly feminized activity: (1) they accentuate traditional markers of masculinity, and (2) they emphasize their heterosexuality by sexualizing their female teammates to other men. Male cheerleaders typically spend hours in the gym, with a particular focus on building biceps and quads, two very visible markers of masculinity. They reference their strength as proof of their masculinity. Comebacks such as this one are common: "You catch a one-pound football. I throw 115-pound women into the air and catch them with no problem!"[23] They emphasize the inherent heterosexuality of coed cheerleading with references to close intimate contact with their female counterparts: "I'm hanging around with some of the hottest, in-shape young ladies that the school has to offer. I'm touching them and holding them in places you can only dream about. Now let me ask, who's gay?"[24] They turn the presumptions about being gay back on male athletes in traditional sports by pointing out they aren't showering naked with other guys or slapping them on their butts when they make a good play.

Both male and female cheerleaders view injuries as badges of honor. But injuries for male cheerleaders are also proof of their masculinity. They proudly cite statistics about cheerleading being second only to football in terms of injuries. "I've endured more injuries from cheerleading than [from] playing rugby but, still, a lot of my colleagues don't understand what's involved in the sport," remarks Lewis Judd, a rugby player turned cheerleader for Team England (winners at the 2018 World Cheerleading Championships). "I regularly turn up to work with black eyes following a night of cheerleading practice."[25]

*Rule #2 for Guys: Do not dance.* The gendered division of labor on the mat often extends beyond stunting and pyramid building. On many cheerleading teams, it is understood that male cheerleaders do not dance, because dancing is seen as too feminine—that is, "too gay." While the women sway their hips provocatively to fast-paced music and shimmy their shoulders and chests, the men often follow the dance routine in the background with some simple moves—called "strong arms"—that one might see in a military parade. If the men don't feel like doing the strong arms, they can pick up a megaphone and yell or throw T-shirts into the crowd. Even smiling is optional for men.

These rules about appropriate masculine performance can be seen in training camps, particularly in the 1990s and early 2000s, as men were just reentering cheer. At cheer camps sponsored by the Universal Cheerleaders Association (UCA), popular in the South, a strict code of gender-specific behavior was enforced. Laura Grindstaff and Emily West quote a UCA instructor's rules for men: "UCA stipulates no toe touches, no girl motions and moves, nothing with hips, no dancing. Once you cross that line and let the guys dance like girls you start losing the masculine image you want to project."[26] Other camps allowed more gender fluidity. At United Spirit Association (USA) camps, popular on the West Coast, male cheerleaders danced, smiled, and performed toe touches. They were encouraged to exhibit a flashier style. Today these institutionalized gender differences are not as pronounced as they once were, for several reasons. UCA, USA, and the National Cheerleaders Association (NCA) are now all owned by one company, Varsity Brands. Competitive cheer has opened doors for male cheerleaders to be more performative, and societal shifts toward nonbinary ways of thinking about gender have made their way into cheerleading as well.

The first two rules in the male cheerleader handbook are specifically aimed at proving one's masculinity and, by extension, heterosexuality, thus disproving stereotypes that only gay men cheer. But what about queer male-presenting cheerleaders? If Netflix's *Cheer* is an accurate portrayal of contemporary coed cheerleading, then it seems to be much more welcoming of gay men than other traditional sports. Eric Anderson's scholarly research on male cheerleaders affirms this perception. He writes, "The emergence of a more inclusive form of masculinity [in cheer] is attributed to many factors, including the structure of the sport; the reduction of cultural, institutional, and organizational homophobia; and the resocialization of men into a gender-integrated sport."[27] The final rule in the unofficial rule book for male cheerleaders speaks directly to cheer as a space for some men to demonstrate and play with a full and diverse range of masculinities.

*Rule #3 for (Queer) Guys: Be out, be proud, and be you!* We discover in season 1 of *Cheer* that La'Darius Marshall, one of the most popular members of the Navarro College cheer team, was bullied in high school because he was gay and a cheerleader. His openness about his sexual identity and his experiences being bullied resonated with many viewers, as did his presentation of gender. His outward appearance exudes traditional masculinity: strong, big muscles, superathletic. His demeanor, particularly with teammates, is stern. He is known for shredding his teammates' confidence with tough criticism and is nonchalant about making a few of his female teammates cry. He is aggressive both on and off the mat. He also loves to smile and dance and be the center of attention. His performances can be flamboyant, sassy, and over-the-top expressive. It is obvious that in cheer, Marshall has found a space to authentically perform his sexuality and gender.

This freedom to do some gender bending, to be out and proud on the mat, is unfortunately not extended to most queer female-presenting cheerleaders, whose invisibility stands in stark contrast to other lesbian athletes or the cheerleaders' gay male teammates. As several media scholars have pointed out, cheerleaders serve as "visual tropes" and a "semiotic shorthand" signifying American femininity.[28] Their appearance in film and television, advertisements, and social media assumes that the audience shares a common knowledge about the multiple, often conflicting meanings of this ambiguous cultural icon:

- Cheerleaders are the popular, smart, pretty girls who represent the most desirable traits in American femininity.
- Cheerleaders are vapid, dumb, uninteresting girls with limited goals, introspection, and depth.
- Cheerleaders are nice, virginal girls and the object of heterosexual male desire because they are so good and unattainable.
- Cheerleaders are sexually promiscuous.

Because these significations exist in tandem, cheerleaders in popular media vary from the pretty, popular girls at the top of the high school food chain, to mean girls, vapid girls, supersexual girls, and (occasionally) superathletic girls. Within these different cheerleader motifs, one theme commonly exists. Cheerleaders are young, white, middle class, suburban, physically attractive, and *straight*. According to Emma Jane (Tom), they "function in [popular] discourse as a sort of litmus test for detecting 'normal,' hetero-focused male desire."[29]

Of course, queer girls do cheer, although they have been rendered invisible in news reports and academic research about cheerleading. Their inconspicuousness makes it all the more important to look at how queer girls are represented in indie films such as *But I'm a Cheerleader* and in more mainstream media such as *Glee*. In both, as Barbara Brickman discussed in chapter 9, the cheerleader's signification as both girly and heterosexual is appropriated and then turned on its head. This disruption not only provides a rich visual and artistic space for experimentation but also forces the audience to question the social construction of normative gender and sexuality and the ways in which those norms are constantly resisted and reshaped. The representation of queer cheerleaders in popular media calls into question the "normal" way of both "doing" cheerleading and "doing" queer.

## Race Matters

Queer girls are not the only cheerleaders missing from cheer teams and in our public imagination of this American institution. Sharita Mathis Richardson, the mother of three All Star cheerleaders, drew attention to the invisibility of Black cheerleaders in 2015 when she formed a Facebook group called Black Girls Cheer and invited five other moms to join. In less than twenty-four hours, Richardson attracted more than 1,000 Facebook followers and 120,000 Instagram followers. It ignited a movement called Black Girls Cheer, which aims to draw attention to discriminatory cheerleading policies and to the underrepresentation of Black girls in cheer.[30] Today the Black Girls Cheer movement has its own website, a documentary of the same name, and a robust network of Black cheerleaders, parents, coaches, and business owners who are challenging the exclusion of Black girls in cheer.[31]

Black girls have always cheered. In the segregated high schools of the 1940s, 1950s, and 1960s, Black female students, like their white counterparts, vied for positions on the cheerleading squad. Making the team was a validation of one's popularity, physical attractiveness, leadership abilities, and femininity. While the types of cheers and styles of cheering differed somewhat at white and Black schools, the meaning of cheerleading was the same.[32] The cheerleader was the highest-status position for a girl, the social equivalent of the quarterback. As discussed in chapter 2, an examination of cheerleading's role in desegregation provides insights into the contradictory and inconsistent ways that racial and ethnic integration occurred in our nation's schools, gymnasiums, and football fields. It also reflects the close interconnectedness of gender, sexuality, and race.[33]

Teena Horn grew up in Jackson, Mississippi, in the 1960s and attended Murrah High School when it was court ordered to desegregate. Teena was selected as a cheerleader that year and recalls the social, cultural, and financial capital the designation conferred:

> Being one of eight Murrah cheerleaders in a school of over a thousand people was probably the biggest thing that could happen to a north Jackson girl. . . . Being a white cheerleader in the 1970s meant entering a closed inner circle of northeast Jackson women and society. Perhaps there was an invitation to the Sub-Debs and the Sub-Deb Ball, which was the high-school version of the pre-debutante.[34]

All eight of the Murrah High cheerleaders, including Teena, were white. The squad wasn't integrated until August 1970, when a Black senior girl was added just before school opened. Teena's account of her cheerleading team reflects a common story from this era of school desegregation. White girls continued to dominate their cheerleading teams. Black girls were routinely excluded from cheerleading. That denial represented more than just a missed opportunity to participate in a fun extracurricular activity. Because the cheerleader was a symbolic signifier of American femininity, Black girls' exclusion from cheerleading was a declaration of their deficit. They weren't pretty enough, charming enough, respectable enough, feminine enough to wear the moniker of the all-American girl next door.

As chapter 2 discusses, the exclusion of Black and Brown girls from cheerleading squads precipitated protests and walkouts throughout the country. In a few places, riots occurred, and in Burlington, North Carolina, a Black student, Leon Mebane, was killed.[35] Parents filed lawsuits against school districts for discriminatory cheerleading policies, and students themselves were often at the helm of these protests. The creation of the Raza Unida Party movement in Texas is partially attributed to a school- and community-wide protest of the underrepresentation of Chicana cheerleaders at Crystal City High School. The integration of cheerleading teams has been largely ignored in the history of school desegregation and the integration of sports. It does not align with the more popular redemptive narrative about how sport transcends barriers of race and class—a story repeated in numerous movies, such as *Remember the Titans*. The myth-like narrative about the seemingly smooth transition to integrated football and basketball teams is the story of American meritocracy in which hard work and athletic skills determine membership, not the color of one's skin. On the other hand, the challenges Black girls have faced in their pursuit of cheerleading reflects the power of institutional racism to determine who belongs and who does not. These historical accounts do not fit well within the colorblind sports narrative—the one that insists everything ends well if we all just come together and ignore race.[36]

When the lack of Black representation on cheer teams was brought to administrators' attention during the school desegregation era, they typically responded with references to fair judging criteria, saying that Black girls lacked the requisite skills and abilities to perform the duties of a cheerleader—that is, they didn't perform militaristic, straight-armed movements; they couldn't do a cartwheel and a split; their dancing was "too expressive," all code for they didn't appear or act white enough. Today, the underrepresentation of cheerleaders of color is still prevalent, as anyone who has ever attended a cheer camp or competition can attest. Like the unspoken rules deployed during school desegregation to ensure that white girls dominated cheer teams, the cheerleading rule book for young women still disadvantages Black girls. The last rule for cheerleaders speaks to this.

*Rule #5: Manage your hair.* In cheerleading, hair matters. Official rules often read like this: "Hair must be secured away from the face and eyes and off the shoulders, such as in a ponytail," or "No nonnatural-colored hair (green, blue, purple, orange, cherry red) is allowed." In 2020, to avoid any confusion about acceptable cheer hair, the Iowa Cheerleading Coaches' Association added twelve clarifications:

1. Hair in a ponytail and bangs (which would have been in the eyes) *secured* away from the face (legal)
2. Hair in a high ponytail that is long and goes down the back (legal)
3. Hair in pigtails or side ponytail that does NOT touch the shoulders (legal)
4. Hair in a low back ponytail at the base of the nape of the neck (legal)
5. Short hair with hair that could be in face *secured* away (legal)
6. Hair that is half up and half down (the back of hair is down, but front and bangs are pulled up and secured) (illegal)
7. Long, ratted hair and/or hair pieces that fall in a cheerleader's face, including the hair of the top person obscuring the vision of the base(s) or spotter(s) (illegal)
8. Long hair in a ponytail high on the crown that allows the hair to fall into the face (illegal)
9. Short hair that brushes the tops of the shoulders (illegal)
10. Hair in a ponytail that's lying on or over the front of the shoulder (illegal)
11. Hair in a side ponytail that goes onto or touches the shoulders (illegal)
12. Hair in pigtails that touches the shoulders (illegal)[37]

Embedded in contemporary discussions of cheerleading hair are many cultural assumptions about beauty, desirability, and femininity.[38] For example, a common rule governing hair in cheerleading states that "hairstyles should not distract from the uniform look of a team." Jacie Scott, a former

Dallas Cowboys Cheerleader, explains what that meant to her as a Black cheerleader: Straighten your hair. "It never occurred to me that maybe I could start over and rock my natural hair as a cheerleader because I hadn't seen that being done."[39]

Erika Carter, who cheered for Northwestern University, was penalized for wearing her hair in braids on game day because her hairstyle didn't conform to the team's official hair policy: "Hair and makeup must be worn in the assigned manner." According to Carter, this meant, "Look like the white, blonde girls on the team."[40] In 2020, Asia Simo, who cheered for Captain Shreve High School in Shreveport, Louisiana, was dismissed from the team because of excessive demerits. Fifteen of the twenty demerits she received related to wearing the "wrong hair," meaning she didn't sport the team's "half up, half down" hairstyle.[41]

Black Girls Cheer has used its platform to call attention to these discriminatory policies and their effects on individual Black cheerleaders, as well as on their lack of representation more broadly. These restrictions place financial pressures (e.g., costly trips to beauty salons) on Black girls that most white cheerleaders do not have to face. More importantly, hearkening back to earlier policies of exclusion during the school desegregation era, these current hair policies coded in seemingly neutral language of team unity and uniformity demand that Black girls accommodate and assimilate to white norms of cheering and appearance. Pushback about hair has resulted in some changes. The US All Star Federation (USASF) recently adopted new appearance rules. In addition to discouraging excessive makeup, big bows, and poufed hair, the rules state, "Hair must be secured off of the face with a simple and unexaggerated style that is adaptable to all diversities."[42]

### Cheerleading as Sport Matters

Sports is one of the primary social institutions for reproducing and maintaining "hegemonic masculinity," a term denoting the socially dominant or "culturally exalted" form of masculinity prized and privileged in society.[43] Hegemonic masculinity idealizes traits typically associated with men, such as assertiveness, competitiveness, limited emotional expression, and power. Sometimes called "toxic masculinity" or "orthodox masculinity," it is built around heteronormative notions of what constitutes a "real" man, thereby excluding men who fail to meet these norms (e.g., queer men, men who appear effeminate, or men who participate in feminine activities) and subordinating women and traits associated with women or the feminine. Men who deviate from these expected norms of masculinity have not found traditional sports a welcoming place, as evident in the invisibility of gay men in football, basketball, baseball, hockey, rugby, and soccer. Taunts of "fag" are meant not only to exclude gay men but also to control the behavior of all men who play sports. Certainly, not all men embody hegemonic masculinity or perform it in their everyday lives. And gender norms and expectations change in response to larger social and cultural shifts. For example, today being a hands-on father who coparents his children is seen by many as indicative of ideal masculinity.

From its inception, sports provided a space for men to revel in the physicality of their bodies. In this sex-segregated space, boys were taught that toughness, imperviousness to pain, pushing the limits of physical exertion, and risk-taking define a "real" man. Sports also provided a safe space for men to bond with each other and to express forms of intimacy (e.g., hugging after a big win) rarely allowed in other contexts. The sacredness of sports as a male institution and as a primary mechanism for socializing boys and men into conventional norms of masculinity was based on the exclusion of girls and women. The traits associated with sports were seen as incompatible with women's "true" nature, and girls and women who wanted to play sports or desired to beat the boys in physical feats were viewed as gender abominations. Their negation in the early world of sports reinforced the belief that segregated spheres for men and women were imperative for the maintenance of gender norms and the social order. Gendered boundaries were not to be blurred.[44]

As chapter 3 discussed, women slowly made strides into the world of sports, but their acceptance was never meant to challenge dominant gender norms. Women were siphoned into a female-only sphere. They were channeled into sports deemed appropriate for building healthy female bodies and minds. If they played the same sport as men, there were different rules, equipment, and uniforms. For decades, female athletes were governed by separate organizations in the United States. Most important to the continuance of hegemonic masculinity, a sports hierarchy was created in which the most prized sports with the highest status and financial rewards and resources were those most closely associated with hegemonic masculinity (e.g., football in the US context). In the contemporary fight for equitable resources, many women's sports seek legitimacy by adopting the masculine conventions (rules, uniforms, athletic performance) of their male sports counterparts. For example, women's basketball is currently enjoying a heyday. Commentators suggest it is because the sport has upped its pace; three-point shots are common, and dunking has now become part of the game, as has taunting on the court. All of these have long been hallmarks of men's basketball.

Sports reifies and reproduces a social order firmly entrenched in essentialized notions of gendered bodies. This is seen in the worldwide organization of sports based on gender segregation. When Title IX passed, it was heralded as a progressive step in the fight for equal rights for girls and women. Women would now have access to a variety of sports; their numbers would compare fairly to those of male athletes, and they would have access to scholarships, facilities, equipment, and safety mechanisms. Title IX was never meant to challenge the separation of men and women in sports. Its rules for determining compliance reflect the belief that physiologically men and women are so different that they naturally must play and compete separately. The hold of the gender binary in sport, steeped in essentialized assumptions about strength, physicality, and natural athletic prowess, is ingrained in sporting culture at almost every level of competition worldwide.

It is important to bring attention to cheerleading's place in the sports hierarchy for several reasons. First, the resolution of the debate around whether cheerleading is a sport has consequences on the everyday lives of cheerleaders, as discussed in chapter 3. It also has significant implications for male cheerleaders. Further, cheerleading is unique in the sports world because its most popular form is coed competitive cheer. If coed cheer continues to flourish, and if it gains formal sports status, it may change the organizational framework of sports to include men, women, and mixed-gender divisions, thus providing more opportunities for men and women to compete together based on ability rather than gender. Lastly, discussions about where cheerleading belongs in the current sex-segregated sports regime introduces a new perspective into current debates about the limitations of the gender binary in sporting culture.

Chatter abounds in the cheer world and in the mainstream media about cheer's possible inclusion in the Olympics. Although less visible in news media, the recent designation of STUNT and acrobatics and tumbling (acro) as National Collegiate Athletic Association (NCAA) emerging sports has also gained attention. For many, this is a celebratory moment in cheer's long fight for legitimacy. But the ramifications of these designations have not been sufficiently discussed, especially the consequences for male cheerleaders and the future format of cheerleading. The NCAA's approval of STUNT and acro was in response to a long battle fought by two competing organizations (USA Cheer and the National Collegiate Acrobatics and Tumbling Association [NCATA], sanctioned by USA Gymnastics) and a federal judge's ruling in *Biediger v. Quinnipiac University* (2010) that cheerleading could not count as a Title IX sport. It is important to note that the formats of STUNT and acro differ from each other, and both differ from what one would see at a UCA, NCA, or Worlds competition. An acro event looks somewhat like a gymnastics meet, minus the hyperfeminized uniforms. There are heats, judges, a halftime, and only two or four teams competing at a meet. The athletes wear numbered jerseys and shorts, similar to women's volleyball. At STUNT events, there are basket tosses, back tucks, toe touches, and tumbling, but no smiling, expressive facial movements, glittery makeup, or bows. And in both, there are no men. STUNT and acro were created specifically to comply with Title IX, as explained on STUNT's website: "USA Cheer created STUNT as an opportunity to increase athletic opportunities for *female athletes*. . . . STUNT will expand participation opportunities for *young women* at the collegiate level by providing an avenue for *female athletes* to use their cheerleading skill backgrounds in a new sport" (emphasis added).[45]

The introduction of a female-only type of cheerleading to count toward being a Title IX equivalency sport has significant implications for male cheerleaders and their future in the sport. A male athlete participating in a female-designated sport typically precludes it from meeting Title IX guidelines. One response from universities has been to offer two different cheerleading teams: the traditional, coed team—which cheers at athletic events, represents the university at public events, and vies to compete for the NCA College Championship—and a girls-only STUNT or acro team. The girls-only team is eligible for the NCAA-related benefits and can potentially (if they're good enough) compete for an NCAA-sanctioned national championship.

The University of Kentucky recently followed this path, adding STUNT to its athletic roster in 2021. The University of Kentucky coed cheerleading team has long been a powerhouse in competitive collegiate cheerleading, winning twenty-four national NCA championships. What will the addition of STUNT mean for the university's traditional coed cheer team? Historically, members of the University of Kentucky's Blue Team (coed) have received scholarships. Will this continue now that STUNT athletes are eligible for NCAA scholarships? If both teams qualify for their respective national championships, will their travel be funded equally? What if both teams win? Is one national championship more prestigious than the other? How will the university's strategic communications division handle the celebratory announcements? Will the University of Kentucky boast that they have two 2026 national cheerleading champs? Will both teams get official national championship rings? Will the university pay for them both? Does this entire scenario seem so out of sync with the rest of the sports world that it renders the current NCAA cheer sport resolution highly problematic?

At the global level, the International Olympic Committee (IOC) granted full recognition to cheerleading in 2021, an important step toward becoming a regular feature at the Olympic Games. But it's unclear what format cheerleading will take *if* cheer ever makes it to the global stage,[46] since the Olympics, like the NCAA, generally adheres to a gendered division of sports. Will we see a men's division, with only male cheerleaders, and a women's division, with only female cheerleaders? Will mixed-gender cheerleading—the format most people assume we will see—be excluded at the Olympics? Bill Seely, president of Varsity Spirit, doesn't think so: "I think it's going to be exciting, and being able to be a part of the Olympics and introducing this co-ed format could have an impact on many other sports. . . . There are all of these other dynamics you're introduced to when you're on a co-ed team that you may not be used to otherwise." He adds, "To the extent that other sports see this and realize they can participate in that, it's fantastic."[47]

Seely's hopefulness that cheer's uniqueness as a coed sport may allow a different Olympic designation, coupled with his comments about its potential impact on other sports, suggests that the binary gender logic of sex-segregated sports is perhaps penetrable. As discussed above, the organization of sports based on a strict gendered binary assumes that men are naturally superior to women in most athletic events, particularly those that rely on muscular strength. As several scholars have pointed out, this "common sense" logic is seldom challenged since men and women rarely compete together in the same sport.[48] Courts, state legislatures, and athletic governing bodies have used this argument to ensure that trans athletes compete in the gendered sports division that reflects the sex they were assigned at birth. The argument is that the possession of male genitals at birth "obviously" and "naturally" gives boys and men an advantage in sports, and thus a trans woman possesses innate abilities that would give her an unfair advantage if she competed in the women's division.

This commonsense argument, as many scholars note, is problematic.

Mary Jo Kane, citing empirical evidence of women outperforming men in a variety of athletic events, calls for a radical transformation of sports based on a sports continuum, which proposes that men and women have varying levels of athletic abilities (from low to high) that transcend gender.[49] This model proffers that if sports were organized differently and women were given the chance to demonstrate their abilities, some women would outperform some men in some sports, even in contact sports.[50] Thus, exclusion based simply on gender is insufficient and unfair. Organizing sports based on a continuum "provides the possibility of seeing sport as a gender-neutral activity in which numerous individuals, some of whom are male and some of whom are female, participate and have varying degrees of ability."[51] Kane proposed the sports continuum thirty years ago. Its effect on the reorganization of sports has been minimal because, as she noted, "it is a threat to one of the most seemingly real aspects of sport: the mutually exclusive oppositional binary."[52] Keeping men and women segregated in the world of sports ensures that men will probably never witness the superior abilities of a woman, and thus the commonsense logic of male superiority is perpetuated.

Coed competitive cheerleading has the potential to reenergize this discussion for several reasons. Mixed-gender competitive cheerleading is relatively new and constantly evolving. Assumptions about athletic superiority (e.g., men are naturally better athletes) and suitability for the team (e.g., only girls cheer) are not as firmly entrenched as in traditional sports with long histories. Globally, cheer is comprised of men and women in relatively equal numbers. They train, practice, and compete together, thus allowing men and women to witness firsthand overlapping abilities and the variance of skills, irrespective of gender. The sport requires a high degree of athleticism, and while traditional gendered roles exist on many teams, the newness of the sport, its playfulness, and the ever-changing criteria for judging performance offers a fluidity, and thus possibilities, different from most sports with firmly entrenched rules, customs, and assumptions about athletic prowess. When gender is no longer the guiding framework for participation in sports, it allows for "alternative gendered practices, shaped by novel experiences of male and female bodies that do not conform to the essentialist categories productive of an immutable sexual hierarchy."[53]

Proponents of coed sports point to the valuable lessons men and women learn when working together. They develop an appreciation of their overlapping and complementary skills. For example, in coed cheer, the base's athletic skill and role on the team is complementary to that of the flyer, not oppositional or hierarchical. Both roles are imperative for the team's success. Further, proponents of mixed-gender sports argue that the benefits of coed skill development and team building help socialize men and women to work together in other contexts. The time seems ripe for discussing the benefits of coed sports as boys' participation in contact sports is decreasing because of growing concerns about their safety and long-term health effects (e.g., brain injuries related to concussions). Mixed-gender play is touted as an antidote to a toxic masculinity many parents find troublesome. The Olympics has begun to offer a few coed events: mixed-gender curling at the 2018 Winter Olympics and shooting, swimming, and table tennis (among several others) at the 2021 Summer Olympics. And one of the fastest-growing sports for middle-aged and older adults is mixed doubles pickleball. To date, there is no powerful coalition calling for and supporting coed sports nationwide. The popularity of coed cheerleading and the possibility that perhaps coed cheer may be recognized as a sport sometime in the future positions cheerleading to be at the forefront of such a movement. Cheerleading seems primed to take a lead in pushing this untapped but potentially flourishing market for coed sports.

## Joy and Hope Matter: To a Cheery Future

Cheerleading was born out of a youthful, unadulterated enthusiasm that led its leaders and followers to literally jump for joy. It was invented by students, for students, and with little interference from adults. Its cheers, its rituals, its traditions were intentionally cultivated to create a community among students—quite different and separate from the staid culture of heady books and rules of comportment. Describing cheerleading's evolution in American sporting culture, Arturo Gonzales notes that its "Jabberwockian permutations [became] a part of the nation's Fall-Saturday tradition, ranging in varying degrees of sanity."[54] Yet throughout its history, critics have questioned cheer's purpose and its timeless appeal. The president of Harvard was so upset by the popularity of cheerleading on his campus in 1911 that he told a group of music teachers gathered at a convention in Boston that cheerleading was a horrid way for students to express emotion; the only thing worse was a "chorus of fog-horns." He viewed cheerleading as ruinous to the "delicate qualities" that universities were trying to develop in their students. *The Nation* responded with its own critical assessment of President Lowell, calling him a "stepping-stone of the dead" who would prefer "three or four opera singers in the grand stands subduing everybody to silence or tears."[55]

All the jumping, yelling, incessant smiling, and chucking people fifteen feet in the air make cheerleading a unique activity that defies easy classification. Consequently, the cheerleader holds a complicated place in American society, as discussed throughout this volume. But one constant has persisted throughout cheer's evolution and its contemporary challenges: its close association with youthful idealism, hope, and joy. This is captured in cheerleading's place in the American lexicon and how frequently it appears in headlines, press reports, and speeches in contexts having nothing to do with sports. "I'd rather be a cheerleader for the country than Mr. Doom and Gloom," President Trump told ABC News in May 2020.[56] Describing President Obama's attempts to pass sweeping healthcare reform, Michael Muskal of the *Los Angeles Times* referred to him as "cheerleader in chief."[57] When California Governor Gavin Newsom threw his support behind Kamala Harris during the 2024 presidential election, one newspaper reported, "Gavin Newsom, Once Joe Biden's Biggest Cheerleader, Inches into the Kamala Harris Campaign."[58]

For the first anniversary of the September 11, 2001, terrorist attacks, the photographer Eddie Adams sought images demonstrating American resiliency in the face of adversity. In his pictorial display in *Parade* magazine, entitled "Our American Spirit," Adams included a picture of high school cheerleaders with the caption "Sheer Energy."[59] His placement of cheerleaders next to photographs of civil rights workers, firefighters, and police officers signifies the cultural importance of cheerleading in our public imagination. Cheerleaders remind us that amid adversity and defeat, better times are just around the corner. They are our national antidote to cynicism and our cultural conveyors of hope and optimism.

We've spent the past thirteen chapters discussing ongoing debates, conflicts, and tensions within the world of cheer: problems with its image, conflicts with Title IX, sexualization, money, monopolies, protests, and representation. So, it may come as a surprise that we end with the conclusion that cheer's resilience and endurance as an essential part of American culture signals a bright future. We may not be able to predict what forms it will take, who will wear the uniforms, and in what contexts it will appear, but cheerleading is not going anywhere. We expect that some cheerleading team fifty or seventy-five years from now will be yelling with as much exuberance and enthusiasm as do cheerleaders today: "We've got spirit! Yes we do! We've got spirit. How about you?"

## Notes

1. “Organized Cheering,” *The Nation* 92 (January 1911): 6.

2. F. B. Kutz, “Cheerleading Rules, Desirable Traits, and Qualifications,” *School Activities*, May 1955, 310.

3. Pamela Grundy, *Learning to Win: Sports, Education, and Social Change in Twentieth-Century North Carolina* (University of North Carolina Press, 2001), 287.

4. Maxine Paetro, “Cheerleader Envy,” *New Woman*, March 1996, 91–93, 142.

5. Kyle Smith, “Relax, It’s OK for Cheerleaders to Look Hot,” *New York Post*, April 27, 2016, https://nypost.com/2016/04/27/relax-its-ok-for-cheerleaders-to-look-hot/.

6. “Cheerleading Constitution,” St. Clair County Schools, https://www.sccboe.org/site/handlers/filedownload.ashx?moduleinstanceid=1676&dataid=6518&FileName=20-21%20ST%20CLAIR%20COUNTY%20CHEERLEADING%20CONSTITUTION.pdf.

7. “Ware Shoals High School Cheerleader Handbook,” 2020–2021, https://core-docs.s3.amazonaws.com/documents/asset/uploaded_file/767540/Cheerleading_Handbook.pdf.

8. *Merriam-Webster.com Dictionary*, “wholesome,” https://www.merriam-webster.com/dictionary/wholesome.

9. Suzette Scholz, Stephanie Scholz, and Sheri Scholz, *Deep in the Heart of Texas: Reflections of Former Dallas Cowboys Cheerleaders* (St. Martin’s Press, 1991), 143.

10. Arturo Gonzales, “The First College Cheer,” *American Mercury* 83 (November 1956): 104.

11. Natalie G. Adams and Pamela J. Bettis, *Cheerleader! An American Icon* (Palgrave Macmillan, 2003), 85.

12. Jane Kenway, Susan Willis, Jill Blackmore, and Leonie Rennie, “Making ‘Hope Practical’ Rather Than ‘Despair Convincing’: Feminist Post-Structuralism, Gender Reform and Educational Change,” *British Journal of Sociology of Education* 15, no. 2 (1994): 205.

13. Naomi Wolf, *Fire with Fire: The New Female Power and How It Will Change the 21st Century* (Random House, 1993), 185.

14. Dan Kindlon, *Alpha Girls: Understanding the New American Girl and How She Is Changing the World* (Rodale, 2006); Susannah Meadows, “Meet the Gamma Girls,” *Newsweek*, June 3, 2002, 44–50; Anita Harris, *All About the Girl* (Routledge, 2004); Anita Harris, *Future Girl* (Routledge, 2004).

15. Harris, *Future Girl*, 17.

16. Natalie G. Adams and Pamela J. Bettis, “Alpha Girls and Cheerleading: Negotiating New Discourses with Old Practices,” *Girlhood Studies* 2, no. 1 (2009): 148–166.

17. Jennifer Baumgardner and Amy Richards, *Manifesta: Young Women, Feminism, and the Future* (Farrar, Straus and Giroux, 2000), 60.

18. Adams and Bettis, *Cheerleader!*, 87.

19. Laurel Davis, "Male Cheerleaders and the Naturalization of Gender," in *Sport, Men, and the Gender Order*, ed. Michael Messner and Donald Sabo (Human Kinetics, 1990), 153–161.

20. Eric Anderson, "Orthodox and Inclusive Masculinity: Competing Masculinities Among Heterosexual Men in a Feminized Terrain," *Sociological Perspectives* 48, no. 3 (2005): 337–355; Michelle Bemiller, "Men Who Cheer," *Sociological Focus* 38, no. 3 (2005): 205–222.

21. "Cheerleading Participation Report," Sports and Fitness Industry Association, 2018, https://www.sfia.org/reports/629_Cheerleading-Participation-Report-2018.

22. Anderson, "Orthodox and Inclusive Masculinity"; Bemiller, "Men Who Cheer"; Laura Grindstaff and Emily West, "Cheerleading and the Gendered Politics of Sport," *Social Problems* 53, no. 4 (2006): 500–518; Adams and Bettis, *Cheerleader!*

23. Adams and Bettis, *Cheerleader!*, 87.

24. Grindstaff and West, "Cheerleading and the Gendered Politics of Sport," 511.

25. "14 Hours Training a Week, 38,000 Spectators, Homophobic Slurs: What It's Really Like to Be a Male Cheerleader," *The Independent*, February 3, 2019, https://www.independent.co.uk/lifestyle/super-bowl-2019-male-cheerleader-atlanta-los-angeles-rams-new-england-patriots-nfla8758721.html.

26. Grindstaff and West, "Cheerleading and the Gendered Politics of Sport," 512.

27. Anderson, "Orthodox and Inclusive Masculinity," 338.

28. Michelle Liu Carriger, "'Cheering Ain't for Show, Y'all': Cheerleaders, Performative Uniforms, and Theatre Affect," in *Sports Plays*, ed. Eero Laine and Broderick Chow (Routledge, 2021), 190–206; Emma Jane, "Is *Debbie Does Dallas* Dangerous? Representations of Cheerleading in Pornography and Some Possible Effects," *Feminist Media Studies* 17, no. 2 (2017): 264–280.

29. Jane, "Is *Debbie Does Dallas* Dangerous?"

30. Will Linendoll, "Black Girls Cheer: How a Mom's Social Media Group Sparked a Movement," *Good Morning America*, March 3, 2020, https://www.goodmorningamerica.com/living/story/blackgirls-cheer-moms-social-media-group-sparked-69294124.

31. Home page, Black Girls Cheer, https://blackgirlscheer.com/; *Black Girls Cheer: The Movie* (Double Good, 2020), https://www.doublegood.com/blackgirlscheer/.

32. For an excellent analysis of differences between white and Black cheerleading styles, see Chelsea Mary Elise Johnson, "'Just Because I Dance Like a Ho I'm Not a Ho!': Cheerleading at the Intersection of Race, Class, and Gender," *Sociology of Sport Journal* 32, no. 4 (2015): 377–394; Adams and Bettis, *Cheerleader!*, 97–99.

33. For an in-depth analysis of how cheerleading played out in the larger context of extracurricular activities during school desegregation in Mississippi, see

Natalie G. Adams and James H. Adams, *Just Trying to Have School: The Struggle for Desegregation in Mississippi* (University Press of Mississippi, 2018), 124–166.

34. Teena Horn, Alan Huffman, and John G. Jones, eds., *Lines Were Drawn: Remembering Court-Ordered Integration at a Mississippi High School* (University Press of Mississippi, 2016), 184.

35. Grundy, *Learning to Win*, 285.

36. Adams and Adams, *Just Trying to Have School*, 124–166.

37. "Expectations for Cheerleaders," Iowa High School Athletic Association, 2020.

38. For a more in-depth analysis of the politics of hair, see Ingrid Banks, *Hair Matters: Beauty, Power, and Black Women's Consciousness* (New York University Press, 2000); Gino Canella, "#BlackIsBeautiful: The Radical Politics of Black Hair," *Visual Studies* 35, nos. 2–3 (2020): 273–284, https://doi.org/10.1080/1472586X.2020.1789501; Tracey Owens Patton, "Hey Girl, Am I More Than My Hair? African American Women and Their Struggles with Beauty, Body Image, and Hair," *NWSA Journal* 18, no. 2 (2006): 24–51; Kay Siebler, "Bonnets, Braids, and Big Afros: The Politics of Black Characters' Hair," *Feminist Media Studies* 12, no. 8 (2023): 4026–4040.

39. Paige Skinner, "Black Cheerleaders Are Calling for Change; Will the NFL Listen?," *Allure*, October 11, 2020, https://www.allure.com/story/nfl-black-cheerleaders-hair-discrimination.

40. Alyssa Johnson, "Marginalized on the Sidelines," *Daily Northwestern*, February 4, 2021, https://dailynorthwestern.com/2021/02/04/in-focus/marginalized-on-the-sidelines/.

41. "Captain Shreve Student Dismissed from Cheerleading Team over Hair," KTBS-TV, February 5, 2020, https://www.ktbs.com/news/captain-shreve-student-dismissed-fromcheerleading-team-over-hair/article_30fac2fc-487c-11ea-a9e0-af438a6dcede.html.

42. US All Star Federation, "2022–2023 USASF Cheer Rules," https://usasfmain.s3.amazonaws.com/Rules/USASF_Cheer_Rules_22-23.pdf.

43. R. W. Connell, *Masculinities* (University of California Press, 1995); Tim Carrigan, R. W. Connell, and John Lee, "Toward a New Sociology of Masculinity," *Theory and Society* 14, no. 5 (1985): 592.

44. Mary Jo Festle, *Playing Nice: Politics and Apologies in Women's Sports* (Columbia University Press, 1996); Natalie Adams, Alison Schmitke, and Amy Franklin, "Tomboys, Dykes, and Girly Girls: Interrogating the Subjectivities of Adolescent Female Athletes," *Women's Studies Quarterly* 33, no. 1/2 (2005): 17–34; Susan Cahn, *Coming on Strong: Gender and Sexuality in Twentieth-Century Women's Sport* (Harvard University Press, 1994).

45. "Overview of STUNT," STUNT the Sport, USA Cheer, https://stuntthesport.org/jh-hs-resources/overview-of-stunt/.

46. The road to an Olympic appearance is long and complicated. The IOC has recognized many sports, and this recognition is an important step toward a potential Olympic appearance. But IOC recognition does not guarantee a straight pathway to the Olympics. For example, the IOC recognized ballroom dancing

(i.e., dancesport) as a sport in 1997, but it has yet to appear in the Olympics, although breaking (breakdancing) did appear in the 2024 Olympics.

47. Jennifer Gerson, "Cheerleading in Olympics Could End the Gendered Debate on If It Is a Sport," *The 19th*, August 4, 2021, https://19thnews.org/2021/08/cheerleading-olympics-could-end-the-gendered-debate-sport/.

48. Mary Jo Kane, "Resistance/Transformation of the Oppositional Binary: Exposing Sport as a Continuum," *Journal of Sport and Social Issues* 19, no. 2 (1995): 191–218; Esther Priyadharshini and Amy Pressland, "Doing Femininities and Masculinities in a 'Feminized' Sporting Arena: The Case of Mixed-Sex Cheerleading," *Sport in Society* 19, nos. 8–9 (2016): 1234–1248.

49. Kane, "Resistance/Transformation of the Oppositional Binary."

50. Nancy Theberge, "'Same Sport, Different Gender': A Consideration of Binary Gender Logic in the Sport Continuum in the Case of Ice Hockey," *Journal of Sport and Social Issues* 22, no. 2 (1998): 183–198.

51. Kane, "Resistance/Transformation of the Oppositional Binary," 207.

52. Kane, "Resistance/Transformation of the Oppositional Binary," 204.

53. Alex Guy Channon, "Enter the Discourse: Exploring the Discursive Roots of Inclusivity in Mixed-Sex Martial Arts," *Sport in Society* 16, no. 10 (2013): 1294.

54. Gonzales, "The First College Cheer," 101.

55. "Organized Cheering," 6.

56. "ABC News Anchor David Muir Interviews President Trump in Arizona," ABC News, May 6, 2020, https://abcnews.go.com/Politics/transcript-abc-news-anchor-david-muir-interviews-president/story?id=70523003.

57. Michael Muskal, "Obama Plays Cheerleader to Push Healthcare," *Los Angeles Times*, November 7, 2009, https://www.latimes.com/archives/blogs/nation-now/story/2009-11-07/obama-plays-cheerleader-to-push-healthcare.

58. CALmatters.org and Alexei Koseff, "Gavin Newson, Once Joe Biden's Biggest Cheerleader, Inches into the Kamala Harris Campaign," *Press Democrat*, August 14, 2024, https://www.pressdemocrat.com/2024/08/14/gavin-newsom-once-joe-bidens-biggest-cheerleader-inches-into-the-kamala-harris-campaign/.

59. Eddie Adams, "Our American Spirit," *Parade*, September 8, 2002, 4–5.

# Acknowledgments

In January and February 2020, I was riding high professionally because of the stunning success of the Netflix hit *Cheer*. Being featured as the cheer historian on the docuseries resulted in a deluge of calls from reporters and documentary filmmakers throughout the world, eager to talk about this hugely popular series and the American institution of cheerleading. My colleague and dear friend, Pam Bettis, and I decided to write a second edition of our 2003 book *Cheerleader! An American Icon*. We were knee-deep in that process when my family received devastating news on March 1, 2020. My husband was diagnosed with Stage IV cancer. The next day we drove from Tuscaloosa to Cleveland, Ohio, for him to receive treatment at the Cleveland Clinic. Two weeks later, he was in surgery and the world shut down because of the coronavirus pandemic. Stuck in the freezing cold of Cleveland, not knowing a person other than my husband, who was convalescing, I abandoned the book project. I didn't have the emotional bandwidth or mental capacity to write a book at that time.

Despite a valiant fight against an aggressive colon cancer, Jim died on October 8, 2021. Amid grieving for him, I picked the book project back up. I needed something to do to fill my lonely days, and writing this book became my salvation. So, there are many, many people to thank who helped me get through this very difficult period. I can only mention a few here, but I hope that I have personally, in the last six years, thanked all of them. If not, here is my collective thank you to my incredible village!

Thanks to Greg Whiteley, executive producer and director of *Cheer*, for getting me back into cheerleading. In 2019, when he asked to interview me for the series, I had not thought or written about cheerleading in years. His enthusiasm for the topic, the smart, realistic series he produced, and the reception *Cheer* received reminded me that cheerleading is worthy of serious examination and planted the seeds that eventually grew into *The Cheer Reader*.

This book is dedicated to my friend, colleague, and coauthor, Pam Bettis. She retired from her position at Washington State University several years ago and decided not to be involved in this book, but our twenty-five-plus years researching and writing about cheerleading—some of which occurred on our back porches over wine and while performing our own renditions of the Herkie jump—are woven throughout *The Cheer Reader*. I thank her for her friendship, her sage guidance, and her unwavering support of me personally and professionally.

Thanks to all the contributing authors of *The Cheer Reader*. I had long respected their work from afar, so it was an honor when they agreed to write a chapter for the book. Thanks for your patience with my endless emails and requests and your quick responses to all my asks. Thank you, Dawn Durante, for directing me to the University of Texas Press. While we never worked together formally, I am very appreciative of Dawn's encouragement of me and the book at a time when I was about to abandon it. I am so happy that I landed with the wonderful team at the University of Texas Press: Sarah McGavick, Lynne Ferguson, Andra Bailard, Elizabeth Winkler, and freelance proofreader Wendy Moore. They have been a delight to work with. Thanks also to the external reviewers, Susan Cahn and Georgia Cervin. They were hands-down the best reviewers I have ever had. When I finally found out their identity, I was gobsmacked because they are scholars for whom I have the deepest respect. If you like this book, read Georgia's *Degrees of Difficulty: How Women's Gymnastics Rose to Prominence and Fell from Grace* and Susan's *Coming on Strong: Gender and Sexuality in Women's Sport* and *Sexual Reckonings: Southern Girls in a Troubling Age*. Thanks to copy editor Abby Webber, who was meticulous, quick, and kind in her critiques and suggestions. Thanks also to Isabelle Bennington, a University of Alabama student and former cheerleader, for her help in establishing a social media presence for this book. I am delighted that our paths intersected in a fortuitous way. The unfortunate part of the publishing process is that relationships are relegated to email exchanges. I wish I could gather the whole editorial team and the contributing authors at my house in Tuscaloosa for a big, old-fashioned Southern celebration where I would feed them my famous chocolate chip cake, Chex mix, and corn dip and play cornhole while drinking margaritas, beer, bourbon, wine, and sweet tea.

Thanks to my University of Alabama colleagues in New College and the Department of Social and Cultural Studies in Education, especially Julia Cherry, John Miller, Barbara Brickman, John Petrovic, Becky Atkinson, Nirmala Erevelles, Ingie Givens, and Doug McKnight. They are not only close, supportive colleagues but also dear friends. Thanks to the Glendale Garden Crew, the best neighborhood anywhere.

I spent countless hours talking about this book to my father, John Guice, who has always believed that I was the smartest, kindest, most beautiful person in the world. I am so lucky to have a father who was a feminist long before any man in the Deep South claimed that moniker. Thanks to my wonderful children and grandchildren, who keep me laughing, grounded, and give me so much joy: Hunter, Alexa, and JK; Rebecca, Zack, Lewis, and Bonnie; and Chris and Suzanne. My late husband, Dr. James Adams, was my biggest cheerleader and was with me every step of this long process—even after he left this earth way too early. I am forever grateful for the thirty-five years I had with him.

# Cheer Notes Answer Key

Cheer Note #2
1E; 2D; 3B; 4A; 5F; 6H; 7C; 8J; 9I; 10G
Bonus answer: Unlike most team nicknames, none end in an *s*.

Cheer Note #3
1F; 2D; 3J; 4A; 5O; 6E; 7L; 8I; 9G; 10K; 11M; 12H; 13N; 14B; 15C

Cheer Note #4
1C; 2E; 3M; 4L; 5J; 6I; 7F; 8D; 9B; 10A; 11H; 12K; 13G

Cheer Note #6
1B; 2C; 3A; 4C; 5D; 6D; 7B; 8C; 9A; 10B

Cheer Note #8
1B; 2A; 3A; 4B&D; 5B

Katie Britt, US senator from Alabama, was named a national Cheerleader of the Year in 2000 and world Cheerleader of the Year and Dance Performer of the Year in 1998 and 1999. Matthew McConaughey is often on the sidelines at University of Texas football games, but he was never a cheerleader in real life. Nor was Will Ferrell, who famously played Craig of the Spartan Cheerleaders on *Saturday Night Live*.

**Lagniappe**

The list of former cheerleader celebrities, politicians, journalists, coaches, and entertainers is impressive. In addition to the answers already given, here are a few more highly successful people who were cheerleaders:

Paula Abdul, Christina Aguilera, Halle Berry, Danielle Brooks, Sandra Bullock, Miley Cyrus, Cameron Diaz, Hannah Einbinder, Dakota Fanning, Fergie, Sally Field, Calista Flockhart, Megan Fox, Kathie Lee Gifford, Teri Hatcher, Faith Hill, Kendall Jenner, Kylie Jenner, Ashley Judd,

Jennifer Lawrence, Jack Lemmon, Blake Lively, Eva Longoria, Susan Lucci, Madonna, Natalie Maines, Reba McEntire, Lela Rochon, Mitt Romney, Cybill Shepherd, Alicia Silverstone, Jean Smart, Snooki, Meryl Streep, C. Vivian Stringer, Chrissy Teigen, Sela Ward, Lainey Wilson, Reese Witherspoon.

# Contributors

**Natalie G. Adams** is coauthor of *Cheerleader! An American Icon* (2003). She is a professor in New College and the College of Education at the University of Alabama. Adams is also coeditor of *Geographies of Girlhood: Identities In-Between* (2005) and coauthor of *Just Trying to Have School: The Struggle for Desegregation in Mississippi* (2018). Her articles on girls and cheerleading have appeared in *Girlhood Studies*, *Sex Education*, *Women's Studies Quarterly*, *Gender and Society*, and *Sociology of Education*. She has been featured in major media outlets, including *Time*, *Newsweek*, *Slate*, *The 19th*, *The Lily*, *Huck*, the *Every Little Thing* podcast, the *Los Angeles Times*, *The Washington Post*, *The Dallas Morning News*, the *Houston Chronicle*, *The Chronicle of Higher Education*, the *Times Education Supplement*, and *Sports Illustrated*. Her work has also been covered in the international press, with coverage in the United Kingdom, Canada, Russia, Spain, France, and more. In addition, Adams appears as the cheer historian in both seasons of the Emmy Award–winning Netflix docuseries *Cheer*.

**Isabelle Bennington** is a recent graduate of the University of Alabama in advertising with minors in general business and women's studies. She began cheering on an All Star team at age nine and for the next ten years participated in both competitive and sideline cheer. After high school graduation, she spent a summer as a Universal Cheerleaders Association (UCA) staff member. During her college tenure, she worked at ACE Cheer Company, where she coached youth tumbling, stunting, and tryout prep clinics and assisted local high schools. In 2024, she was awarded the Elizabeth Meese Memorial Award in Research from the University of Alabama's Department of Gender and Race Studies for her paper "Cheerleading, the Gendering of Sport, and How Femininity's Historical Lack of Value Is Harming Athletes." Now a cheer coach at Buckeye Cheer Elite, Bennington also manages social media for the Cheer Professors.

**Barbara J. Brickman** is a professor of media and gender studies at the University of Alabama. Her work has appeared in *Camera Obscura*, *Journal of Film and Video*, *Discourse*, and *Journal of Popular Music Studies*. She is the author of *New American Teenagers: The Lost Generation of Youth* *in 1970s Film* (2012), *Grease: Gender, Nostalgia and Youth Consumption in the Blockbuster Era* (2018), and *Suffering Sappho! Lesbian Camp in American Popular Culture* (2023), which was recognized with the 2024 Judy Grahn Award for Lesbian Nonfiction. She is also the founder and director of the Druid City Girls Media lab in Tuscaloosa, Alabama.

**Zoie Comer** is a member of the Alabama State Bar. A recent graduate of the University of Alabama School of Law, Zoie was a Capstone Scholar, senior editor of the *Law and Psychology Review*, and a member of the Order of Barristers. She is a summa cum laude graduate of Mississippi State University with a major in wildlife, fisheries, and aquaculture and minors in French and chemistry.

**Amira Rose Davis** is an assistant professor in the Department of African and African Diaspora Studies at the University of Texas at Austin, where she specializes in twentieth-century American history, with an emphasis on race, gender, sports, and politics. Davis is currently completing her book manuscript, "'Can't Eat a Medal': The Lives and Labors of Black Women Athletes in the Age of Jim Crow" (University of North Carolina Press). Davis is cohost of the feminist sports podcast *Burn It All Down* and the host of season 3 of *American Prodigies*, "A History of Black Girls in Gymnastics." She is also coauthor of *Go, Wilma, Go! Wilma Rudolph, from Athlete to Activist* (2024), a children's book, cowritten with Michael G. Long.

**Laura Grindstaff** is a professor of sociology at the University of California, Davis, with affiliations in cultural studies and performance studies. Trained in ethnographic and textual analysis, she studies American media and popular culture with a focus on gender, race, and class inequality. She is the author of the award-winning book *The Money Shot: Trash, Class, and the Making of TV Talk Shows* (2002) and the coeditor of two editions of the Routledge *Handbook of Cultural Sociology*.

**Lauren C. Hindman** is an assistant professor in the Department of Management and Entrepreneurship at Hofstra University. Her research focuses on issues related to diversity, equity, and inclusion in the sports industry, particularly the gendered experiences of employees in sports organizations.

**Michelle Inderbitzin** is an associate professor of sociology in the School of Public Policy at Oregon State University. Her work and research center around juvenile justice, prison culture, and transformative education. She is a frequent instructor and volunteer in state prisons and youth correctional facilities. She is the lead author of *Deviance and Social Control: A Sociological Perspective* (3rd ed., 2012) and has received numerous awards for her teaching and engagement, including the Pacific Sociological Association's Distinguished Contribution to Sociological Praxis Award (2016) and the American Society of Criminology's Teaching Award (2017).

**Caitlyn M. Jarvis** is an assistant teaching professor of strategic communication and advertising in the Communication Studies Department at Northeastern University. Jarvis's research addresses the intersection of organizational and health communication through attention to new media, identity, and resilience.

**Amy Moritz** is a former sportswriter and full-time lecturer at St. Bonaventure University. She earned her bachelor of arts in journalism and mass communication from St. Bonaventure and her master of arts in humanities at the University at Buffalo.

**Stanley J. Murphy** is an attorney in Tuscaloosa, Alabama, and a member of the bars of Alabama, Florida, the District of Columbia, and the US Supreme Court. He is former senior counsel for the University of Alabama System and is an adjunct professor at the University of Alabama School of Law, where he teaches advanced seminars on higher education and civil immunity law.

**Lauren R. Nowosatka** is a doctoral candidate in physical cultural studies in the Department of Kinesiology at the University of Maryland. A former high-level gymnast, Nowosatka's research draws on personal experience and combines her scholarly interests in sporting femininities, safe sport, and media representation. Her master's thesis examined constructions of femininity and empowerment in the reality television show *Dallas Cowboys Cheerleaders: Making the Team*. Her doctoral dissertation examines the conceptual underpinnings of safe sport in contemporary American sporting culture.

**Dwaine Plaza** is a professor of sociology in the School of Public Policy at Oregon State University. He has written extensively on the topic of Caribbean migration within the international diaspora, and his publications have focused on such topics as return migration, migration and settlement practices of Caribbeans, second-generation acculturation, cultural celebrations, and immigration policy in Canada, where he grew up. He also publishes extensively in the area of race and gender relations in the United States. Plaza is coeditor of *Carnival Is Woman: Feminism and Performance in Caribbean Mas* (2019) and *Higher Education Beyond COVID: New Teaching Paradigms and Promise* (2023). His passion for the sociology of sport comes after decades of mentoring and teaching Division I athletes at Oregon State University.

**Paulina A. Serrano** is the Carlos E. Castañeda Postdoctoral Fellow with the Center for Mexican American Studies at the University of Texas at Austin. Her interests include twentieth-century US history, gender, race, sport, and citizenship. Serrano's current book project, "¡Deportistas! Mexican Women, Sporting Citizenship, and Belonging in Twentieth-Century America," locates the histories of sportswomen of Mexican ancestry to highlight their contributions to community formation, grassroots organizing, and institution building across and within US borders. Her research has been funded by the American Association of University Women (AAUW) and the Institute for Citizens and Scholars, formerly the Woodrow Wilson Foundation.

**Ashleigh N. Shields** is an assistant teaching professor in the Department of Public Health and Health Sciences and the Department of Communication Studies at Northeastern University. Shields's research explores the intersection of health and interpersonal communication through attention to disclosure, listening, and stigmatized health topics.

**Kathleen Stanley** is a retired senior instructor of sociology at Oregon State University. Her courses were wide-ranging, with many focusing on gender issues in society and popular culture.

**Emily West** is a professor of communication at the University of Massachusetts Amherst. She studies popular culture, digital platforms, and promotional culture. She is the author of *Buy Now: How Amazon Branded Convenience and Normalized Monopoly* (2022) and coeditor, with Matthew P. McAllister, of *The Routledge Companion to Advertising and Promotional Culture* (2nd ed., 2023).

# Index

www.ingramcontent.com/pod-product-compliance
Lightning Source LLC
LaVergne TN
LVHW090741300826
846729LV00004B/80

* 9 7 8 1 4 7 7 3 3 4 5 7 7 *